Seamus Heaney

Seamus Heaney

Searches for Answers

Eugene O'Brien

Pluto  Press

LONDON • DUBLIN • STERLING, VIRGINIA

First published 2003 by Pluto Press
345 Archway Road, London N6 5AA
and 22883 Quicksilver Drive, Sterling, VA 20166–2012, USA

Distributed in the Republic of Ireland and Northern Ireland
by Columba Mercier Distribution, 55A Spruce Avenue,
Stillorgan Industrial Park, Blackrock, Co. Dublin, Ireland.
Tel: + 353 1 294 2556. Fax: + 353 1 294 2564

www.plutobooks.com

British Library Cataloguing in Publication Data
A catalogue record for this book is available from
the British Library

ISBN 0 7453 1735 9 hardback
ISBN 0 7453 1734 0 paperback

Library of Congress Cataloging in Publication Data
O'Brien, Eugene, 1958–
    Seamus Heaney : searches for answers / Eugene O'Brien.
       p. cm.
Includes bibliographical references.
    ISBN 0–7453–1735–9 (hardback) — ISBN 0–7453–1734–0 (pbk.)
    1. Heaney, Seamus—Prose. 3. Northern Ireland—In literature.
 3. Northern Ireland—Intellectual life. I. Title.
    PR6058.E2 Z799 2003
    828' .91408—dc21

                                                                   2003005381

10   9   8   7   6   5   4   3   2   1

Designed and produced for Pluto Press by
Chase Publishing Services, Fortescue, Sidmouth, EX10 9QG, England
Typeset from disk by Stanford DTP Services, Northampton, England
Printed and bound in the European Union by
Antony Rowe, Chippenham and Eastbourne, England

For Áine, Eoin and Dara

Contents

Acknowledgements

At this juncture, I would like to record a number of debts accrued in the writing of this book. Roger van Zwanenberg at Pluto Press has been supportive of this project from the outset and for this I thank him. At an initial stage in the planning of this book, Bruce Stewart gave support and advocacy when both were needed, and for this, and for much support over the years, I thank him. My colleagues in the Department of English at Mary Immaculate College, University of Limerick have also been most helpful in easing my load through their efficiency and professionalism, thus leaving me free to complete this text, and for this, and much else, I am most grateful. Eoin Flannery took time off from his own research to read a final draft, and provided perceptive comments as well as correcting errors – I hope to do the same for him.

Tony and Sinead Corbett proofread the final draft at quite short notice and enriched the text, at both the level of the signifier and the signified, with their perceptive comments and suggestions. They have read all of my previous work and I would like to thank them for their help, recommend them for their intelligence, wonder at their perseverance, and warn them that there's more to come.

I would also like to thank Tracey Day and Ray Addicott for their thorough, intelligent and painstaking reading of the typescript, and for the many suggestions and corrections they made. The book is all the better because of them.

Finally, my debts to my wife Áine are many and various but I would chiefly thank her for her ongoing encouragement of this and other projects, past, present and hopefully future, her sharp proofreading, her teasing out of ideas, her frequent reality checks, and most of all, for continuing to put up with me. My two sons, Eoin and Dara were central to this project, as to so many others, and Paul and Katie continue to inspire.

I would like to thank Faber & Faber and Farrar, Strauss & Giroux for permission to quote from the works of Seamus Heaney.

Introduction

In 1997, Seamus Heaney published a review of Roy Foster's *The Apprentice Mage*, the first volume of his biography of William Butler Yeats, in *The Atlantic Monthly*. In this review, Heaney wrote about both biographer and subject in terms which have no small bearing on this book, and its *raison d'être*. To write a book about Seamus Heaney, one must, of necessity, declare one's *raison d'être* from the outset as with over 30 books devoted to his work, the field is in danger of becoming over-ploughed (indeed I have already ploughed some earlier furrows myself). Any further exploration of Heaney must, *de facto*, suggest its relation to, and difference from, this body of critical work, if it is to justify its existence. That the majority of these studies of Heaney have been beneficial to any understanding of his work is a further problem – as this book cannot be offered as a necessary corrective to previous critical errors. However, the poet has, to date, been fortunate in his critics, therefore that avenue is also closed.

So, if this book is to justify its place on the shelves, what then does it bring to Heaney studies that has been heretofore lacking? In a time-honoured manner in literary studies, and validated by the words of Shakespeare that one can 'by indirections find directions out' (*Hamlet*: II, I), I will advance my thesis via Heaney's book review. In terms of what Heaney has to say about both Foster and Yeats, this review serves as an index to the reasons for my writing this book, as well as suggesting the critical niche which it hopes to fill. Contrary to many studies of Heaney which see him as obsessed with the past, I will be arguing that his work, both poetry and prose, is, on the contrary, oriented very much towards the future.

Writing about Roy Foster, Heaney makes the following points with regard to his position within Irish historical studies in particular and Irish cultural studies in general. He notes that Foster is 'identified as the most influential "revisionist" among contemporary Irish historians, which is to say that he, like his subject, has often been at the centre of the culture wars'. He goes on to discuss the nature of this revisionism noting that it attempts to revise the default nationalistic narrative of Irish history as a teleological emergence of the 'Gaelic nation from foreign domination, culminating in the reinstatement of native government and the official recognition of the native language and majority religion after Irish independence was gained, in 1921' (Heaney 1997). This narrative, it is argued, suppresses other strands or varieties of Irishness 'and is therefore detrimental to any move toward a more politically workable, culturally pluralist future for the country, north and south' (Foster 1997: 158). It is Foster's participation in this ongoing, and sometimes fraught, process, that Heaney sees as being of value. Revisionism participates in what might be called the deconstruction of a monological historical narrative, bringing out the strains, fractures, aporias and antinomies that have been attenuated by the narrative sweep.

Indeed, part of my thesis in this book will be that from a philosophical, and arguably methodological standpoint, this type of revisionism is allied to deconstruction, specifically the work of Jacques Derrida, who also focuses on neglected strands of discourses in order to bring out other narratives, histories and perspectives; as he puts it 'marginal, fringe cases' are important to the deconstructive project as they almost 'always constitute the most certain and most decisive indices wherever essential conditions are to be grasped' (Derrida 1988: 209). That Heaney should see Foster as ideally suited to write Yeats's biography is also significant in terms of his own intellectual orientation. That he should be so affirmative of Foster's revisionist project indicates an identification with a thinker who has engaged with the increasing complexities of socio-cultural identity that have become definitive of the situation in Northern Ireland over the past 30 years. That he should use this notion of 'cultural pluralism' to adequate Foster with his subject, Yeats, is highly significant in terms of Heaney's own orientation on these issues. As Heaney points out:

> Nobody, therefore, was better qualified to write this book, which follows Yeats into his fiftieth year, through a period of Irish history when all the questions about national and cultural affiliation that have come so desperately to the fore again in Northern Ireland were being lived through in the rest of the country at both private and public levels and leaving their indelible mark on Irish life. But it was precisely because these crucial tensions had come to the fore that Yeats, at fifty, began to set himself up as the representative Irish poet of his times – one whose ancestors included not only a soldier who had fought for William of Orange at the Battle of the Boyne at the end of the seventeenth century but also a

country scholar who was friends with the revolutionary Robert Emmet at the beginning of the nineteenth. By invoking these figures in 1914, in the introductory verses of a volume significantly titled *Responsibilities*, Yeats was reminding his Irish readership that he took the strain of both the major ideologies that were exacerbating Irish political life in that critically important year. (Heaney 1997: 158–9)

For Heaney, then, *The Apprentice Mage* saw a congruence between two Irish intellectuals – Foster and Yeats – both of whom were keen to avoid a singular, monocular vision of Irishness and instead to embrace a more pluralistic and complicated construction of what it means to be Irish. Revisionism involves pluralising the narrative of history and Yeats, too, was involved in such a process. Discussing the mooted destruction of Nelson's Pillar, in 1923, Yeats argued that the monument 'should not be broken up' as it represented the 'feeling of Protestant Ireland for a man who helped to break the power of Napoleon'. Interestingly, Yeats goes on to explain his reasons for his view, noting that the 'life and work of the people who erected it is part of our tradition', and concluding his remarks with the telling assertion: 'I think we should accept the whole past of this nation and not pick and choose' (*Evening Telegraph*, 25 August 1923). The unravelling of different strands is again a feature of this perspective.

That Heaney should be attracted by such complex and creative allegiance to a notion of a revisioned Ireland, and that he should also be attracted by the intellectual position of Foster, serves as an index of his own commitment to a similar range of ideas. Throughout his writing, in both poetry and prose, he will stress the duality and necessity for interaction and intersection of notions of selfhood and notions of alterity. As he put it elsewhere: the locating of one's identity in 'the ethnic and liturgical habits of one's group' is all very well, but for that group to 'confine the range of one's growth' and 'to have one's sympathies determined and one's responses programmed' by that group, is clearly a 'form of entrapment' (1985: 6–7), an entrapment which defines place and identity in extremely narrow terms, and which is a polar opposite of the discourse of poetry as Heaney sees it. As Heaney puts it in *The Redress of Poetry*, poetry has to be 'a working model of inclusive consciousness. It should not simplify' (1995a: 8), and this desire to express the complexity of inter-subjective relationships is the connecting thread that binds Heaney, Foster, Yeats and, I would also suggest, Derrida.

All of these writers have endeavoured to avoid those 'forms of entrapment' of which Heaney spoke and instead, have looked for broader symbolic enunciations of individual and cultural identity, and in his *Atlantic Monthly* review, he stresses this admirable aspect of Yeats as icon:

> As a Yeats, he belonged to the respectable stratum of Protestant Irish society that owed its position and power to William of Orange's victory and its consequences – the establishment of an Anglo-Irish ascendancy and the institution of penal laws against the Catholic population. So as a Yeats he might have been expected to support the cause of the union of Ireland with the other British nations under the English crown. But as an Irish poet who had written a manifesto aligning himself with Irish Nationalist precursors such as Thomas Davis and James Clarence Mangan, as the author of the early, inflammatory 'rebel' play *Cathleen Ni Houlihan*, as the chief inventor of the Celtic Twilight and a founding member of the Abbey Theatre, which claimed to be the country's national theatre, Yeats had long been creating a vision of Ireland as an independent cultural entity, a state of mind as much as a nation-state, one founded on indigenous myths and attitudes and beliefs that pre-dated not only William of Orange but even Saint Patrick himself. (Heaney 1997: 159)

The idea of the nation as a 'state of mind' is a recurring trope in contemporary cultural discourse. Heaney has made the point in his sequence 'Squarings' from *Seeing Things*, that places are always open to different naming paradigms; indeed that places are created by such paradigms:

> In famous poems by the sage Han Shan,
> Cold Mountain is a place that can also mean
> A state of mind. Or different states of mind
>
> At different times. (1991: 97)

It is this embracing of the difference that is at the heart of the nation that further unites these writers as they all, in different ways, look to more pluralistic and complex structurations of society and culture. Not seeing nationhood or identity as either predestined or given, instead they see it as something to be created through language and imagery, and I would suggest that Heaney and Derrida follow Yeats's idea of the importance of a dialogue between notions of selfhood and notions of alterity. Ireland as a 'state of mind' is a concept that is transformative of the givens of identity, in any ideological group, and it is this ongoing transformation that will take the strain of conflicting ideologies and, possibly, create new structures which will allow these ideological and cultural positions to interact, intersect and enter some form of dialogue with each other which may allow for some dissipation of the conflict.

It is with this idea of taking the strain of conflicting and diverse ideological positions that I return to the question posed in the first paragraph of this introduction, as to the *raison d'être* of this book. I think, in the light of Heaney's comments on Foster and Yeats, that a strand of his thinking can be traced which engages with these notions of complexity of identity, hybridity and liminality in terms of the situating of the text of selfhood within the context of one's cultural associations and predications. His praise of the methodology used by Foster also contains the glimmerings of my own *modus operandi* in this book, as I will offer parallel analyses of Heaney's poetry and prose, the latter being a glaring lacuna in what might be termed 'Heaney studies' over the years. Until now, I would suggest, Heaney's prose has been generally used as a preparatory gloss on his poetry; it has never been subjected to any sustained critique in terms of its role in Heaney's overall project. This book will redress this balance by taking specific themes in his writing, most notably concerned with issues of identity, belonging, ideology and the role of the aesthetic with respect to the political, and examine them through a sustained study of both his poetry and his prose.

Finally, the connections I have made between the disciplines of historical revisionism and deconstruction presage another thematic strand of this book, namely the adequation of the ideas of Heaney and Derrida with respect to the notions of reading, writing, cultural discourse and ideology. If nothing else, this articulation has the virtue of being an unploughed part of the Heaney canon, and it also demonstrates, as I hope to show, that Heaney needs to be addressed as a cultural thinker as well as an artist in terms of his involvement in themes so seminal to the cultural narration of a contemporary form of Irishness. In both his poetry and his prose, Heaney partici-pates in a transformative discourse which exfoliates the fixed ideological positions of Catholic-nationalist-republican and Protestant-loyalist-unionist by probing their borders, their points of limitation. By then locating these within broader and more expansive contexts, Heaney's writing transforms points of closure into points of opening to the other. Working at the level of the individual consciousness, Heaney gradually creates the plural, complex and fluid 'state of mind' of an Ireland which is open to its future.

At the end of his 'Frontiers of Writing' essay, Heaney quotes from Roy Foster's earlier book *Paddy & Mr. Punch*, citing the idea that we 'need not give up our own claims on Irishness in order to conceive of it as a flexible definition. And in an age of exclusivist jihads to east and west, the notion that people can reconcile more than one cultural identity may have much to recommend it' (Foster 1993: xvi–xvii). It is this complexity of perspective that attracts Heaney to Yeats, and which, I will suggest, creates a strand in his work which enacts Colin Graham's concept of deconstructing Ireland:

> The conclusion which this book edges towards is that 'Ireland' stages its own deconstruction and that at every turn the idea unravels and reforms itself, always in anticipation of the next act of definition and criticism which, like this one, will be inadequately applied to it. (Graham 2001: x)

'Revisionism', 'deconstruction', 'different states of mind' 'flexibility of definition' or pluralism: what all of these terms have in common is a desire to enunciate the complexity of Irish culture and society through the different strands of identity and to focus on the creation of this plural form of identity instead of being fixated on the givens of the past. It is this ongoing theme that will be discussed in the coming chapters.

Chapter 1 deals with the theories of selfhood and alterity that run through Heaney's prose writings. These are seen as being organised around some central questions posed in *Preoccupations* as to the role of poetry within society and culture. The chapter also examines the interaction and intersection of tropes of selfhood and alterity in Heaney's writing as well as his focus on the emancipatory aspects of writing. Heaney addresses these questions, in both poetry and prose, throughout his writing. The second chapter deals with Heaney's theory of poetry, specifically in terms of the dialectical interchange between different identitarian positions in Northern Ireland. Connections are made between his experience of internal exile and that of Derrida in Algeria, with these concrete images of travel and crossings used to extrapolate a particular strain in the work of both writers as they create plural and complex structures within which the binary oppositions can interact and inform each other, in the name of what Heaney describes as the need to accommodate 'two opposing notions of truthfulness simultaneously' (1985: 4). Poetry as a vehicle for the achievement of such a structure is examined in poems from *The Haw Lantern, Seeing Things* and *The Spirit Level*, as well as in essays from *Preoccupations*, where his notions of 'continuous adjudication' and a 'field of force' are first expressed.

Chapter 3 focuses on the transformative effect which poetry can bring to reality and actuality in terms of subverting, and amplifying, the givens with which our culture presents us. This chapter discusses the effects of poetry as a dialectical structure on both writer and reader, looking at the title essay and 'Frontiers of Writing' in *The Redress of Poetry*, as well as at his Nobel lecture *Crediting Poetry*. Parallels between Heaney and Derrida in terms of concepts of identity, responsibility, liminality and the fluidity of borders will also be discussed.

The fourth chapter examines the transformative interaction of poetry and politics, examining the creative ambiguity in the phrase 'government of the tongue', and then developing this analysis to examine some of his poetry and prose which attempt to transform signifiers which have a hegemonic attachment to a particular tradition into indices of plurality and complexity. Connections are made between his work and that of Derrida and Emmanuel Levinas. These include some of the placename poems from *Wintering Out* as well as the almost programmatic example of a poem involving the interaction of self and other: 'The Other Side', read in tandem with 'The Pitchfork' in *Seeing Things*. 'The Flight Path', from *The Spirit Level*, is read in terms of a transformation of the individual in terms of political allegiance.

The fifth chapter deals with the deconstruction of notions of place, particularly with how placenames specifically associated with nationalist ideology, are recontextualised in order to open different paths of signification. These names are significant in terms of the Heaney canon – Toome, Mossbawn, Glanmore – and are read in terms of Derrida's presence/absence conceit, and in terms of Heaney's own resonant image of a creative space which stood where a chestnut tree had stood, an image traced from an essay in *The Government of the Tongue*, through some poems in *The Haw Lantern*. This reading of absence as a creative source is paralleled with Maurice Blanchot's *The Space of Literature*.

The sixth chapter parallels the fifth by deconstructing different aspects of language which have been associated with a particular tradition in Northern Ireland. By examining different signifiers that would seem to have a nationalist or Gaelic association, and by teasing out Heaney's deconstruction of this aspect of their etymology as he brings the signifier into the ambit of the other tradition, his ongoing pluralisation of language is foregrounded. Specifically, the complexity of language as it is experienced in art is discussed, ranging through Heaney's poetry and prose.

Chapter 7 examines the influence and interaction of Heaney's work with that of another Nobel Prize-winning Irish poet, one with whom he has often been compared. I refer, of course, to William Butler Yeats. Heaney has written of his debt to Yeats, and in this chapter, we will examine the ethical similarities between these writers in terms of their views on the role of the aesthetic with respect to the politic, as well as in terms of their attitude to the complexities of identity. The Nobel lectures of each writer will also be compared in terms of their attitudes to the place of writing in society.

In his essay 'Vision and Irony in Recent Irish Poetry', published in *The Place of Writing*, Heaney stresses the relationship between the poet and his or her cultural context in ideal terms: 'as poets, they comprehend both the solidarities of their own group and the need to subvert them' (1989: 49). It is this complexity of response that will be the *terminus ad quem* towards which Heaney's ongoing searches for answers will be directed.

1 'Preoccupying Questions': Heaney's Prose

To say that Seamus Heaney's work is academically popular would be an understatement. There are, to date, over 30 books completely devoted to the study and analysis of his writing, and to list the number of articles and chapters on Heaney would probably be a book-length enterprise in itself.[1] Given that Heaney is a Nobel Prize winner, as well as being one of the most popular poets currently writing in English, and given that he reaches a global audience, this profusion of academic attention should come as no surprise. However, what is surprising is that, in all of these books, there is not one which is devoted to a sustained study of his prose writings, and how these writings are central to his overall project.

Many critics refer to these essays and lectures in terms of providing some form of explicatory or contextual commentary on his poems. For example, Elmer Andrews, in his Icon Critical Guide (1998) to Heaney's work, makes frequent use of his prose in order to explain the backdrop of many of the poems.[2] The same is true of Neil Corcoran's study where he sees Heaney's second collection of essays, *The Government of the Tongue*, as a companion to some of the poems in *The Haw Lantern*, with 'the essays sometimes fleshing out in discursive terms what the poems encode more obliquely' (Corcoran 1986: 138). Ronald Tamplin uses a passage from the end of 'The God in the Tree', from *Preoccupations*, to enable a reading of Heaney's poem *In Gallarus Oratory* (Heaney 1969: 22), noting the contrast of light and dark in the passage, and significantly commenting that this contrast can be seen 'even more clearly in the poem' (Tamplin 1989: 33), thus making the supplementary status of the prose explicit. Andrew Murphy uses passages from *Preoccupations* as a gloss in his readings of *Requiem for the Croppies* (Murphy 2000a: 31–2),[3] while almost all of the other studies of his poetry use the prose as a supplementary point of reference. These are just a selection of examples of this usage of Heaney's prose in academic writing: there are numerous others.[4]

I think it is clear, then, that the received critical wisdom here is to treat Heaney's prose as a kind of piecemeal supplement to his poetry.

9

The essays and lectures are seen to provide a privileged commentary where the poet can discuss his art in terms which will cast greater light upon it. Even in reviews or articles which purport to discuss the prose itself, the terminology and attitude is suggestive of just such an approach. Thus, in writing about the essays, Thomas Docherty feels obligated to see them as constituted by a 'poetic' logic (1997: 148). It is as if, were Heaney not a poet, then these essays and lectures would be of less worth: they are not 'stand-alone' pieces. In a similar fashion, Bernard O'Donoghue, in an article on *The Government of the Tongue*, makes the point that some of the best reviews of this book 'read it enlighteningly in relation to the general political poems in *The Haw Lantern*' (1994: 181).[5] In a review of *The Government of the Tongue*, the Irish writer and critic Colm Tóibín saw the essays as underscoring this view of Heaney as poet, noting that it was 'as though he needs to insist that he is not a critic, or a prose-writer, but a poet trying to clear space for himself' (1988). This approach to Heaney's prose is by now endemic, with the essays and lectures being seen as a commentary on the poetry, and also as texts which can usefully shed light on individual poems, or on biographical or thematically related detail and incident in Heaney's own life.[6] In general the readings of Heaney's prose all seem to share this perspective.

At this juncture, my own perspective needs enunciation. I see his prose as central to his developing project. Far from being a meta-commentary on his poetry, it is a seminal aspect of his work, providing parallel expressions and explorations of the themes that have been ongoing in his writing. I would suggest that Edward Mendelson's remark, about *The Government of the Tongue*, that the book was less miscellaneous than it appeared, could validly be applied to his prose in general (1988: 726), though the faint praise that is to be found in the phrasing of this remark further strengthens the view of the prose as very much second best in the Heaney canon.

In terms of offering a reading of Heaney's essays, I would offer his own reading practice as a useful paradigm. In *The Government of the Tongue*, he discusses the work of the Polish poet Zbigniew Herbert, and as befits one whose academic rite of passage was undergone when 'practical criticism held great sway' (Heaney 1980: 13), there is a close, in places line-by-line, examination of passages from three works by Herbert. These are *Barbarian in the Garden*, *Selected Poems* and *Report from the Besieged City and Other Poems*. What is interesting, in the context of our discussion, is that *Barbarian in the Garden* is a collection of prose writings, 'ten meditations on art and history which masquerade as travel writing' (Heaney 1988: 55). Heaney does not see these essays as a metalinguistic gloss on the poetry; nor does he see them as separate, in terms of thematic concerns, from Herbert's poetry; rather he sees them as another enunciation of the thematic, aesthetic and ethical imperatives that ground Herbert's work.

The same standards can be applied to Heaney's own beginnings as a prose writer. In the foreword to *Preoccupations*, he makes the following points:

> I had a half-clarified desire to come to poetic terms with myself by considering the example of others, and to try to bring into focus the little I knew....I hope it is clear that the essays selected here are held together by searches for answers to central preoccupying questions: how should a poet properly live and write? What is his relationship to be to his own voice, his own place, his literary heritage and his contemporary world? (1980: 13)

In this quotation, Heaney outlines the *raison d'être* of the essays in the book: I would argue that one could also see this quotation as outlining the *raison d'être* of his entire *oeuvre*. I would make two points about this assertion. Firstly, it demonstrates the centrality that Heaney ascribes to his prose writing, seeing it as a meditation on art and poetry, and as a coming to terms with his own voice through a consideration of other poets, what he terms, borrowing from Auden, 'breaking bread with the dead' (1980: 14). From the outset, this is no piecemeal series of disparate essays and reviews; instead it is a bringing 'into focus' of his concerns about the notion of 'art'; it is an enunciation of, what one might tentatively term, given its early placement in the Heaney canon, an aesthetic theory.

I use the term 'theory' advisedly, tracing its etymology from the Greek *theoria*, meaning 'to look at', and keeping in mind Heaney's own metaphor of bringing his knowledge 'into focus'. This new sense of looking at poetry, in terms of the study of other poets, initiates a theoretical perspective that underwrites all of his prose as opposed to just this book. In this context, the theoretical perspective that is in the process of being heuristically wrought is coterminous with the views of Christopher Norris, who describes theory as being 'capable of providing a better, more adequate conceptual grasp of experiences that would otherwise belong to the realm of pre-reflective "commonsense" knowledge' (1991: 13). Surely this is what Heaney is setting out to achieve in *Preoccupations*, and by extension in his other books. He is taking his own work, and the work of other writers who have in some way helped him to write, and is taking up 'a critical distance from the data of first-hand subjective understanding' (Norris 1991: 12). In this context, O'Donoghue notes, correctly in my view, that Heaney's writing can be connected with 'mainstream English critical theoretical tradition' since Coleridge (1994: 148),[7] and I would see this connection as a far better contextual placement of Heaney's prose than that of Corcoran, who entitles his chapter on the prose 'Heaney's Literary Criticism' (1998: 209–33).[8]

Secondly, this quotation attests to the teleology of his project, namely the 'searches for answers' to those central preoccupying questions which are cited above. This is foregrounded by the deictical *glissement* in the above quotation, a *glissement* which is thematically significant in terms of his prose. He begins using the personal pronoun, first person singular: '[a]ll that *I* really knew about the art was derived from whatever poetry *I* had written and from those poets who had helped *me* to write it. *I* had a half-clarified desire to come to poetic terms with *myself*' [*my italics*]. It is clear that Heaney himself, and his work, are both the subject and object of this particular search for answers. His writing will focus on his own work, and on the work of others in terms of how they have helped him to come to poetic terms with himself. Interestingly, though, the second part of the quotation demonstrates the deictical progression from the personal to the general, with the teleological object of the searches for answers now becoming 'the *poet*', and *his* relationship with voice, place, literature and society: 'how should a *poet* properly live and write? What is *his* relationship to be to *his* own voice, *his* own place, *his* literary heritage and *his* contemporary world?' [*my italics*]. In this context, Heaney is being provoked by questions similar to those discussed by Derrida in terms of the form and function of literature. Pondering on his response to the question, Derrida traces his thinking as follows, as he comes back to the question:

> 'What is writing in general?' and, in the space of writing in general, to this other question which is more and other than a simple particular case: 'What is literature?'; literature as historical institution with its conventions, rules etc., but also this institution of fiction which gives *in principle* the power to say everything, to break free of the rules, to displace them, and thereby to institute, to invent and even to suspect the traditional difference between

nature and institution, nature and conventional law, nature and history. Here we should ask juridical and political questions. The institution of literature in the West, in its relatively modern form, is linked to an authorization to say everything, and doubtless too to the coming about of the modern idea of democracy. (1992a: 37)

The similarity between both writers in terms of their attitudes to the value and purpose of literature is striking, and further connections between their thinking will be traced in the later chapters of this work. Both writers probe the interstices between the literary and the political, Derrida examining the constitutive function of a literature which sanctions and enhances debate and discussion, while Heaney examines the relationship of the literary to notions of place, heritage and the contemporary world. No less than Derrida, he is probing the epistemological status of the literary as well as examining the inter-actions of the literary text with the cultural and societal context.

In short, what is attempted in his various prose pieces is nothing less than a theory, or epistemology, of poetry in particular and writing in general, what Bernard O'Donoghue calls, speaking specifically of *The Government of the Tongue*, Heaney's *ars poetica* (1994: 135). I would suggest that such a project is the result of the 'searches for answers' that have set in motion his prose writings in the first place. In this study, I will be focusing on what I consider to be the main prose-writings of Heaney's career thus far: *Preoccupations: Selected Prose 1968–1978* (1980); *Among Schoolchildren* (1983); *Place and Displacement: Recent Poetry of Northern Ireland* (1985); *The Government of the Tongue: The 1986 T. S. Eliot Memorial Lectures and Other Critical Writings* (1988); *The Place of Writing* (1989), *The Redress of Poetry: Oxford Lectures* (1995), *Crediting Poetry* (1995), his Nobel lecture and the most recent summative collection *Finders Keepers* (2002), which also includes some new material. I will trace Heaney's *ars poetica* through all of these books, concentrating on his evolving discussion of how a poet should live and write, a discussion framed by the different relationships between a poet and his or her voice, place, literary heritage and society. I will also make connections between these essays and the themes of his poetry, seeing both genres as different ways of progressing his ongoing search for answers to those preoccupying questions.

I will argue that the concerns and themes that various critics have discussed in his poetry are also to be found in his prose. To see what Helen Vendler terms his 'vivid, metaphorical and intelligent prose'

(1998: 5) as merely a metalinguistic commentary, or as some form of necessary background research, is to mistakenly transform generic considerations into epistemological ones. In the essays of the books cited, one finds ongoing parallel discussion of some of the central concerns of Heaney's poetry: the nature of Irish identity; the difficulty of writing about place, given the historical and cultural baggage that always accrues; the relationship of poetry with politics; the ethical questions that are intimately connected with aesthetic enterprises; the influence of European and world perspectives on his own work, and on the whole notion of Irishness in general, the influences of other writers from different traditions on his work; the special relationship with the work of Yeats, and, finally, the attempt to set up a fluid spatial metaphor of an Irishness, which one might term negative dialectical, as it combines the multifarious traditions, cultures and ideologies that have been thrown together historically.

Underwriting all of these concerns, or preoccupations, is the ongoing attempt to bring into focus some form of theorisation of the aesthetic, to take up some form of critical distance so as to better understand the mode of knowledge that is operative within art and which, by extension, is operative through poetry and prose in terms of the socio-political sphere. What emerges in these essays is a sophisticated approach to poetry, an approach which grants the internal laws of language and aesthetics which are applicable within the domain of poetry, but which at the same time demonstrates a growing awareness of the need to reconcile what he terms 'lyric celebration' (1988: 12), and its concomitants 'the phrase or cadence which haunts the ear and the eager parts of the mind' (1980: 61), with the demands of an ethical imperative which 'the poet may find as he exercises his free gift in the presence of the unfree and the hurt' (1988: xviii). This sophisticated aesthetic is brought about by a complex dialectical approach, which sets up what in German is termed an *Auseinandersetzung*, a confrontation wherein one can gain a greater understanding of each term, as well as of the relationship between them.[9] It will become clear that it is on this relationship, what Andrew Murphy terms the 'conflicting demands of Song and Suffering' (2000a: 1), and its effect on the individual categories, that Heaney's critical focus will be directed.

For Heaney, the epistemological force of poetry is complex and multilayered, involving the granting of voice to different perspectives, as well as setting up cognitive and intellectual structures which allow for their interaction. His careful readings of other texts always gesture towards such constructs, where the dialectical oscillation between the different perspectives creates a field of force wherein it is the relationship between the different perspectives that is the main focus of his 'searches for answers', and we can see this type of reading in action in an early example from *Preoccupations*.

In an essay entitled 'In the Country of Convention', about a collection of English pastoral verse,[10] he is critical of what he sees as an oversimplification of response on behalf of the editors to the notion of what they term 'the pastoral vision'. Barrell and Bull see this vision as being ultimately false, because it posits a simplistic unhistorical relation between the land-owning class and the workers, which mystifies and obscures the actuality of working conditions. Heaney notes the influence of Raymond Williams on this point of view,[11] and goes on to criticise this 'sociological filleting of the convention' as being guilty of a 'certain attenuation of response' which curtails the consideration of the poems as 'made things' as 'self-delighting buds on the old bough of a tradition' (1980: 174).

The complexity of his position may not seem at first obvious in this essay; there is a polarity seemingly set up between what we might term intrinsic and extrinsic, or aesthetic and sociological criticism. Indeed, 'In the Country of Convention' does not figure in many discussions of Heaney's work;[12] nevertheless, I would argue that here, in embryo, are to be found two of the defining facets of his aesthetic epistemology, namely a fluid dialectical movement of thought, and an awareness of the complicated interaction of text and context, demands which lead writing towards a position of some complexity. So, while deploring the simplification of response, Heaney is also willing to grant the benefit of sociologically driven criticism as 'a bracing corrective' to what could prove an 'over-literary savouring' of the genre as a matter of 'classical imitation and allusion' (1980: 174). He is obviously not against extrinsically driven criticism *per se*; rather he is against any form of 'attenuation of response', any thinning of the plurality and complexity of the field of force which should be set up in the process of his teleological searches for answers. He sees the relationship between the internal dynamics of the poems, and their reflection, refraction, and transformation of external societal and cultural factors, as far too complex to allow the 'Marxist broom' to sweep aesthetic considerations aside in favour of the societal and economic.

Instead, Heaney's notion of the relationship between text and context is far more complex and fluid. It could be seen as an example of the rhetorical figure of anastomosis, as cited by J. Hillis Miller in *The Ethics of Reading*, in terms of notions of 'penetration and permeation'. Miller is also speaking about the relationship between text and context, and sees this notion of context as hovering 'uneasily' between 'metonymy in the sense of mere contingent adjacency and synecdoche, part for whole, with an assumption that the part is some way genuinely like the whole' (1987: 6). It is here that he cites the trope of anastomosis, adverting to Joyce's verbal example 'underdarkneath'[13] as well as Bakhtin's view of language as a social philosophy which is permeated by a system of values 'inseparable from living practice and class struggle' (1973: 6–7).[14] One could just as easily see 'con-text' as a similar case, with one word, 'text' penetrating or permeating the other, 'context'.[15] Here both words intersect and interfuse, but perform the dialectical action of remaining separate as well as blending.

Heaney's reading sets up a further contextual aspect of this dialectical structure which, far from attenuating our response, will thicken and enable it. Heaney laments the decision of the editors not to print translations of Theocritus, Virgil, Horace, Mantuan, and Marot,[16] as these were the 'informing voices that were "modified in the guts of the living"' (1980: 175), which underwrote the pastoral poetry of Spenser, Milton, Pope and Thomson as they attempted to 'adorn and classicise' the native literature. He feels that such a 'classical penumbra' was automatic cultural capital for these writers, and thinks it a pity that the 'ancient hinterland, the perspectives backward, are withheld' (1980: 175). Here, the textual-contextual anastomosis becomes more intricate, as this withholding delimits our reading of the pastoral genre, and of the specific English writing of this genre, as well as the complexities inherent in the title of the book.

This level of contextual cultural and linguistic complication is also to be found throughout Heaney's poetic development. One thinks of the early placename poems 'Broagh' and 'Anahorish', where the dialectical linguistic evolution from the native Irish words *'anach fhíor uisce'*, meaning 'place of clear water' and *'bruach'*, meaning 'riverbank' is traced through their eponymous transliterations, into a form of language that is shot through with both the native Irish and the colonising English languages. In these poems, the dialectical movement between different cultural significations is instantiated in the desire to see the placename 'Anahorish' as translated into: 'My "place of clear water"' (1972: 16), and in a similar movement in the first line of 'Broagh' which translates the title as 'Riverbank' (1972:

27). Of course, no Irish or English dictionary will validate these 'translations' as the placenames are Anglicisations and transliterations of the original Irish words as opposed to translations. What they signify is a dialectic, a movement between languages which is creative of a new sense of English with an Irish influence. Herman Rapaport makes this point in connection with Derrida, noting that for Derrida, 'language isn't entirely masterable to perfection; therefore one always senses that one is, however slightly, a stranger or foreigner to it' (2003: 31), and Heaney, in his poems dealing specifically with language, takes this position fully on board.

In 'Traditions', one of Heaney's 'most discussed anthologised pieces' (Crotty 2001: 201), the same process is to be found. The poem begins with an overt symbol of colonisation in sexual terms:

> Our guttural muse
> was bulled long ago
> by the alliterative tradition. (1972: 31)

However, it progresses from this direct binary conflict to more nuanced notions of linguistic diffusion, as the Irish are seen to be 'proud' of their 'Elizabethan English', with some 'cherished archaisms' actually being 'correct Shakespearean' (1972: 31).[17] The interaction is further complicated in the lines which speak of consonants 'shuttling obstinately / between bawn and mossland' (1972: 32). As will be seen later in this discussion, the two nouns of the second line are overdetermined signifiers in the Heaney canon, deriving as they do from the name of his early home, Mossbawn. Each term has a meaning in Irish and in English, and Heaney will attempt to articulate these oppositions in a manner which will create a hybrid identity. Throughout his work, Heaney does not privilege one meaning over the other. Instead, meanings interact, gesturing towards a new fusion of languages and culture, and paralleling the trope of anastomosis already discussed.

In the final section of 'Traditions', and the plural number of this noun is significant in the light of this reading of Heaney's work as plural in terms of its searches for answers, another linguistic and cultural tradition is grafted onto the givens of Irish identity. In answer to the most quoted question in Irish studies, MacMorris's 'What ish my nation?' (Shakespeare, *Henry V*: II, ii, 124), Heaney cites the words of Joyce:

> And sensibly, though so much
> later, the wandering Bloom
> replied, 'Ireland,' said Bloom,
> 'I was born here. Ireland.' (Heaney 1972: 32)

In this stanza, a Hungarian Jew states his claim to an Irishness that must accommodate him as he was born in Ireland. In this seemingly simple juxtaposition of Shakespeare and Joyce, Heaney is in effect setting out a paradigm of identity which is pluralistic, ethically driven and which refuses to be hidebound by hypostasised traditions and instead, remains open to the voice and language of the other who may come into contact with the self. There is a transformative imperative at work here, as the Ireland to which Bloom lays claim is in effect transformed by that very claim into a locus of plural identity. The adverb 'sensibly' carries a weight within this poem, as it defines an obligation to embrace change which is gradual as opposed to violent.

In the appropriately entitled 'A New Song', Heaney seems to develop this consensual paradigm of linguistic and cultural interaction, as instead of one tradition being 'bulled' by another, an image of a more gentle form of sexual intercourse is posited:

> But now our river tongues must rise
> From licking deep in native haunts
> To flood with vowelling embrace,
> Demesnes staked out in consonants. (1972: 33)

This new song is a paradigm of Heaney's own developing attitude to the linguistic and cultural context that surrounds all texts. Just as the notion of English pastoral is being deconstructed in his essay, so too are the seeming simplicities of the Irish-English historical conflict offered to ongoing critique in his poetry. The language that had been foisted upon Ireland as an apparatus of colonisation is also the language through which Joyce gave voice to a new sense of Irishness, a new song in which Irishness became redefined.

What is set out as *The Penguin Book of English Pastoral Verse* (Barrell and Bull 1975), with all the canonical, imperial, and culturally homogeneous connotations that are implied by the proper adjective '*English*', becomes something different when placed in a dialectical relationship with the classical antecedents to which he refers. Such external influences, in this case, far from attenuating the response to the lyrical impulse of the pastoral, thicken our reading of these works by complicating and interrogating how '*English*' this genre actually is. This 'perspective backwards' is also a perspective outwards, pointing up the dependence of what is seen as the English poetic canon on generic and conventional borrowings from continental Europe. It is also a perspective inwards, as these extrinsic features have had a major influence on stylistic and thematic considerations, as well as on the aesthetic objectives of the genre. Here, the anastomosis between text and context is enacted in the permeation and intersection of the poems in the book and the poems which preceded them; of the English language and Latin and French; of Latin and French and translation; of classical pastoral convention and the English version of it and finally, of the texts that are present in the book, and those enabling translations from the classics, which are absent.

Throughout Heaney's poetry, I would argue, there is a process of ongoing recontextualisation of language at work. As his career develops, there is an increasing level of linguistic plurality to be found in his writing. Translation has become an increasingly important aspect of his canon with translations of complete texts from Polish, Anglo-Saxon, French, Latin, Greek, Italian and Irish, as well as snippets from a number of other European languages. In his latest collection of poetry, *Electric Light*, one finds an increasingly polyglot range of allusions. In 'Known World', for example, he describes his return flight from a poetry festival at Struga, in Macedonia, in a highly polylinguistic style:

> I kept my seat belt fastened as instructed,
> Smoked the minute the *No Smoking* sign went off
> And took it as my due when wine was poured
> By a slight *de haut en bas* of my headphoned head.
> *Nema problema. Ja.* All systems go. (Heaney 2001: 22–3)

The 'I' of this poem is clearly influenced by his European context, and the linguistic and cultural anastomosis is a metaphorical enunciation of an increasingly complex sense of identity within Heaney himself.

This complex interrogation of the categories of text and context calls to mind a similar interrogation in the work of Jacques Derrida who, in *Limited Inc.*, has noted that 'nothing exists outside context', and that consequently, the 'outside penetrates and thus determines the inside' (1988: 153).[18] Derrida has made a similar point in

Positions, where he speaks of how each seemingly simple term is marked by the trace of other terms, so that the 'presumed interiority of meaning' is 'worked on by its own exteriority. It is always already carried outside itself' (1981a: 33). Heaney's project will also demonstrate a view of poetry which stresses the transformative and interpenetrative mode of action through which poetry achieves its ends of breaking down opposed binary positions.

Keeping these points in mind, when we return to the title, 'In the Country of Convention', we realise that this title is, like the essay, less simple than it might seem. Analogously, the country being described by the placenames 'Broagh' and 'Anahorish' is similarly complex: at first glance, it is an ur-Ireland, but ongoing investigation underlines the traces of the context of colonisation on both placenames, and, by extension, on English as it is spoken in Ireland. Similarly, in *Preoccupations*, while the country in question is England, as denoted by the proper adjective of the subtitle, '*English* Pastoral Verse', the essay draws out the connotations of the diverse influences, literary, linguistic and political, that are present in the pastoral convention. The constituent factors of this genre are not English, but Latin and French in language, as well as in tone and theme. The 'convention' of the title derives from classical pastoral literature, but as translations of this literature are absent, the presentation of the 'country' in question is consequently attenuated.

As much of the poetry shares Thomson's notion of 'England as an after-image of Augustan Rome' (Heaney 1980: 178), Heaney has accurately pointed out the weakness of the book, while at the same time providing a strong reading of the genre itself through an interrogation of this absence. Thus, Heaney allows the classical context to imbricate his reading of the English texts in the book, and both present text and absent context permeate and penetrate each other in a fuller exploration in the essay than is given in the book itself. Heaney's reading can be seen, in the terminology of Mikhail Bakhtin, as heteroglossic, in that different voices and different languages are allowed to confront each other and achieve some kind of dynamic interaction, or dialogisation (Bakhtin 1981: 263).[19]

Hence Heaney pluralises the title of the essay so that the 'country of convention' opens its borders to other countries, other languages and other literary traditions. Just as Heaney's reading of this book sees text and context interpenetrate each other, so, by implication, the genre of English pastoral has also set text and context in a dialectical relationship, a relationship which ultimately calls into question the separateness of the English poetic canon as such. Heaney's reading of conventionality has become unconventional in its dislocation of the ground on which the epistemological premises of the book are based. In this reading there is an obvious similarity with a reading by Derrida of Shelley's *The Triumph of Life*. Here, Derrida also questions the borderlines of a text, suggesting that a text is no longer:

> a finished corpus of writing, some content enclosed in a book or its margins, but a differential network, a fabric of traces referring endlessly to something other than itself, to other differential traces. Thus the text overruns all the limits assigned to it so far (not submerging or drowning them in an undifferentiated homogeneity, but rather making them more complex, dividing and multiplying strokes and lines). (1987: 84)

This is precisely the process of reading undertaken by Heaney in this essay; he takes the assumptions imposed by the title and format of the book, points to the attenuations of response that the selection criteria impose, attenuations that have an analogous relationship to the Marxist broom and sociological filleting already mentioned, and proceeds to make them 'more complex, dividing and multiplying strokes and lines'. He furthers this process towards the end of the essay by wondering whether the temporal and spatial limits imposed by the editors on poets who were included in the book are valid.

He questions whether the editors' 'brisk dismissal' of the further possibilities of pastoral are well-founded, and goes on to suggest valid reasons for the inclusion of other writers – Edward Thomas, Hugh MacDiarmid, David Jones, A. E. Housman – and also wonders about Louis MacNeice's eclogues which 'represent the form as an enabling resource' (1980: 180). Finally, he further extends the limits of his critique by multiplying some 'strokes and lines' which figure as political borders, and asks whether such seminal works as Synge's *Aran Islands* (pastoral),[20] Kavanagh's *The Great Hunger* (anti-pastoral), and Montague's *The Rough Field* are 'not to be regarded just as "occasional twitches"' before finishing the essay with the ironic question 'Or are these latter works held at bay in the term "frontier pastoral"?' (1980: 180). Conceptually, this notion of a frontier has resonances of Derrida's idea of the fluid and permeable borderlines of a text: both writers stress the value of writing in terms of breaking down rigid lines of demarcation and instead, suggesting that writing in general, and poetry in particular, exerts a deconstructive leverage over such positions of fixity.

This final irony is instructive, as his earlier dialectical interpenetration of text and context demonstrated that the English pastoral had already crossed temporal, political and linguistic frontiers in appropriating Latin and French translations from classical antiquity into a specifically English landscape. However, to adopt another 'perspective backwards', the origin of the master trope of the pastoral was, as Barrell and Bull (1975) have noted, the Eden myth, which, together with classical dreams of a Golden Age 'lies behind most versions of pastoral' (Heaney 1980: 175). Here again, frontiers of language and culture have been crossed by the genre. So his question is, why stop at this particular frontier? If the genre has been sufficiently fluid to engage with the classics and the Bible, perhaps it is also capable of engaging with more modern sensibilities.

The frontier, denotative of a spatial binary opposition between one notion of place and another, functions here as both a borderline of the anthology, and at the same time, as a point of possibility which will allow the 'English' pastoral as genre, to develop. In a further expansion of these limits, this development would necessitate an ongoing problematisation of the notion of Englishness in the title, as now, some form of 'Irishness' would be included. Of course, as Heaney has already noted, the final poem in the anthology is Yeats's *Ancestral Houses* (Heaney 1980: 177), so there has already been a crossing of the 'frontier pastoral'. It becomes clear, then, that his reading of the conventions of the pastoral becomes quite unconventional in its implications and in its reading practice. What we see are what Hillis Miller, in his discussion of anastomosis, terms a variety of 'crossings, displacements, and substitutions, as inside becomes outside, outside inside, or as features on either side cross over the wall, membrane or partition dividing the sides' (1987: 7), and I will argue that such transgressive and transgenerative crossings of frontiers are a central feature in Heaney's epistemology of poetry.[21] Indeed, Derrida, in 'Living On: Borderlines' probes the epistemology of the border between text and context in a broadly analogous manner, as he talks about borders in terms of permeability, noting that no context is 'saturatable any more', and that 'no border is guaranteed, inside or out' (1987: 78).[22]

Hence, for Heaney, the two poles of an opposition, as exemplified here by text and context, are never simply set down in isolation; nor are they placed in a dialectic which produces a definite synthesis.

Instead, his work produces readings which set up a relationship which is fluid and interactive, and in which both terms interact and reflect each other.[23] This relationship is what Theodor Adorno would term a *Kraftfeldt* (force-field), which contains transactional and dialectical interplay of different, and sometimes opposing, forces, and which is comprised of juxtaposed clusters of changing elements that, according to Martin Jay, 'resist reduction to a common denominator, essential core, or generative first principle' (1984: 15).

In a manner that is strikingly analogous to the thinking of Heaney, Derrida has described a similar process, in *Positions*, where what he terms 'undecidables' inhabit an opposition, 'resisting and disorganising it, *without ever* constituting a third term, without ever leaving room for a solution in the form of speculative dialectics' (1981a: 43). The answers which Heaney's enabling searches find are often similar 'undecidables', which encourage us to probe the interstices of the text, and the 'network of textual referrals to *other* texts' where each term is 'marked by the trace of another term' (Derrida 1981a: 33). Politically, this makes Heaney's writing highly significant as he is attempting, in both poetry and prose, to problematise simplistic concepts of identity, language and culture and instead, and by extension, to set up more fluid and complex structures where borders and limits are transformed and transgressed. Such a reading is certainly at odds with the consensus opinion of 'famous Seamus' whose work has been criticised for being a published form of 'private musing', something which is seen as far removed from any political stance (Fennell 1991: 33). However, as I will demonstrate, such readings do not take full account of the scope and complexity of Heaney's thought and writing.

To most readers, the articulation of the work of Heaney with that of Theodor Adorno, Mikhail Bakhtin and especially with that of Jacques Derrida would seem unusual, but in this study, I will show that, in terms of the central activity of Heaney's prose, there are parallels in terms of the activity of reading. There are many similarities between Heaney's preoccupying questions, and the complex reading and writing processes through which he conducts his searches for answers, and what has become termed as critical theory. This is particularly true of the work of Derrida, and a seminal aspect of this study will be the demonstration of the similarity between the theoretical projects of both writers. As well as an approach which breaks down static positions and oppositions into more fluid and economic dialectical structures, they each value a sense of responsibility to notions of alterity, and an ethical imperative towards inter-subjective truth and justice. They each also stress the importance of notions of 'play' in any system, if that system is not to become hypostasised.

Hillis Miller has made the telling assessment that deconstruction is 'nothing more or less than good reading' (1987: 10), and in a recent book on Derrida, Julian Wolfreys goes on to amplify this by suggesting that 'good reading' may well be reading which 'never avoids its responsibility, and which never falls into reading by numbers' (1998: 16). In his response to the issues and texts in his prose, Heaney's plural searches for answers means that there is never any question of reading by numbers, or of forcing texts and contexts to bend to a preconceived agenda. I would suggest that for Heaney, the notion of attenuation, of making one's response thinner, more reductive, more simple, comes close to Wolfreys's notion of 'reading by numbers'. Heaney's essays always grant the heterogeneity and complexity of the issue under discussion, and in the following chapters, I will analyse his treatment of a number of important themes in his own writing, but more importantly, in terms of writing in general, or what I have already termed a theory of poetry. In his own poems, such heterogeneous notions of identity have been a feature from the very beginning. In *Death of a Naturalist*, such liminal intersections are to be found:

> Did sea define land or land the sea?
> Each drew new meaning from the waves' collision.
> Sea broke on land to full identity. (1966: 47)

It is my contention that his work is driven by just such an integrative dimension, and this is to be found in his theory of writing, his view of the relationship between poetry and politics, his teasing out of the location of the place of writing, his comments on Irish identity, and the complexity inherent in both terms, his relationship with his fellow Nobel Laureate William Butler Yeats, his views on the ethics of writing, his sense of openness to a placing of Irishness in a broader, European context and finally, his complex symbolisation, set out in *The Redress of Poetry*, of a shape, the quincunx, which gestures towards the fluid, reflexive and complex resolution of form and theme that may provide some of the results of his 'searches for answers' to those central pre-occupying questions. This shape represents the combination of the dialectical interaction of different perspectives and the complexity of perspective and understanding, which I suggest are the hallmarks of Heaney's writing. In terms of permeation of text and context, of fluid and intersecting borders, of frontiers which are multiple and inclusive, this structure is mimetic of Heaney's epistemology of writing in general and poetry in particular: it is his *Kraftfeldt*, his field of force wherein the binary oppositions that structure the parameters of identity can be contextualised and transformed. As Blanchot observes, art embodies this transformative potential:

> In the world things are *transformed* into objects in order to be grasped, utilised, made more certain in the distinct rigor of their limits and the affirmation of a homogeneous and divisible space. But in imaginary space things are *transformed* into that which cannot be grasped. Out of use, beyond wear, they are not in our possession but are the movement of dispossession which releases us both from them and from ourselves. (1982a: 131)

Blanchot, like Heaney, sees part of the function of art as the transformation of the given perception of reality. The function of imaginary space, a concept akin to Heaney's field of force, is the transformation of the actual, and the creation of an alternative paradigm of truth and integration.

He sees poetry as a 'source of truth and at the same time a vehicle of harmony', and in terms of writing in Northern Ireland, this truth is achieved by being 'true to the negative nature of the evidence' while at the same time showing 'an affirming flame' (1995a: 193). The complex dialectical force of poetry is, for Heaney, a recusant one in terms of simplistic political or literary allegiance. Writing about an early poem of his own, 'The Other Side' (1972: 34–6), Heaney describes how a Presbyterian farmer waits until his Catholic neighbours have finished their prayers before calling in to the house. He notes that this poem was not 'fundamentally intended as a contribution to better community relations...it was about a moment of achieved grace between people with different allegiances rather than a representation of a state of constant goodwill in the country as a whole' (1995a: 194). Here, art attempts to redress, in its own way, the polarities of the political. As he puts it, the frontier between different forms of knowledge, or politics, or ideology 'is for crossing' (1995a: 203); and it is in the interstices of the weft caused by these polysemic crossings that the searches for answers are conducted. He develops this point in *Finders Keepers*:

the poem went on to play with the notion of separation, of two sides of the march drain being like the two sides of the divided community of Northern Ireland – two sides divided by the way they pray, for example, and in little subtle but real ways...by the way they speak. The poem, however, ended up suggesting that a crossing could be attempted, that stepping stones could be placed by individuals who wanted to further things. (2002: 57)

These stepping stones (and we will discuss this image at greater length in Chapter 6), served as points of liminality which allowed access to different influences; they formed a type of fluid border crossing or frontier.

The notion of the frontier also figures in his collection *The Haw Lantern*, where a poem entitled 'From the Frontier of Writing' 'evokes all the emotions entailed in the experience of oppression and also finds in that experience an analogue for the growth of conscience and consciousness' (Tobin 1998: 231). This poem, which explores the connection 'between the real and the written, experience and its representation' (Molino 1994: 191), is structurally formal, with four tercets describing a physical roadblock which then becomes transposed into a metaphor for the power of writing to transform the contextual conditions that brought it into being originally. He speaks of the 'tightness and nilness' round the 'space' as the troops 'inspect' the 'make and number' of the car, and also notes that 'everything is pure interrogation' before he is freed to go on his way (Heaney 1987: 6). The political context of this poem, the experience of being stopped at a military roadblock is balanced by four 'almost identical tercets' in which 'the poet is self-halted' (Vendler 1998: 115) at the frontier of writing. Perhaps the most important aspect of this poem is the notion of 'pure interrogation', as it is only through an ongoing self-questioning of the self by the other that any form of ethical role for poetry can be fully set out. The second part of the poem features the poet self-consciously writing about the experience of the first part, and Heaney has spoken of the poem's thematic imperative in an interview with Thomas Foster, an imperative which focuses specifically on the notions of borders and frontiers:

There's a poem called 'From the Frontier of Writing,' which uses an encounter at a roadblock, a kind of archetypal, Ulster, Catholic situation. It turns it into a parable for the inquisition and escape and freedom implicit in a certain kind of lyric poem. You know, you cross the bar and you're free into that other region. I would say that the American experience may have confirmed and assisted what I think always happens anyway as you get towards your fifties, that is a certain rethinking of yourself, a certain distance from your first self. (Foster 1989: 132–3)

For Heaney, writing has become an activity which is governed by a self-questioning, a sense of recognising the context that is creative of much of the self, yet which can also be transformed by the recreated text of the self: 'And suddenly you're through, arraigned yet freed.' He sees art as at least offering 'a vision of possible order and harmony' (Mathews 1997: 164). Interestingly, in the context of a reading of Heaney's work predicated on his ongoing searches for answers, the trope of a journey is a strong connective between the experience of the roadblock 'guarded unconcerned acceleration' and the aesthetic recreation of that experience 'the black current of a tarmac road' (Heaney 1987: 6). As Henry Hart tellingly observes, Heaney's 'inclusionary strategies ultimately indict the exclusionary ones being practiced around him' (Hart 1992: 187), and it is to these inclusionary strategies, which see frontiers or borders as liminal areas where different strands of identity can be interrogated and transformed that I now turn.

2 'Continuous Adjudication': Binary Oppositions and the Field of Force

If the searches for answers to Heaney's preoccupying questions are to be posed with any degree of consistency, then the notion of poetry *qua* poetry must be explored. His complication of the anastomosis between 'text' and 'context', already discussed in the introduction, is a pointer towards the type of knowledge which he will see poetry as possessing and projecting. In the title essay of *The Government of the Tongue*, Heaney cites the critic C. K. Stead, in conjunction with Osip Mandelstam, in terms of their criticism of the 'purveyors of ready-made meaning', and he goes on to talk about a verse 'like a metrical piston, designed to hammer sentiment or argument' into its readers. Such a poetics, with a 'strong horse-power of common-sense meaning' (1988: 91) is not what Heaney has in mind when he is speaking about poetry, or attempting to set out some form of *ars poetica*. As he puts it in *The Redress of Poetry*, poetry has to be 'a working model of inclusive consciousness. It should not simplify' (1995a: 8). One can also bring into the equation the work of Maurice Blanchot in this context. Blanchot sees one of the seminal functions of literature as literature as being that of interrogation of the norm: 'Let us suppose that literature begins at the moment when literature becomes a question' (1981: 21), and Heaney will go on to question some of the most central givens of his culture in his ongoing search for answers. Perhaps the verb is more significant than the noun in this phrase as it is the search, the process, as opposed to the answers, the product, that will concern us. As Blanchot observes, commenting on the imperative to write, the writer must: 'start immediately, and, whatever the circumstances without further scruples about beginning, means or end, proceed to action' (1981: 24). This is because, like Heaney, he feels that poetry is in essence a matter of contradiction, an 'extreme intensity of mysteries, interrogations and oppositions' (1995: 123).

Indeed simplification is the antithesis of what Heaney sees as the force of poetry, both in terms of writing and reading. If poetry is to be of value, he notes, it must avoid the 'consensus and settlement of

28

a meaning which the audience fastens on like a security blanket' (1988: 122). The problem with such a view of poetry is that the very complexity and ambiguity that are part of the force of poetry are denied and etiolated. If he is to find any answers to those initial questions in *Preoccupations*, dealing with how a poet should 'properly live and write' and analysing his relationship to 'his own voice, his own place, his literary heritage and his contemporary world' (1980: 13), then he must set out some theory of how poetry works. Hence, in this chapter, we will look in more detail at points already adduced in the introduction. If the 'security blanket' of a consensual meaning is seen as something to be avoided, perhaps the best way to proceed is not by throwing off the blanket altogether, but instead, to examine more closely the weft and weave of the textile of the blanket in order to bring out the intersections, joins and interfusions that create the blanket in question. Indeed, one is reminded of Declan Kiberd's concluding image in *Inventing Ireland*, wherein he speaks of the 'green flag' that once had been wrapped around Cathleen Ni Houlihan being replaced by: 'a quilt of many patches and colours, all beautiful, all distinct yet all connected too. No one element should subordinate or assimilate others: Irish or English, rural or urban, Gaelic or Anglo, each has its part in the pattern' (Kiberd 1995: 653).

This is also true of Heaney's own writing, as in both poetry and prose, he probes the nature and epistemology of poetry itself. In *Death of a Naturalist*, and *Door into the Dark*, there are poems about 'silent tradesmen' which are intended as 'models for the poet: as he celebrates them, so they in turn guide and sanction his craft' (Morrison 1982: 31). The transforming effect of poetry on language, identity and perception is analogous to the transformations wrought by these figures in their own world. Hence in 'The Diviner', the moment when water is discovered is imaged in strongly verbal terms: 'Spring water suddenly broadcasting / Through a green aerial its secret stations' (1966: 36), while in 'Thatcher', as the silent thatcher puts on a new thatched roof, he is seen as 'pinning down his world', and stitching together the different pieces of straw into a 'sloped honeycomb', leaving his audience 'gaping at his Midas touch' (1969: 20). In 'Churning Day', the notion of art as transforming reality is again an important trope, as 'gold flecks / began to dance', and the raw materials become 'coagulated sunlight' (1966: 21). The poetic subtext is foregrounded by the butter being compared, in the final section of the poem, to 'soft printed slabs' (1966: 22).[1]

Here, the seeming opposition between reality and representation, or between the non-literary and the literary is interrogated by the craftsmen as poetic archetypes. It is not that these are seen as 'folksy' but rather that they participate in the field of force within which poetry is operative. At no stage is poetry seen as in some way removed from the world; instead, its mode of operation is transformative in that it changes our perception of that world. All of the active subjects in these seemingly simple poems are operative within their environment, and responsible for significant developments and changes therein. This is a paradigm which will be further developed as Heaney's art develops. As in his seminal poem 'Digging', where spade and pen become analogues of each other, a revisioning of action is at stake, and the dichotomy between physical and intellectual labour, while not subsumed, nevertheless is encompassed within a new structure where the perspective has changed, and the binarism is recontextualised within a more fluid structure, like Kiberd's woven patchwork quilt.

In terms of such a weave, the mode of its creation is that of a loom with a shuttle which moves back and forth creating the solidity of the blanket through the intermeshing of the skeins of threads. This metaphor is relevant to Heaney's own theoretical processes as in his earlier writing, the dialectical cut and thrust of poetry is a major theme. In *Preoccupations*, for example, one of the main discursive strategies that Heaney undertakes in his discussion of texts or their socio-political contexts, is the uncovering of binary oppositions.[2] Much of Heaney's thought revolves around such dualisms and binarisms. Writing about different types of poetry, he speaks of masculine and feminine strains (1980: 34), and later he divides the activity up into craft and technique (1980: 47). Still later, speaking of the work of Wordsworth and Yeats, he invokes Valéry's definition of two kinds of poetry, *les vers donnés* and *les vers calculés* (1980: 61), and he goes on to contrast the poetry of Wordsworth and Yeats in terms of the binaries of 'complaisance' and 'control' (1980: 71). Writing about Ireland, and the political situation in Ulster, he uses a similar vocabulary, seeing Ireland as associated with the feminine and England with the masculine. He also sees the tension between poetry which is 'secret and natural' and the world in which it must make its way 'that is public and brutal', and notes the opposition between the 'old vortex of racial and religious instinct' and 'the mean of humane love and reason' (1980: 34). In Heaney's poetry, such structures also inhere: one thinks of the bipartite divisions in *Wintering Out, North,*

Seeing Things, and *Electric Light*; of the Greek/Trojan binarism in *The Cure at Troy*, of the Irish/English binarisms of *Beowulf*, of the pagan/Christian conflict in *Sweeney Astray*, of the north/south binarisms that feature in *Field Work* and of the general tendency to look at different sides of an issue: 'Two buckets were easier carried than one / I grew up in between' (1987: 5).

Neil Corcoran, speaking of these, notes what he calls a 'tendency to over-schematic or even specious binary thinking' (1986: 230), and seems to see it as a type of defect in Heaney's writing. Possibly because such binarisms call to mind the work of Derrida, Corcoran is inclined to see them as negative, given his placement of Heaney's prose in the mould of New Criticism, which in turn, he sees as descending from Romanticism. In this vein, he goes on to deplore Heaney's occasional use of terms such as 'empowered', 'heuristic' and transgressive' seeing them as in some way a dilution of the 'individuality of Heaney's critical lexicon' (1986: 228).[3] For Corcoran, Heaney's 'critical consciousness of Wordsworth makes his basic conceptions of poetry essentially Romantic ones' (1986: 229).[4]

To take this standpoint is to attenuate the complexity of Heaney's own poetic epistemology. It is also to deny Heaney's work as part of the theorising of literary studies that was coterminous with Heaney's own education in literature and his writing career. The influence of structuralist and poststructuralist theory, with its overt use of examinations of cognitive, linguistic and societal structures in terms of binary oppositions, has clearly been operative in Heaney's own mindset. Instead of locating him in terms of the new critics, it would seem more valuable to see him as participative in the theoretical project of re-envisaging the role of literature in terms of political and ethical effects. Heaney's binarisms, far from being overschematic, instead attempt to give value to the alterity of experience, and of poetic experience in particular. Corcoran, by attempting to place Heaney's writing in a Romantic–New Critical paradigm as opposed to a Modernist–Postmodernist one, misses the interaction of these binarisms that is so important to the structure of Heaney's thinking. For Heaney, the notion of poetry as a mode of knowledge is one which partakes of multiple perspectives, as evidenced in his polyglossic enunciation of different voices in *North*.[5] To write about the experience of Northern Ireland, without succumbing to sectarian atavism is, of necessity, to inhabit some form of binarism. Such binarisms however, are used dynamically and constructively, as opposed to statically, to create the complex weave of interconnections and intersections which are the results of his searches for answers.

This becomes clear when we look at the primal binarisms that define Northern Ireland – Catholic and Protestant; nationalist and unionist; republican and loyalist; Irish and British; green and orange – and examine how these are treated in the Heaney aesthetic. He has given us an educative insight into the development of this type of thought-process which highlights the dynamic oscillatory structure that defines his transformative notions of dialectical knowledge. To put it another way, what Corcoran is describing may be imagined as the security blanket which was adduced earlier in our discussion; a simple covering device with little complexity attached, on first sight. However, Heaney will demonstrate that, on closer inspection, this woven material is comprised of numerous criss-crossings and inter-sections of threads which face in different directions, processes analogous to the complexities of dialectical thought.

In *Among Schoolchildren*[6] Heaney spoke about a great-aunt of his, Catherine Bradley, and about an example of her school needlework, from 1843. This included the following verse, embroidered on her 'sampler':

> Ireland as she ought to be
> Great glorious and free
> First flower of the earth
> First gem of the sea. (1983a: 6)

The embroidery beneath this verse was of a shamrock, the traditional symbol of Ireland, but 'squeezed to the right of the verse' were the words 'God Save the Queen' (1983a: 6). Here the prevalence of binarisms in Heaney's thought is embodied on a piece of Ulster linen. Is the imperative here, stressing how Ireland 'ought' to be, inclining to the notion of being free of British influence, as signified by the shamrock, or else of being free as part of the union between Great Britain and Ireland, as signified by the rubric 'God Save the Queen'?

Throughout this pamphlet, and in *Place and Displacement*, Heaney stresses the bifurcation of ideologies and identities that have marked his growth. From learning about Jane Austen, Tennyson and Lawrence and from attending sherry parties at the house of a professor in Queen's University who hailed from Oxford,[7] to acting with the Bellaghy Dramatic Society, and playing the parts of a United Irishman and Robert Emmett (1983a: 7),[8] we see someone who is being influenced by both the Irish and British aspects of Ulster culture. In many cases, such binarisms were expressed in antagonistic tones of self and other, or us and them. For Heaney, as he puts it, the exposure to aspects of both cultures, brought about an uncertainty in terms of cultural and ideological identification.[9] The physical oscillation between weekly exposure to English literature, 'the elegances of Oscar Wilde and the profundities of Shakespeare' and the weekend, with its religious devotions in the chapel, and acting as *fear a' tigh* at the GAA *ceilidhs*[10] has its psychical and identificatory effect in a number of questions which are broadly coterminous with those preoccupying questions with which we began our discussion. Heaney asks:

> Was I two persons or one? Was I extending myself or breaking myself apart? Was I being led out or led away? Was I failing to live up to the aspiring literary intellectual effort when I was at home, was I betraying the culture of the parish when I was at the university? (1983a: 8)

In this discussion, Heaney is probing the conditions of subjectivity and identity, as the 'I' of the poem is caught between different forces which must, of necessity, change and alter it. As Derrida has pointed out, all subjects are imbricated in this play of signification:

> Nothing – no present and in-*different* being – thus precedes *différance* and spacing. There is no subject who is agent, author, and master of *différance*, who eventually and empirically would be overtaken by *différance*. Subjectivity – like objectivity – is an effect of *différance*, an effect inscribed in a system of *différance*. (Derrida 1981a: 28)

For Derrida, the subject is constituted in language by this 'economy of traces' (1981a: 29), and he goes on to say that the economic aspect of *différance* confirms that the speaking subject is constituted by the division from itself, through the movement of *différance*, in language, and to agree with Saussure that language, which consists only of differences, 'is not a function of the speaking subject' (Derrida 1981a: 29). Heaney, by his exposure to different linguistic and cultural discourses, feels himself pulled in different directions, and finds that the seeming core of his identity has become fractured.

Given the linguistic context of this sense of fracture in subjectivity, it would seem that language can also be the vehicle where such
a sense of fracture can be seen as positive, allowing for development
and change within the parameters of identity. The differential aspects
of language and meaning, the lack of teleology in discourse, is what
is being explored by Heaney, and this locates his work within the
postmodern and poststructuralist paradigms in terms of a wariness
about the referentiality of language: as Jacques Lacan has observed
that 'we are forced, then, to accept the notion of an incessant sliding
of the signified under the signifier' (Lacan 1977: 154). Hence, there
is strong theoretical warrant for Heaney's musings on the different
traces of his origins and modes of identity.

This view of the poet as being situated within a linguistic and social
matrix has important implications for textual study, implications
that have been summarised by Roland Barthes when he sees texts as
sites of hermeneutic intersection rather than the release of a single
'theological' meaning (Barthes 1979, in Lodge 1988: 170). The 'I' (and
here, there are major implications for the lyric 'I'), stands at the axis
of signifier and signified, a split being, never able to give its position
a full presence. The unconscious play with meaning is revealed,
according to Freudian and Lacanian theory, in dreams, jokes and art.
The subject of the enounced is never fully able to stand in for the
subject of the enunciation who in turn is never able to give full,
conscious expression to him or herself through language. Heaney's
interrogations of subjectivity and language are very much in keeping
with this theme of the creation of subjectivity through language.

The preconditions which set up this questioning are defined in
terms of spatial and temporal oscillations. Temporally, he spent the
weekdays of term at Queen's University studying English literature
and becoming enculturated into the middle-class, literary, cultured
ethos that is signified by 'sherry parties on the Malone Road'. At
'weekends and during the holidays' he was immersed in Catholic,
rural, Gaelic, nationalist social and cultural *mores*. Spatially, he
oscillated between city and country, Belfast and Bellaghy, the
academy and the parish. This physical movement, constituted in
time and space, serves as a paradigm for the psychical and cognitive
motion of what I term Heaney's epistemology of poetry. It informs
statements which see the poet as being 'displaced from a confidence
in a single position by his disposition to be affected by all positions,
negatively rather than positively capable' (1985a: 8) as transgressive
in terms of experiential knowledge and epistemological paradigm.

In terms of temporal and spatial movements in different directions, there is an immediate similarity between Heaney's psychic and cultural subjective bifurcation, and Derrida's notion (and neologism) of *différance*. Derrida has coined this term, substituting an *'a'* for the second *'e'* of *'difference'*, to explain what he sees as the deconstruction of meaning in terms of a simple self-presence. His point is that, in any system, the meaning of each individual element is neither unified nor self-present. Instead, it is created through a twin process of differentiation from other elements and a deferral until some point of closure. For example, in the practice of reading, the meaning of any one term is different from the others, and deferred until the end of a clause, or of a sentence, or of a paragraph or of a book. As Derrida puts it, 'no element can function as a sign without referring to another element which itself is not simply present'; hence this interweaving results in each element being constituted 'on the basis of the trace within it of the other elements of the chain or system' (1981a: 26). The *'a'* in *différance* denotes the temporal and spatial dimensions of the term which are so similar to Heaney's oscillation, what Derrida terms '*différance* as temporisation, *différance* as spacing' (1982: 9).

It is obvious that such a process is analogous to what is being described by Heaney in his description of being pulled in different directions in terms of seeking cultural norms of meaning. The difference between Belfast and Bellaghy is enunciated in spatial and temporal vectors; the persona of Heaney himself is being created by the differential pulls of both, as well as by a constant process of deferral in terms of a final flash of self-present knowledge. The opposing forces were taking him in different directions, but were also setting down the parameters of a cognitive structure which comes close to that of *différance*. Geoffrey Bennington makes the point that *différance*, if thought of as a force, can only be seen in terms of the 'tension between at least two forces' (Bennington and Derrida 1993: 82). In Heaney's case, it is the differential interaction between the forces signified by Belfast and Bellaghy that help to form his notions of poetry as a cognitive structure which is capable of including different forces. When we come to examine his notion of poetry as a field of force, we will see that this field is analogous to Derrida's suggestion that when speaking of the different terms of an identity, be that of the self, or of a culture, then 'each of the terms must appear as the *différance* of the other, as the other different and deferred in the economy of the same' (1982: 17). In terms of

Corcoran's discussion of the binary oppositions in Heaney's writing, what is becoming clear is that a deconstructive position is being introduced wherein the binary oppositions themselves are less important than the process of their interaction, an interaction that will become transformative of the context within which these oppositions exist.

Such identificatory oscillations and bifurcations are also definitive in terms of Derrida's notion of selfhood, living in Algeria, but speaking French, and, as the following passage will indicate, this constitutes a further connection between the thought of both of these writers. Derrida, while living in Algeria, learned French as his only language and yet was acutely aware that 'all of this came from a history and a milieu that were not in a simple and primitive way mine' (Derrida 1995: 120). Derrida's notions of *différance*, and his breaking down of seeming unities and totalities, has much in common with Heaney's view of poetry as the articulation of different forces within some form of structure which can reveal more aspects of the self to the self. In this sense, Heaney's cultural hybridity has definite similarities with that of Derrida. Derrida's sense of alienation from the given matrix of identity: 'the Frenchman of France was an other' (1995: 204) has much in common with Heaney's view of being led out or led away. In *The Other Heading*, Derrida speaks of himself as someone 'not quite European by birth' (1992b: 7), and goes on to pose the question as to whether one is 'more faithful to the heritage of a culture by cultivating the difference-to-oneself (*with oneself*) that constitutes identity' (1992b: 11).

In a passage that is remarkably similar, Heaney too speaks of feelings of strangeness and alienation in connection with place and language. Writing in *Preoccupations* he points out that he has maintained a notion of himself 'as Irish in a province that insists it is British' (1980: 35), and goes on to further underscore his sense of difference in the following statement:

> I speak and write in English, but do not altogether share the pre-occupations and perspectives of an Englishman. I teach English literature, I publish in London, but the English tradition is not ultimately home. I live off another hump as well. (1980: 34)

Here, we see the similar sense of the *Unheimlich* invading the seeming certainties of the *Heimlich*. Both writers inhabit a liminal space which allows them to see difference, rather than sameness, as a criterion of definition in terms of notions of singular and communal identity.

Both writers, in other words, have taken a physical progression, Heaney from County Derry to Belfast, and Derrida from Algeria to France, with its attendant cultural problematics, and transformed it into a cognitive dialectical epistemology of identity. This progression from physical movement to dialectical cognition is a feature of 'Digging', the opening poem of *Death of a Naturalist* and the first poem where he felt his 'feelings had got into words' (1980: 41). Here the experiential practice of digging into earth becomes transformed into an epistemological paradigm of an artesian imagination as well as of an unearthing of new experiences through the process of upturning the givens of the surface so as to create 'opened ground', in terms of ideas and worldviews.[11] In other words, rather than seeing the act of writing as merely descriptive of the actuality of experience, both Heaney and Derrida instead see writing as creative of the contexts of that experience. This poem also signifies the importance of a particular relationship with memory in Heaney's writing.

Hence, his dialectical relationship is the defining factor in his epistemology of poetry in that it allows him to set up transformative and transgressive structures which he sees as answering his own complex position in terms of the knowledge or truth-claims of poetry. That Heaney figures his growth to maturity in this lecture through such binary oppositions does not place him as some sort of proto-deconstructionist, nor does it presage some form of 'reading by numbers' schematicisation of experience.[12] Instead, such binarisms, as we will see, are part of a dialectical mode of thought which is ethical in its mode of operation. To be affected by all positions is to acquire some form of negative knowledge inasmuch as one can see that neither position has a monopoly on truth or right, and also that one has some form of ethical responsibility to this other; it involves a responsibility to the thought of the other. It also involves an ongoing process of critique, what John D. Caputo calls a questioning dialogue of homologia by heterologia (1993: 113).[13]

Ethics, in the sense of the word as used by Emmanuel Levinas, envisions a sense of responsibility to the other, to forms of alterity which are outside the self, as a primary facet of human discourse.[14] Derrida has made the point, in *Of Spirit*, that the origin of language is responsibility (1989a: 132) in the sense that to speak is to speak to someone else, to assume a responsibility of addressing some other person. In a binary opposition, something is defined in terms of the other, and as such, can be placed in an ethical context by taking note of the differences and connections between self and other. It is what Heaney terms the notion of 'needing to accommodate two opposing notions of truthfulness simultaneously' (1985: 4), the very condition which has been emblematically rendered in Catherine Bradley's embroidery sampler, where 'two value systems, which now explode daily, are lodged like dormant munitions' on one piece of Ulster linen (1983a: 6).

I would suggest that Heaney's writing will dislodge these positions so as to bring out the etymological senses of 'munition' as a fortification ('*munitio-onis*') and as ammunition, but also its cognate term 'muniment', meaning a document entailing rights or privileges. Two sets of fortified rights and privileges are exactly what is signified by the shamrock and the slogan on the sampler, and both have munimental designs on the notion of 'Ulster' in that piece of Ulster linen. By dislodging these fortifications, Heaney is, symbolically, bringing these documents into dialectical interaction. It is worth keeping in mind that the term 'dialectic' originates from the Greek '*dialektos*', meaning discourse or conversation. The verb διαλεγοηαι (*dialegomai*) means 'to converse', but δια (*dia*) means 'through', or 'against' or 'because of', and λεγο (*lego*) means 'to speak', so there is another oscillation set up etymologically. The sampler is a mimetic example of this process in Heaney's epistemology of writing, as he sets up an oscillation between the two positions found on this piece of Ulster linen, an oscillation which parallels his physical oscillation, and which will allow these sets of rights and privileges to 'speak through' or 'speak against' or 'speak because of' each other in a structure which embodies what we have already seen of *différance*.

The proper adjective 'Ulster' is significant here. In *Place and Displacement: Recent Poetry in Northern Ireland*,[15] delivered in 1984, Heaney makes it clear that to be a writer in Ulster is to be very much in two minds, to be 'in two places at once', to be aware that he or she belongs to a place 'that is patently riven between notions of belonging to other places' (1985: 4). This view of place as inhabited by oppositions pulling in different directions puts an obligation, or responsibility, on the writer to delineate the positions – ideological, social, political and cultural – of his or her own grouping (self), as well as that of the 'other', in a place where the whole population are adepts in the 'mystery of living in two places at one time' (1995a: 190). To define the identificatory parameters, the muniments, of each group is not as simple as it might first seem, as there are complex equations and intersections which are both mutually exclusive and at the same time, mutually intertwined. These notions form parts of the weave that his dialectical *mentalité* will outline.

Ulster, as he notes, is just such a complex series of threads in this weave. As he puts it, the nationalist will 'wince at the Union Jack and "God Save the Queen" as tokens of his place in the world', but for the unionist, with whom the nationalist conducts his daily life, these emblems have 'pious and passionate force' (1985: 4).[16] Heaney goes on to demonstrate the further complex imbrications and dualities of identity in Northern Ireland:

> The fountainhead of the Unionist's myth, springs in the Crown of England, but he has to hold his own in the island of Ireland. The fountainhead of the Nationalist's myth lies in the idea of an integral Ireland, but he too lives in an exile from his ideal place. Yet while he has to concede that he is a citizen of the partitioned British state, the Nationalist can hold to the physical fact of his presence upon the Irish island, just as the Unionist can affirm the reality of political realm of the United Kingdom even as he recognises the geographical fact that Ireland is his insular home.[17] (1985: 5)

Here we do not see Corcoran's notion of schematic binaries at work; instead we see the careful delineation of a complex series of oppositions which are placed in an evolving structure which attempts to set up some form of dialectical conversation between them. There is a careful weighing of the nuances of each position, seen in terms of its similarity with the other side of the equation. As Hans-Georg Gadamer puts it, the presence of the other 'before whom we stand helps to break up our own bias and narrowness' (1981: 26), and this can be seen as part of Heaney's searches for answers. There is no attenuation of either position here; both sets of oppositions are placed within a structure which allows them to interrogate each other.

Simon Critchley has argued that there is a 'duty' in Derrida's terms, to produce a reading that commands respect insofar as it opens an 'irreducible dimension of alterity' (1992: 41), and I would suggest that Heaney's thought is aimed at achieving such a respect for alterity. His binary oppositions invariably interact and intersect so as to create some form of text or structure wherein they can mutually inform each other. This is not to say that Heaney is setting out to create some post-Hegelian synthesis which will 'lure the tribal shoals to epigram / And order' (1975: 59). As we have already seen, in both his reading of the genre of pastorality and of the multiform notions of identity in Northern Ireland, he realises that such simplicity of synthesis is just not possible, given the many layers and levels which construct the complex weave which dialectical shuttling sets up. The many layers interact at different levels as they attempt to give figuration to the different interstices as nodal points in the delineation of the knowledge that poetry, and the reading of poetry, can bring to bear on issues of life and art. Hence, his readings of poetry and of notions of identity, share the same complex structurations, and strive to produce an epistemology of poetry which does justice to the complexity and ethicity that are central to its operation.

In his poetry, this probing of the structurations of meaning has been a constitutive strand from the beginning. In 'Alphabets', in *The Haw Lantern*, Heaney has traced the progression from reality to representation in terms of a sign-producing function, beginning with his father making a shadow 'like a rabbit's head' with his 'joined hands', and with the letters of the alphabet being compared to objects from his early known world:[18]

> Then draws the forked stick that they call a Y.
> This is writing. A swan's neck and swan's back
> Make the 2 he can see now as well as say.
>
> Two rafters and a cross-tie on the slate
> Are the letters some call *ah*, some call *ay*. (1987: 1)

The pre-given nature of these signs, the seeming naturalness of their adequation with the known world is gradually deconstructed as the poem progresses. Different writing systems – Gaelic, Latin, Greek, Merovingian – take their place within his developing consciousness, inscribing their differential structures within his sense of self, and further broadening the field of force which becomes the 'I' of the poem. Whereas at the beginning, systems of signification were seen in terms of the experientially familiar, by the end of the poem, the familiar objects of his home are now envisaged through the sign-systems which have been part of his education:

> Balers drop bales like printouts where stooked sheaves
>
> Make lambdas on the stubble once at harvest
> And the delta face of each potato pit. (1987: 3)

By the end of the poem, the notion that our selfhood is predicated by our language and systems of discourse is made explicit as an astronaut is seen as looking back at the earth from space in terms of its being an 'aqueous, singular, lucent O' (1987: 3). Here, there is a desire to escape from the binary logic through some form of contextual framework which foregrounds the arbitrariness of language and the constructedness of reality and ideology.

Historically, Heaney's preoccupation with binaries and dualities can be traced back to formative poetic and rhythmic experiences, which he discusses in *Preoccupations*. In *Mossbawn*, he points out the different types of poetry that influenced him, beginning with rhymes from his schooldays featuring a character called Neddy McGuigan or Dirty-Faced McGuigan who 'pissed in the Quigan / The Quigan was hot / So he pissed in the pot', as well as more ideologically centred rhymes: 'Up the long ladder and down the short rope / To hell with King Billy and God bless the Pope' (the answer to this being 'Up with King William and down with the Pope') (1980: 25). Here, the sectarian divide is captured in what might be termed subcultural poetry, but interestingly both traditions are set down together. Indeed, the rhythmic and prosodic similarity of the two couplets sees both traditions as placed in a mutually defining, if antagonistic, structure, with King William being defined in contradistinction to the Pope, and vice versa. The same mutuality of definition is clear from the other two poems quoted, one suggesting that 'Paypishes' (Catholics) should be 'cut in two' with the answering verse suggesting that it is 'red, white and blue' which should be 'torn up in two' (1980: 25). This type of oppositional writing is also found in early stages of Heaney's work, as in 'Docker', where the eponymous Protestant worker ('The only Roman collar he tolerates / Smiles all round his sleek pint of porter') is seen as violently opposed to his other: 'That fist would drop a hammer on a Catholic' (1966: 41). The same perspective is clear in 'Orange Drums, Tyrone 1966', where self and other are conflictually defined, with the lambeg drum, an instrument traditionally associated with Protestant celebrations of William of Orange's victory in the Battle of the Boyne in 1690. In this poem, as in the rhymes being discussed, there is little complication or interrogation; instead the other is defined in terms redolent of evil and disease:

> It is the drums preside, like giant tumours.
> To every cocked ear, expert in its greed,
> His battered signature subscribes 'No Pope'. (1972: 68)

The binary perspective is writ large in this poem, with the image chain leaving no room for any interaction or intersection between selfhood and alterity.

We seem to be back in the weave of Catherine Bradley's sampler here, with the binarisms being sketched out in bold lines of difference, and the memory of the poet oscillating between them. In this case, we might, perhaps, agree with Corcoran's criticism of the flatness of the binary opposition, and the overschematic nature of the verses. Here, there seems to be no sense of dialectical interaction between the two. This is because these rhymes are separate from the present tense of the voice of the essay. The 'I' describing these poems is not involved in any of them; they are remembered from a distance, and serve as signifiers of a childish sense of rhyme, which merely enunciates the sense of the group to which the rhymester belonged. There is no sense of responsibility or adjudication between the positions; each set of rhymes delineates the security blanket of each tradition. To recall an earlier comment from *The Redress of Poetry*, this type of poetry is *not* 'a working model of inclusive consciousness'; here, this type of poetry *does* simplify; self is self, other is other and there can be no middle ground between them.

In an essay entitled 'Christmas, 1971', a more complex interaction is foregrounded by the voice of the poet himself as the *locus* of the interaction. Writing about the role of the artist in the face of the political confrontation in Belfast in 1971,[19] Heaney again sees the situation in terms of binaries, but now, we see a far more dynamic structure of thought, as well as a more ethical concern with the correctness of the choices being made. He says that he is 'fatigued by a continuous adjudication between agony and injustice, swung at one moment by the long tail of race and resentment, at another by the more acceptable feelings of pity and terror' (1980: 30). Here, the physicality of the original oscillation between cultural and ideological poles is restated in the verb of motion 'swung'; the poet is struggling to control these forces of 'race and resentment' as opposed to those of 'pity and terror', as they swing him from one to the other, giving him little chance to pause in a space between.

Perhaps the most important words in this passage are 'continuous adjudication'. The interaction of active and passive voices in this passage outlines the complexity of the struggle that is ongoing within the culture, and within the poet. There are two levels involved here, both of which reflect back on each other. Firstly, he is involved in continually adjudicating between agony and injustice, and the nature of the stated weariness is that while attempting to exercise the cognitive faculty of judgement, he is also (and here we see the second level) being 'swung' by events over which he seems to have no control, the external political and violent actions which occurred in Belfast in 1971.

That the adjudication here is continuous would imply that the terms are never finally defined, in contradistinction to the perspective of 'Docker' or 'Orange Drums, Tyrone 1966'. An example of the poetic exemplification of this paradigm is to be found in one of Heaney's later translations, *The Midnight Verdict*. In this poem, Heaney demonstrates how differential and fluid his notions of selfhood are. Speaking about the impulse to translate, he notes:

> The three translations included here were all part of a single impulse. 'Orpheus and Eurydice' was done in June 1993, just before I began to prepare a lecture on *Cúirt an Mheán Oíche* (1780) for the Merriman Summer School. Then, in order to get to closer grips with the original, I started to put bits of the Irish into couplets and, in doing so, gradually came to think of the Merriman poem in relation to the story of Orpheus, and in particular the story of his death as related by Ovid. The end of *The Midnight Court* took on a new resonance when read within the acoustic of the classical myth, and this gave me the idea of juxtaposing the Irish poem (however drastically abridged) with the relevant passages from Ovid's *Metamorphoses*. (2000a: 11)

In this case, the notion of a poetry that should not simplify is the imperative behind this fluid structure. Structurally the book is a triptych, with Ovid framing the two sections from Merriman, a structure he first used in *Field Work* in the poem entitled 'Triptych', and the fluidity of the interaction between Greek and Irish myths is synecdochic of the mature Heaney's notion of art as a field of force which can contain oppositional and parallel structures. Just as in 'Alphabets', different structures of signification became part of the selfhood of the 'I' of the poem, so now, different cultural myths serve to locate atavisms and oppositions within a broader context. The importance of this structure, highlighted by the adjective 'continuous' in the term 'continuous adjudication', is that it is fluid, dialectical and transformative. It is the relational intersubjectivity of these structures that makes them paradigmatic of Heaney's concept of the force of writing in general, and of poetry in particular.

At a further level of discourse, the atavisms which are ratified by a group consciousness, those of race and resentment, are placed in a binary opposition with those of pity and terror, terms which also have a literary resonance. The terms 'pity' and 'terror' are, of course, part of Aristotle's definition of tragedy in his *Poetics*,[20] but they are also to be found in James Joyce's *A Portrait of the Artist as a Young Man*. In the fifth chapter, Stephen tells Lynch that: 'Aristotle has not defined pity and terror. I have.' He goes on:

> Pity is the feeling which arrests the mind in the presence of whatsoever is grave and constant in human sufferings and unites it with the human sufferer. Terror is the feeling which arrests the mind in the presence of whatsoever is grave and constant in human sufferings and unites it with the secret cause. (1916: 178)

Hence, Heaney's continuous adjudication is a multiform complex process, adjudicating between different political, ideological and ethical choices, while at the same time, adjudicating between the different fields of force of 'pity and terror'. Hence there is a question as to whether he is speaking about pity for victims and terror in the face of atrocities, or whether he is speaking about the Joycean aesthetic categories that Stephen is torturously working out, and their role within the context of Belfast in 1971? Is it possible that the 'secret cause' of which Stephen speaks is what Heaney, in *Kinship*, refers to as the 'appetites of gravity' (1975: 43), namely an unadjudicated yielding to the gravitational pull of the tail of race and resentment? Perhaps the terror here is that he feels the racial resentment overcoming the emotions of pity for victims who are not part of his own group. Is there here the dawning of the consciousness that, at some level, he is part of a group, of a 'we' or 'us' for whom the 'other' will always be a focus of our terror but never a recipient of our pity?:

> And you, Tacitus...
>
> report us fairly,
> how we slaughter
> for the common good
>
> and shave the heads
> of the notorious,
> how the goddess swallows
> our love and terror. (1975: 45)

For the voice of this poem, there is no process of adjudication, continuous or otherwise; here there is complete symphysis between agony, injustice, race, resentment and terror on the part of the 'I' of the poem, with possibly Tacitus providing some degree of pity.[21]

The organic figuration of these emotions, in a nexus of blood-sacrifice to a personified notion of the land, is hardly accidental, as many theories of race stem from an anthropomorphisation of characteristics and places so as to construct a *mythos* of the self.[22] Heaney's metaphor of being 'swung' by the 'long tail' represents the atavistic, visceral emotions that were rife in Belfast at this time. Members of Heaney's own community were slaughtering for the 'common good', even as he was writing, and this internecine violence, itself both caused by, and creative of, a binary opposition, foregrounded questions about the nature and function of art. The issue under adjudication appears to be that seminal preoccupying question: 'how should a poet properly live and write?' in such times (1980: 13); an issue which, in its probing of the relationship between politics and aesthetics, reminds us of the earlier anastomosis between text and context.

The etymology of 'adjudicate' helps to clarify the issue at this point. Stemming from the Latin *'judicare'*, the original composite was *'jus'* (law) and *'dicere'* (to say), the word highlights Heaney's difficulty in continually attempting to 'say the law' of proper aesthetic, ethical and political action in the face of a violent contemporary context.[23] Of necessity, such adjudication will be dialectical, it will create a *locus* for the enunciation of the concerns of self and other without necessarily succumbing to the atavisms of either group. As he puts it, the locating of one's identity in 'the ethnic and liturgical habits of one's group' is all very well, but for that group to 'confine the range of one's growth, to have one's sympathies determined and one's responses programmed' by that group, is clearly a 'form of entrapment' (1985: 6–7), an entrapment whose consequences are enunciated clearly in the lines already cited from *Kinship*, and whose prevalence is clear from the 'swung by the tail' metaphor, as individuals become trapped in ideological atavisms.

His adjudication on this issue is first spoken in an essay aptly entitled 'Feeling into Words', where he teases out the different roles of a poet who is attempting to 'properly live and write'. He points to a crucial period, when the 'original heraldic murderous encounter between Protestant yeoman and Catholic rebel'[24] was 'initiated again' in the Summer of 1969, in Belfast.[25] In this *context*, the epistemology of the *texts* of poetry became clear and consisted of becoming a 'search for images and symbols adequate to our predicament' (1980: 56). The performative nature of this activity, a 'search' as opposed to a destination, resonates with his original 'searches for answers', and is qualified directly in terms of what such symbols and images should *not* be:

> I do not mean liberal lamentation that citizens should feel compelled to murder one another or deploy their different military arms over the matter of nomenclatures such as British or Irish. I do not mean public celebrations or execrations of resistance or atrocity – although there is nothing necessarily unpoetic about such a celebration, if one thinks of Yeats's 'Easter 1916'.[26] (1980: 56)

The difficulty Heaney has with both of these epistemological positions is that they both demand a suspension of the faculty of adjudication, and of the notion of searches for some form of inter-subjective truth. In both of the above positions, poetry is very much in the service of the actual; it functions as, at best, reportage, and at worst, as a sort of poetic licence for the barbarities of sectarian hatred.

In the first of these, poetry is attenuated in that it must maintain the note of lamentation which precludes any spontaneous joy or creativity on the part of the writer. As Heaney puts it in *The Government of the Tongue*: 'art does not trace the given map of a better reality but improvises an inspired sketch of it' (1988: 94). Liberal lamentation is of necessity, *post factum*, it is dependent on the actual material situation of politics and violence. In this sense, it is mimetic of one of the meanings Heaney suggests for his resonant title *The Government of the Tongue*, where the tongue is governed by the quotidian, where one is told to govern one's tongue, with the implication of a '*denial* of the tongue's autonomy and permission'. Here, ironically, liberal lamentation, a lamentation that seems to achieve a position of transcendence with respect to the sectarian atavisms of race and resentment, actually allows such atavisms to dictate the nature of such liberal discourse. For a poet or writer, such an epistemology can leave poetry in a 'relatively underprivileged situation, requiring it to take a position that is secondary to religious truth or state security or public order' (1988: 96).

As we have seen in the introduction, such simplifications of writing and reading are the very attenuations that Heaney wishes to avoid, as they in no way facilitate any complex searches after answers.

This attenuated view of poetry suggests that answers must be in response to events, and hence, will be dictated by those events. Similarly, such a position excludes any mythological dimension to poetry. As Heaney demonstrated in *North*, an exploration of the *mythos* that underwrites sectarian constitutions of identity can be a powerful tool in the unpacking of such identities.[27] He sees the role of writing as more than such an event-driven response which must be belated with respect to actuality.

The second position with which he takes issue is that of poetry as a celebration or execration of resistance or atrocity. Such a position places the poet firmly within his or her group or *mythos*. Here the hortatory or execratory role of the poet consists in articulating the monological vision of the tribe or group, without any notion of different perspectives or different standpoints. This monocular vision, which is at the core of *Kinship*, is creative of the subjectivities of the group. It is a vision which achieves the entrapment of consciousness already noted, as the growth of the individual is canalised by the ethnic and liturgical vision of the group. Such a position of immanence removes any power of critique from the writer, and also attenuates the complexity of any political or identificatory conflict. It denies any notion of dialectical complexity in terms of the relationship of the 'I' to the 'we'. Writing about the poetry of Osip Mandelstam, and the memoir of his life, *Hope Abandoned*, written by his wife Nadezhda, Heaney cites her views on the notion of the 'we', the community. She notes that the relationship between the 'we' and the 'I' is dialectical and fluid: '[t]o find its fulfilment, the "I" needs at least two complementary dimensions: "we" and – if it is fortunate – "you"' (1988: 76). These dimensions external to the 'I' yet also connected to it, define a notion of subjectivity that is central to Heaney's notion of the function of art.

This notion is complex, transformational, and plural in its mode of action. As he has put it elsewhere, for him, 'the "I" of the poem is at the eye of the storm within the "I" of the poet' (1985: 4), and this dialectical interaction between the seeing eye, and the subject, the 'I', is what rings true about the 'inspired sketch of reality' already mentioned as the provenance of art. The causal anastomosis between 'eye' and 'I', between vision and subjectivity, signifies an important aspect of Heaney's poetic epistemology. To see others, whether 'we' or 'you', and to take into account our relationship with them, is to embody an ethicity of writing wherein the otherness of the other is taken into account. For Heaney, this broadening of the subject is central to how poetry should achieve its aims and goals. In Gadamerian terms, it is the presence of the other which helps to 'break up our own bias and narrowness' (1981: 26). The narrowness of vision already mentioned is precisely what is being critiqued here. This monocular perspective is the antithesis of Heaney's notion of how a poet should properly live and write.[28] A single perspective will produce attenuated vision with the resultant attenuated subjectivities which can see slaughtering 'for the common good' as a defensible position. The creation of a complex and self-aware 'I' which is aware of its constituent givens but which is also conscious of the role of agency, is a crucial element in Heaney's aesthetic.

The importance of this complexity and plurality of vision that Heaney associates with poetry is underlined by his return to this image of the 'I' and the 'eye' in *The Redress of Poetry*. In an essay entitled 'Joy or Night: Last Things in the Poetry of W. B. Yeats and Philip Larkin', he is writing about Yeats's poem *The Cold Heaven*, and sees in this poem a 'sense of answerability, of responsibility' and goes on to add that 'the "I" of the poet as a first person singular, a self-knowing consciousness, is brilliantly and concretely at one with the eye of the poet as a retina overwhelmed by the visual evidence of infinity and solitude' (1995a: 149). Here again, the conflation of the subject with vision is central to Heaney's aesthetic epistemology. Answerability and responsibility to the other are central to his notion of the constitutive vision of poetry.

This dialectic between 'I' and 'eye' is an example of the rhetorical figure of a metalepsis, the creation of an effect through a remote cause. For Heaney this metaleptic structure allows him to express the complexity of vision that poetry can bring about. As I have already noted, such an epistemology is the very antithesis of simplistic and attenuating notions of subjectivity. To 'see' is to see the other, to create the 'I' with these objects of vision in mind is to act ethically. In this sense, Heaney's notion of art is broadly similar to that of Emmanuel Levinas who sees art as a 'relation with the other' (1989: 143), a position opposed to that of speaking exclusively for one's own group. Such monocularity of vision which, in turn, leads to a monological notion of subjectivity, suspends his notion of adjudication, and instead allows the poet to be swung by the tail of racial hatred.

Hence, Heaney's denial of the validity of these two different methods of providing 'images and symbols adequate to our predicament' is an example of litotes in that through describing what these images and symbols should not be, he is gesturing very much in the direction of what he sees as their correct mode of being. He agrees that there is a profound relation between 'poetic technique' and 'historical situation' (1985: 7). However, he refuses to allow the former to become either dependent on, or subservient to, the latter. Heaney's epistemology of poetry will attempt to avoid these attenuations and entrapments, and I will quote the passage at length:

> I mean that I felt it imperative to discover a field of force in which, without abandoning fidelity to the processes and experience of poetry as I have outlined them, it would be possible to encompass the perspectives of a humane reason and at the same time to grant the religious intensity of the violence its deplorable authenticity and complexity. And when I say religious, I am not thinking simply of the sectarian division. To some extent the enmity can be viewed as a struggle between the cults and devotees of a god and a goddess. There is an indigenous territorial numen, a tutelar of the whole island, call her Mother Ireland, Cathleen Ni Houlihan, the poor old woman, the Shan Van Vocht, whatever; and her sovereignty has been temporarily usurped or infringed by a new male cult whose founding fathers were Cromwell, William of Orange and Edward Carson, and whose godhead is incarnate in a rex or Caesar resident in a palace in London. What we have is the tail-end of a struggle in a province between territorial piety and imperial power. (1980: 56–7)

The term 'field of force' is interesting because it signifies a fluid, mobile structure which is composed of many interacting parts, and which posits the dialectical interaction of different forces. In physics, the term defines the space through which a force, or forces, operate, and clearly for Heaney, such a space is what constitutes the epistemological force of poetry. In this space, this force-field, he will encompass these two different forces, humane reason and religious intensity, and in some way cause them to co-exist, if not in harmony, at least in some form of structure which allows them to penetrate each other in some form of anastomosis which is specific to poetry as genre. Once again, the notion of movement, of forces operating and intersecting, is crucial here.

Such a force-field, or constellation, to use another term of Adorno's, borrowed from Benjamin,[29] results in a dialectical process which constantly oscillates without ever reaching any Hegelian *Aufhebung*. This term, best understood in terms of Benjamin's homology 'ideas are to objects as constellations are to stars' (1977: 34), allows for a non self-present form of identity, which can encompass different ideas and forces, just as a constellation can encompass many different stars. Keeping in mind the plural number involved in Heaney's searches for answers to those preoccupying questions, it becomes clear that when some *answers* are found, they generate other *questions* and so the complexity of the process is constantly regenerated. In the context of the argument being put forward in this study, it is more than interesting that Derrida, too, has made use of this term 'field of forces' in a broadly similar context (1985: 168) in describing the multilayered nature of a text wherein different ideologies and perspectives co-exist in a creative tension. In Blanchot's terms, such a structure is paradigmatic of what he terms the 'space of literature' in that different poles of oppositions are placed in a structure which sees them 'quitting themselves and detaining each other together outside themselves in the restless unity of their common belonging' (1982a: 200).

For Heaney, this notion of space is especially important in the political context which frames much of his work. In an essay entitled 'Cessation 1994', he is writing about the conditions in Northern Ireland that predated the IRA ceasefire that was called on 31 August 1994. He recalls the 'early days of political ferment in the late sixties' and also the 'energy and confidence on the nationalist side' and a concomitant 'developing liberalism – as well as the usual obstinacy and reaction – on the unionist side', and goes on to say that the 'border was becoming more pervious than it had been' (2002: 45). One of the more significant memories he recalls is his own participation in an artistic initiative, and particularly significant is the name given to this enterprise in the context of our discussion:

> I remember in particular feeling empowered...by a week on the road with David Hammond and Michael Longley in May 1968 when we brought a programme of songs and poems to schools and hotels and libraries in unionist and nationalist areas all over Northern Ireland. The programme was called 'Room to Rhyme' and I thought about it again last Wednesday. (2002: 45)

Here the space of literature becomes actual in both the programme of activities and in its title. The sense of movement across Northern Ireland, through both communities, as well as the notion of this movement creating, literally, a space for literature, is highly symbolic in the light of Heaney's searches for answers to those central pre-occupying questions. The creation of a space for poetry allows poetry the chance to become operative within the community and also to attempt to transform that community through its particular usage of language, at both the level of the signifier and that of the signified. What this 'room' managed to achieve was a place, or space, for some recognition of an Irish dimension within the official culture of Northern Ireland.

There is no sense of a return of the repressed here, as was found in the ongoing IRA campaign; rather there is a sense of a more complex understanding of the dynamic that is created by the interaction of both traditions within this room to write, or the space of literature. As Heaney puts it:

> Which is to say that 'diversity' is beginning to be recognised and to find its expression long before it became a buzz word. Small changes of attitude, small rapprochements and readjustments were being made. Minimal shifts in different areas – artistic, educational, political – were beginning to effect new contacts and new concessions. The fact that I felt free to read a poem about the 1798 rebels to a rather staid audience of middle-class unionists was one such small symptom of a new tolerance. (2002: 46)

The role of the arts in the creation of this more diverse climate of feeling should not be underestimated. In retrospect, Heaney can see that small changes, often at the level of the individual, are the building blocks of what can become seismic shifts, if given enough time and enough space. The activity of reading poems to diverse audiences is in no way seen as creative of the climactic moment, in 1994, when the IRA ceasefire was called. However, what was achieved in this 'Room to Rhyme' was the opening an opportunity for plurality and this is precisely the point made at the close of this essay:

> The cessation of violence is an opportunity to open a space – and not just in the political arena but in the first level of each person's consciousness – a space where hope can grow. And I mean hope in the sense that Vaclav Havel has defined it, because it seems to me that his definition has the kind of stoical clarity that should appeal to every realist in the north, Planter or Gael, Protestant or Catholic, optimist or pessimist. Hope, according to Havel, is different from optimism. It is a state of the soul rather than a

response to the evidence. It is not the expectation that things will turn out successfully but the conviction that something is worth working for, however it turns out. Its deepest roots are in the transcendental, beyond the horizon. (2002: 47)

Thus, when, in *The Cure at Troy*, we hear that oft-quoted phrase from the chorus that:

> once in a lifetime
> The longed-for tidal wave
> Of justice can rise up,
> And hope and history rhyme. (1990: 77)

It is this Havelian perspective that is being promulgated. In this context, the space of literature, the room to rhyme, the field of force, the complexity that is created by poetry, all cohere in the sense that they provide an opportunity to work for the values of humanity and understanding despite the chaos that is going on around them.

The shape of his field of force, or constellation, is hinted at in his essay on Osip Mandelstam, where he cites approvingly Mandelstam's notion of the purity of poetry as being like making Brussels lace, an activity which involves 'real work' but whose 'major components, those supporting the design, are air, perforations and truancy' (Heaney 1988: 84). Here, the dialectic of presence and absence, the importance of the shadow as well as the substance, are stressed. The similarity with Derrida's articulation of all communication being achieved through *différance* and the trace is clear. Derrida sees language as functioning through an 'economy of traces', and in an interview with Julia Kristeva, goes on to explain his view of a 'new concept of writing' wherein 'no element can function as a sign without referring to another element which itself is not simply present'. In other words, the elements of the system are structurally dependent on elements which are never 'simply present or absent', and are the results of an interweaving between presence and absence. It is this 'interweaving, this textile', which produces the 'text' (Derrida 1981a: 26). It is ironic that, via Derrida, we are now back in the realm of Catherine Bradley's sampler, and the oscillatory imagery of the loom as it creates the Ulster linen of her sampler. As already noted, this is far from the security blanket of oversimplistic meaning; this weaving, this text(ile) is redolent of the original anastomosis discussed in the introduction, namely that of text and context.

The transformative potential of such a weaving is signalled in 'Markings' in *Seeing Things*. This poem describes a childhood football game with 'four jackets for four goalposts', and goes on to describe this very physical experience, with a transformative moment occurring in the second stanza of the opening section, as the light died, the children kept on playing because 'by then they were playing in their heads'. As he notes:

> Some limit had been passed,
> There was fleetness, furtherance, untiredness
> In time that was extra, unforeseen and free. (Heaney 1991: 8)

The interweaving of actuality and imagination is clear at this point as a physical experience is internalised and seen as a paradigm for the process of imagination. The self, in this poem, becomes that field of force of which Heaney has been speaking:

> All these things entered you
> As if they were both the door and what came through it.
> They marked the spot, marked time and held it open. (1991: 9)

The idea of the self as being both the entrance for alterity and in a way now composed of that same alterity is crucial here. Self is now that entity wherein limits can be passed, and new aspects of identity created through the entrance of 'all these things'. The self, as field of force open to different influences and transformed by these influences, is what is being both explored and at the same time created in this poetic text.

Indeed, the similarity of Derrida's notion of text with Heaney's constellatory 'field of force' is striking. Both writers see meaning as constructed in terms of a dialectic of presence and absence, and they both conceive of a 'text' as constructed of a weave of differences. Derrida gives the name 'trace' to the part played by the radically other within the structure of difference that is language. This, Gayatri Spivak notes, can be called an economy – 'not a reconciliation of opposites, but rather a maintaining of disjunction. Identity constituted by difference is economy' (1976: xlii). Hence, Heaney's appropriation of Mandelstam's Brussels lace metaphor describes a similar economy in that what is present is supported by 'air, perforations and truancy'. It is in the interstices of this economy, this field of force, the places where different forces intersect, that Heaney sees the force of poetry.

Much of his later poetry is suffused with such imagery, and with suggestions that the epistemology of poetry is best understood in terms of its enunciation of such elements in a field of force. Hence, Heaney will attempt to create a force-field, a constellation, a text-context anastomosis in his later poetry as he constantly strives to avoid simplification and instead offer a model of a developed consciousness. Through the use of vastly different contexts, the consciousness, the 'I' of the poem, gradually develops intertextually. In 'The Golden Bough', Heaney translates form Virgil's *Aeneid*, and invokes the chants of the 'Sibyl of Cumae' who made the cave echo with 'sayings where clear truths and mysteries / Were inextricably twined' (1991: 1). The idea that truth is a construct made up of interacting texts is one which would seem to be drawn from his earlier experiences – it is a construct wherein binary oppositions are fused in a structure which concentrates on the 'twining' of 'truths' and 'mysteries'. Similarly in 'The Point', there is a field of force created between the child playing football and the ball itself in his description of the game: 'Was it you // or the ball that kept going / beyond you' (1991: 10), as memory blurs subject and object into a complex image of process. This point is also made in 'The Pulse', the second poem from 'Three Drawings', poems about fishing, where he speaks of 'pure duration' to describe the 'effortlessness / of a spinning reel', before going on to describe the image of the fisherman in terms of a fusion of image and shadow, light and reflection, person and water:

> Then after all of that
> Runaway give, you were glad
>
> When you reeled in and found
> Yourself strung, heel-tip
> To rod-tip, into the river's
> Steady purchase and thrum. (1991: 11)

The third image of this triptych, itself emblematic of the concept of the field of force and structure of tension of which we have been speaking, 'A Haul', describes a new context for the fishing trope, reverting to the Norse mythology of *North*, and recalling Thor's and Hymer's fishing for 'the world-serpent itself'. In this context, the escape of the serpent and the resultant loss of the 'haul' resulted in a surprising sense of plenitude as Thor 'felt at one with space', and this state is seen in simile as reminiscent of 'some fabulous high-catcher / coming down without the ball' (1991: 12). Process and activity are seen as the desirable factors here, creating a field of force or economy where self-definition is due to the interaction with the world, as opposed to a sense of imposition of selfhood on the world.

The following poem advances the fishing motif as a meta-trope on the purpose and function of poetry. Such a trope has a history in an Irish literary context, as it stems from Yeats's programmatic poem 'The Fisherman', wherein the power of poetry to encapsulate different forms and emotions is central to its thematic development. Yeats concludes this poem by telling of how he will address all of his work to this imaginary audience:

> A man who does not exist,
> A man who is but a dream:
> And cried, 'Before I am old
> I shall have written him one
> Poem maybe as cold
> And passionate as the dawn.' (Yeats 1979: 167)

Heaney is also using the technique of fishing, a casting into otherness and a tenuous connection with that which is outside the self, as an image of the fluid and transforming nature of poetry. Given our concern with the idea of binary oppositions, and with the desire to create structures which, as Derrida also implies, can alter and allow these to interact differentially within a new context, this poem is highly significant.

In his poem, dedicated to another poet, Ted Hughes, Heaney speaks of different sounds which 'took side', clearly indicating different forces in a debate or argument. Both sides of this binary opposition are voiced in the poem, personified as fishermen with different styles of casting: one whose cast went 'whispering' while in the case of the other 'a sharp ratcheting went on and on'. Both then voice conflicting opinions, with the 'I' of the poem torn between them, as one says 'Watch it! Be severe' while the other says: 'Go with it! Give and swerve. / You are everything you feel beside the river'. Here would seem to be a *locus classicus* of the binary oppositions of which we have been speaking, with the subject of the poem being torn between the conflicting perspectives. However, the final stanza of the poem functions metapoetically in its creation of a fluid structure which encompasses both perspectives in a way which makes the 'I' of the poem more complex and thoughtful through his exposure (not a term used innocently) to the different voices:

> I love hushed air. I trust contrariness.
> Years and years go past and I do not move
> For I see that when one man casts, the other gathers
> And then *vice versa*, without changing sides. (1991: 13)

In a manner that recalls Catherine Bradley's sampler, the poem gestures towards that inclusivity of consciousness that Heaney has come to valorise as part of the function of the aesthetic in society. The poem creates an economy in the sense already defined by Spivak: it is a not a reconciliation of opposites, but rather a maintaining of disjunction. Identity constituted by difference is such an economy.

Time and again, Heaney's poems are creative of these fields of force wherein different strands are woven together in structures which are transformative of actuality 'Who ever saw / The limit in the given anyhow?' (1991: 46). This *Kraftfeldt* is imagined again and again in his writing as he tries to capture structures which will allow for the different aspects of opposition but which will, at the same time, transform them through dynamic interaction. So, in the aptly titled 'Wheels within Wheels', speaking of pedalling a 'bike' by hand as it was turned 'upside down', and specifically of the spinning wheel, he creates just such a transformative structure:

> I loved the disappearance of the spokes,
> The way the space between the hub and rim
> Hummed with transparency. (1991: 46)

Here, through a process, the elements, brought into dynamic interaction, become altered and almost transparent. Such developments at the level of the individual consciousness, are what poetry can achieve.

In 'Weighing In', in *The Spirit Level*, the same sense of oppositional interaction and a notion of flux is conveyed: 'and everything trembled, flowed with give and take' (1996: 17). Indeed, the very title of this volume inscribes a sense of balance and adjustment to the pulls of different forces in an attempt to maintain some form of equilibrium: 'only as long as the balance holds' (1996: 18). This sense that the individual who has been exposed to the aesthetic can become more complex and more reactive to external forces is a constant of Heaney's work, but especially of his later work. Thus in 'Postscript', he can say: 'You are neither here not there, / A hurry through which known and strange things pass' (1996: 70), and can make the parallel point in 'Tollund' that he can feel 'footloose, at home beyond the tribe' (1996: 67), a line which immediately complicates notions of identity and home as well as almost casually suggesting that personal identity need not be trammelled by that of the tribe or the group.

He is interweaving different aspects of his heritage, language and history into a new context, a context which is also operative within his own *oeuvre*, as the title 'Tollund' refers analeptically to 'The Tollund Man', while the quoted line about being at home beyond the tribe, echoes one of his most emblematic early lines: 'lost, unhappy and at home' (1972: 48). Here, in terms of the altered context, Heaney can progress his 'continuous adjudication', and be both beyond the tribe and at home, a point which is almost a contradiction of the imperative that drives the voice of the tribe in 'The Tollund Man' where there was massive identification between the self and the group consciousness, what Sidney Burris terms the reconciliation of 'Republican dreams with the realities of occupation' (1990: 90). His initial connection with this bog figure was his similarity with aspects of Heaney's personal and Irish past: 'he looks like an ancestor' (Haffenden 1981: 57). However, in the present poem, a totally altered context speaks, not of mythic connections which valorise some form of originary myth of presence, but instead he now sees the place as 'hallucinatory and familiar', and instead of foregrounding the mythic connections, now talks about 'light traffic' in a discourse of normalisation, a discourse which is progressed by his juxtaposition of a 'scarecrow' and a 'satellite dish'.

As a paradigm of his ongoing contextualisation of oppositions within new structures, this poem exemplifies how Heaney creates his differential structures. Gesturing towards the mythopoeic impulses of 'The Tollund Man', Heaney goes on to describe a symbol of Iron Age Denmark in 'Tollund' in a manner replete with postmodern irony:

The scarecrow's arms
Stood open opposite the satellite

> Dish in the paddock, where a standing stone
> Had been resituated and landscaped,
> With tourist signs in *futhark* runic script
> In Danish and in English. Things had moved on. (1996: 69)

He is writing of the present, a present in which the past has become commodified in terms of its tourist potential. Brooding mythic imagery of sacrificial bog victims, and what Peter McDonald sees as one of the seminal tropes of Northern Irish poetry, the 'the attractions, and liabilities, of "home"' (1997: 114) have been consigned to the past, a past which can be reified and 'resituated' like the 'standing stone' and which is no longer a driving force within the present: things had 'moved on'.

The continuous adjudication between past and present has resulted in this most fluid of poems, a poem which decentres the placename 'Tollund' and instead makes it more of a spectral entity, as those who walk 'abroad' there are like 'ghosts' ready to make 'a new beginning' (Heaney 1996: 69). In 'The Swing', the close of the poem embodies this dialectical interaction between the demands of history and the developing complexity of an individual response to those demands. Describing the swing which he used as a child, the poem closes as follows:

> We all learned one by one to go sky high.
> Then townlands vanished into aerodromes,
> Hiroshima made light of human bones,
> Concorde's web migrated towards the future.
> So who were we to want to hang back there
> In spite of all?
>   In spite of all, we sailed
> Beyond ourselves and over and above
> The rafters aching in our shoulderblades,
> The give and take of branches in our arms. (1996: 49)

The notion of the aesthetic as a means of sailing 'beyond ourselves' is one which Heaney probes throughout his work. Whereas the binaries that initiated his continuous adjudication are historically contextualised, he is now able to transcend these by placing them in a constellation, and by talking on the complexities of both sides through a form of exposure of self to other and vice versa. It is

through the interweaving of the historical and the personal, an interweaving flagged by the anadiplosis of the lines:

> In spite of all?
> > In spite of all, we sailed
> Beyond ourselves

that this is brought about.[30] Here, the semantic sequence is that of
question and answer: the fact that the question is verbally identical
to the answer symbolises the complexity of the issues that are at
stake, when an individual interacts with the societal and historical.
For Heaney, such complexity is part of the structure and function of
poetry. As he puts it in 'The Redress of Poetry', the work of George
Herbert can symbolise what he calls: 'fully realised poetry', a poetry
where: 'the co-ordinates of the imagined thing correspond to and
allow us to contemplate the complex burden of our own existence'
(1995a: 10).

The value of Herbert's mind, for Heaney, is that he is able to take
the binary oppositions of his culture, and Heaney cites a number of
these: 'creator/creature, heaven/earth, soul/body, eternity/time,
life/death, Christ/man, grace/guilt, virtue/sin, divine love/courtly
love' (1995a: 10) and offer them to 'structural animation'. As Heaney
puts it:

> What might be called the DNA pattern of Herbert's imagination is
> fundamentally a matter of up-down, criss-cross motion, reversals
> effected with such symmetry that they are experienced as culmi-
> nations, tensions so thoroughly exercised and traced home that
> they return the system to relaxation, dialogues so sinuous that
> they end with speakers ready to start again, sometimes from dia-
> metrically opposed premises. (1995a: 10)

This, I would suggest, is paradigmatic of Heaney's structural sense: a
constellation, a force-field, a dynamic and balanced process wherein
the self is made more complex. In the next chapter a further
dimension of his epistemology will be examined, a dimension
wherein the transformative aspects of poetry become the focus of
our attention.

3   'Writing in the Sand': Poetry and Transformation

In the title essay of *The Government of the Tongue*, Heaney is discussing the 'paradox of poetry and of the imaginative arts in general' (1988: 107) and muses on the efficacy of poetry. He says in one sense, the efficacy is 'nil – no lyric has ever stopped a tank'; however, in another sense he sees its efficacy as 'unlimited' and goes on to cite the metaphor of Jesus' writing in the sand – 'in the face of which accusers and accused are left speechless and renewed' – as an example of the status or force of poetry. Quoting from Chapter Eight of John's Gospel, he cites Jesus' writing, in the face of the scribes and Pharisees who were accusing the woman caught in adultery. He sees poetry as analogous to this writing, a 'break with the usual life but not an absconding from it' (1988: 108). This notion of a break brings us back to the interstices of the field of force, those airy truancies of Brussels lace which were just as important as the designs which they supported. In terms redolent of Derrida's notions of difference and the trace, Heaney speaks of the epistemology of poetry as paralleling the writing in the sand, a process which is ephemeral in the extreme. As he puts it, poetry does not promise a solution to either 'accusing crowd' or 'helpless accused':

> Instead, in the rift between what is going to happen and whatever we would wish to happen, poetry holds attention for a space, functions not as distraction but as pure concentration, a focus where our power to concentrate is concentrated back on ourselves. This is what gives poetry its governing power. At its greatest moments it would attempt, in Yeats's phrase, to hold in a single thought reality and justice. (1988: 108)

Here we see different but parallel statements about the field of force. Poetry can be the space through which reality and justice can operate, not overtly in the political sphere, but in terms of influencing the writer and the reader; he goes on to describe poetry as 'more a threshold than a path' and sees it as one which is 'constantly approached and constantly departed from', and which affects reader and writer by the experience of being 'at the same time summoned and released' (1988: 108). The oscillatory nature of this dialectical movement demonstrates the complexity of the forces acting on both reader and writer. Indeed, Bernard O'Donoghue makes the telling point that this book 'remains intent on thresholds and crossings throughout its formally very different parts', citing the title of the Dante translation, 'Crossings', as emblematic of the book itself (1994: 120).

The importance of this Yeatsian example for Heaney is further underscored by its use in *The Redress of Poetry*.[1] Once again, it features in a discussion wherein Heaney is stressing the force of poetry and its epistemological nature, and once again, this is expressed in a dialectical *modus agendi*. He cites the original location of this quote, the introduction to *A Vision*, where Yeats notes that his 'systems' while at times deemed by him to be 'taken literally', are now seen as 'stylistic arrangements of experience', comparable to the cubes of Wyndham Lewis and the ovoids of Brancusi which have 'helped him to hold in a single thought reality and justice' (Heaney 1995a: 150).[2] Heaney goes on to juxtapose this with a quotation from Lady Dorothy Wellesley's recollection of a conversation with Yeats on the topic of life after death.

After a colloquy on his beliefs, she wryly commented that he seemed to be coming very close to a Roman Catholic position, whereupon Yeats's retort was 'a splendid laugh' (Heaney 1995a: 150–1).[3] For Heaney this laugh is an expression of a 'frame of mind which allowed the venturesomeness of a supernatural faith to co-exist with a rigorously sceptical attitude' (1995a: 151), and he goes on to exfoliate this Yeatsian notion of poetry in a series of oscillatory metaphors. He sees the laugh as the 'comic expression of a tragic perception', and goes on to cite Richard Ellmann's view that Yeats had perceived of the possibility that 'reality was desolation and justice a figment', a perception imaged by Ellmann in terms of life as a cornucopia being undermined by the notion of life as an empty shell.[4] For Heaney it is this dialectical ability to encompass these notions of faith and scepticism, comedy and tragedy, immanence and transcendence that makes Yeats a great poet. As he puts it, it is because of Yeats's 'fidelity to both perceptions and his refusal to foreclose on either that we recognise in him a poet of the highest attainment' (1995a: 151).

It is the fluidity and complexity of this Yeatsian constellatory structure that Heaney admires. The possibility that the writing in the sand will last only until the next gust of wind is the necessary context out of which the text of hope and affirmation can be achieved, if only briefly. In Heaney's own writing, we see a repetition and an invocation of this dialectical *Kraftfeldt* in his introductory essay to *The Government of the Tongue*. Writing about 'The Interesting Case of Nero, Chekhov's Cognac and a Knocker',[5] he demonstrates the value of his field of force in terms of its emancipatory power, and here he evinces a far more confident belief in the force of poetry as being able to achieve some form of effect on an individual consciousness. He is speaking of the 'achievement of a poem' which he sees as a sense of release, and of how, when the lyric achieves its 'buoyant completion' and the 'timeless formal pleasure comes to fullness and exhaustion' there occurs in the writer something which is 'equidistant from self-justification and self-obliteration', and this sense of release and momentary stasis is expressed in terms of the eponymous title of the collection. The 'tongue, governed for so long in the social sphere' (and he uses the phrase 'by nice obeisance to one's origin within the minority or the majority', a phrase that has particular, though not exclusive, resonances with Northern Ireland), is 'suddenly ungoverned' as it gains access to a condition that is 'unconstrained' and while 'not being practically effective, is not necessarily inefficacious' (1988: xxii). In this instance, we see the mode of thought which allows Heaney, like Yeats, to hold two emotions in one cognition. The epistemology of poetry is described in terms of the oscillating binarism that we noted in Catherine Bradley's sampler, and in the metaphor of Brussels lace, with its dialectical series of interstices and weavings.

As Heaney put it in the first Yeatsian citation, poetry is more of a threshold which is constantly approached and departed from, as both reader and writer undergo the experience of being 'at the same time summoned and released' (1988: 108). Heaney's epistemology of poetry focuses on the dialectical forces of space and time, presence and absence, movement and stasis, in an attempt to delineate the transgressive and transformative effects of poetry, if not on the body politic, then certainly on the body individual, the individuated consciousness which is seeking those answers to preoccupying questions. In the space created by poetry between what is going to happen and what we would like to happen, between the actual and the desired, it focuses our attention on ourselves. Ultimately, as already noted in terms of the relationship between the 'I', the 'you' and the 'we', poetry creates a dialectical questioning of the 'I' by the 'I'; it allows our 'power to concentrate', to be 'concentrated back on ourselves' (1988: 108).

In his 'writing in the sand' metaphor, Heaney discusses the efficacy of such activity; on the one hand, he sees that poetry doesn't stop tanks; on the other, it may alter the mindset that is sending in those tanks. Ironically, it is the very ephemerality of poetry, the writing in the sand, that gives it any sense of lasting force, it is 'the imagination pressing back against the pressure of reality' (1995a: 1). However, the force is microcosmic as opposed to macrocosmic; it has no direct effect on the political, but it has the effect of altering the individual consciousness of both writer and reader. In terms of the relationship between writing and politics, he sees the 'purely poetic force of words' as 'the guarantee of a commitment which need not apologise for not taking up the cudgels since it is raising a baton to attune discords which the cudgels are creating' (1985: 7).

We have come a long way from Corcoran's notion of over-schematic or specious binary thinking. Instead we see the complicated construction of the field of force, the constellation, the economy, all of which describe the epistemology of poetry in terms of the creation of a space wherein and where through different forces can operate. This *Kraftfeldt* can be traced back to the spatial and temporal oscillation already adduced in this chapter: it is a cognitive transformation of a physical progression, and the notion of movement is seminal to Heaney's epistemology of poetry.

As we have seen, there is a clear relationship between poetry and reality; it is the nature of this relationship that Heaney puts in question. He is unwilling to see poetry as merely a reflection of a preordained reality as this would negate the imaginative and creative aspect of art. As he puts it: 'when a rhyme surprises and extends the fixed relations between words, that in itself protests against necessity' (1995a: 158). In terms of the issues under discussion in this chapter, namely the scope and nature of Heaney's epistemology of poetry, the verbs in this phrase are telling. Rhyme is seen as a force which is transformative of the 'fixed' relationships between words, a point which can serve as a synecdoche of Heaney's view of the force of poetry in general: 'it is essential that the vision of reality that poetry offers should be transformative, more than just a print-out of the given circumstances of its time and place' (1995a: 159). Time and time again, this trope surfaces in Heaney's writing as he describes the transformation of reality within the individual consciousness. When speaking of sliding on ice, he describes the sensation as being like:

> A farewell to surefootedness, a pitch
> Beyond our usual hold upon ourselves. (1991: 86)

Once again, the transformation of selfhood is the key to this image, and by extension, to the imperatives underlying so much of his writing.

It is through some form of transfiguration of the actual that poetry achieves it epistemological goal, and this transfiguration must occur at the level of the individual, be it reader or writer, as opposed to the societal or communal. Through the new relationships between points of fixity (once again, we are transported back to the weave of Catherine Bradley's sampler of Ulster linen, with its oscillation between the shamrock and emblem), individuals are encouraged to reattune their consciousness, to be 'forwarded' within themselves. What he means by this is that in the most illuminating poetry what is at work is the mind's capacity to 'conceive a new plane of regard for itself, a new scope for its own activity' (1995a: 160). This new plane has a relationship with the actual, but is in no way governed by it, and it also has the ability to encompass different forces within its field of force, and to posit answers, in some way, to the questions raised by the actual.[6]

In terms of these answers, we need look no further than Heaney's specific discussion of the role of poetry as an answering, the title essay in *The Redress of Poetry*. Here the notion of redress encompasses the dialectical field of force which, I have argued, is the shape of Heaney's epistemology of poetry. In the introduction to this book,[7] Heaney stresses the notion of poetry as capable of encompassing different perspectives, a point which is by now a *sine qua non* of his view of poetry. Describing a poem by George Herbert, and one of his own works from 'Squarings',[8] Heaney notes that both works are about 'the way consciousness can be alive to two different and contradictory dimensions of reality and still find a way of negotiating between them' (1995a: xiii). This notion of negotiating is precisely what is meant by his comment that rhyme 'surprises and extends' the fixed relationships between words, and it is with this transgressive aspect of his field of force that our discussion of his aesthetic will conclude. To revert back to Corcoran's point, Heaney's binary thinking necessitates some form of connection between the binarisms, and this connection will in some way change the relationship between them, at least in the consciousness of writer and reader.

In Poem VIII of 'Lightenings', Heaney speaks of a ship appearing in the air while the monks of the medieval monastery of Clonmacnoise were 'at prayer'. The air seemed to be the proper element of this ship, as an anchor was dropped which 'hooked itself into the altar rails' (1991: 62) and paradoxically, a crewman who 'shinnied' down the rope was in danger of drowning in air unless he was released back to the ship. The monks duly released the anchor and the crewman 'climbed back / Out of the marvellous as he had known it' (1991: 62). Here notions of the marvellous and of safety are predicated on the different perspectives from which one comes; in the poem air is both marvellous and dangerous, as, by implication is water. Heaney's aim here is to affirm that:

> Within our individual selves we can reconcile two orders of knowledge which we might call the practical and the poetic; to affirm also that each form of knowledge redresses the other and that the frontier between them is there for the crossing. (1995a: 203)

This idea of crossings and transfers between different positions and epistemologies is also shared by Derrida who notes that texts are usually approached through the metaphor of a type of translation and goes on to speak about the 'procession of one language into another' and the resulting movement of this procession 'over the border of another language, into the language of the other' (1987: 77). I would suggest that both writers, while examining the context of binary oppositions on which much of Western thought is predicated, take the additional step of setting in motion a complex structure wherein these binary oppositions are rendered dynamic, and the focus will be on their intersubjective relationship and the dynamics of that relationship as opposed to the elements of the binary opposition seen as static polar opposites.

For example, earlier we discussed Heaney's use, in *Preoccupations*, of masculine and feminine as synecdoches of different types of poetry, and of different types of socio-cultural identity. However in a following essay, he strives to find an answering shape which will set up some kind of transformative dynamic between the two. He finds this in the poetry of Hopkins, whose poems were conceived as 'the crossing of masculine strain on feminine potential' (Heaney 1980: 95), and he also finds a shape for part of his field of force, noting that 'the Church fathers perceived the sign of the cross in the figure of a man and woman splayed' (1980: 97). Here, a chiasmatic pattern of reversal and transformation is the *terminus ad quem* towards which Heaney's binarisms are directed, a point noted in the previous chapter with respect to the writing of Herbert, whose work contains 'within itself the co-ordinates and contradictions of experience' (Heaney 1995a: 12).

A similar point can be made with reference to his earlier binary view of Ireland and England, as he attempts to see poetry as a constellation wherein both can be set in dialectical and transformative interchange: 'I think of the personal and Irish pieties as vowels, and the literary awarenesses nourished on English as consonants. My hope is that the poems will be vocables adequate to my whole experience' (1980: 37). The word 'vocable' usually refers to the form, as opposed to the meaning of a word, and has connotations of calling, deriving from '*vocare*', meaning 'to call'. Hence, he is striving for a new formal shape which can encompass the differing identities and forces with which he is dealing, and also, to initiate a calling to the other, to initiate a response to that call, and again, we are on familiar ground in terms of an adequation of the thought of Heaney and Derrida. In an interview with Richard Kearney in 1981, Derrida made the point that deconstruction is itself a 'positive response to an alterity which necessarily calls, summons or motivates it...a response to a call' (Derrida 1981c: 168). The ethical similarities are clear; both writers seek some forms or structures which facilitate dialogue with the other, and response to the call of the other. For Derrida, this structure is deconstruction; for Heaney it is poetry; for both, it is a structure which values the interplay of differences. Writing in 'Structure Sign and Play in the Discourse of the Human Sciences', Derrida stresses the double nature of deconstruction in a manner analogous to Heaney's view of the complex structuration of poetry. Speaking about the 'event' that has taken place in the development of the study of structure, Derrida explains that the exterior form of this event would be 'that of a rupture and a redoubling' (1978: 278).[9] The notion of a rupture followed by a redoubling is indicative of a more complex structure in terms of layers, as well as of the imperative to rebuild following the initial deconstruction. Heaney and Derrida both follow their interrogations of simplistic positions of identity and ideology by this very restructuration and redefinition of such positions.

Thus, in 'Exposure' in *North*, Heaney stresses, in litotes, that he is 'neither internee nor informer'. Instead, he takes on the complex role of an 'inner émigré', one who is still part of his culture but existing at a physical 'It is December in Wicklow' (1975: 72), and existential 'weighing / My responsible *tristia*' (1975: 73) distance from it, taking on the persona of a 'wood-kerne', one who has crossed over from the old Gaelic order into the life of an outlaw. Embodying a movement away from simplistic identifications with singular ideological positions: 'His gift like a slingstone / Whirled for the desperate' (1975: 72), Heaney instead takes on a position similar to that of the earlier cited complex notion of selfhood in 'Markings', assuming the position of one who is capable of 'feeling / Every wind that blows' (1975: 73). This position is a recurring trope in his poetry, as he conflates different spatial, temporal and epistemological positions in an increasingly structured sense of selfhood:

> Strange how things in the offing, once they're sensed,
> Convert to things foreknown;
> And how what's come upon is manifest
>
> Only in light of what has been gone through. (1991: 108)

He increasingly sites the 'I' of his poems in terms of being at a crossroads or intersection of different traditions: 'I swim in Homer' (1991: 36), and sees the desired role of the poetic persona as located in such points of intersection:

> Air and ocean known as antecedents
> Of each other. In apposition with
> Omnipresence, equilibrium, brim. (1991: 80)

For Heaney, the balance and process of containing and encompassing different positions is clearly of central importance. The idea of a brim, border, margin or edge, as a teleological point is important especially in the context of the structure in which this poem appears.

In *Seeing Things*, the second section of the book is comprised of a sequence entitled 'Squarings':

> In this sequence, each poem has the same shape: all are twelve lines long and divided into four versets of three lines each, a form which recalls the Dantean *terza rima*, without its interlinked rhyme

scheme....There are four shorter sequences within the larger one: 'Lightenings', 'Settings', 'Crossings', and the concluding sequence 'Squarings' itself. Each of these contains twelve poems: so that the shape of the sequence as a whole is a kind of geometrical 'squaring': 4 x 12 x 12. (Corcoran 1986: 173–4)

Hence fluidity of structure and transformative perspectives are central to this sequence, as both structurally and thematically, it embodies the notion of a field of force as envisaged by Heaney, Adorno and Derrida. Tobin suggests that the ethical function of such a sequence is clear from its insistence that 'the created order of any world exists meaningfully only in relation to the world of the other' (1998: 258), and it is this ongoing interfusion of differences that is at the core of this sequence, and indeed, of much of Heaney's later work.

At this juncture, I would transpose a comment of Henry Hart's, on *The Haw Lantern*, where he notes that in this book, Heaney[10] 'negates age-old prejudices in order to affirm the productive interplay of differences' (Hart 1992: 7), and sees it as more aptly applying to Heaney's theory of poetry in general. The 'productive interplay of differences' is, it seems to me, Heaney's methodology of achieving his searches for answers; to borrow a phrase from Augustine, of making truth (*facere veritatem*), of crossing over positions 'out to another side' (Heaney 1995a: xiii) so as to glean some notion of the other, in order to better inform and create one's own sense of truth. Heaney has coined the term 'the frontier of writing' for this notion of poetry, and the ethical imperative that drives this idea of poetry as a crossing to the side of the other, and of being a connection as well as a point of difference between self and other, is very much in keeping with the central preoccupying question of how a poet should 'properly' live and write.[11]

The concept of borders is also stressed in Heaney's essay 'Something to Write Home About', where he discusses memories of paddling in the Moyola river, and seeing an image of 'Terminus, the god of boundaries', and interestingly in the context of our discussion, he images this god in terms of space once again. The Romans kept an image of this god on Capitol Hill and the interesting point about this image is that 'the roof above the image was open to the sky':

...as if to say that a god of the boundaries and borders of the earth needed to have access to the boundless, the whole unlimited height and width and depth of the heavens themselves. As if to say that all boundaries are necessary evils and that the truly desirable condition is the feeling of being unbounded, of being king of infinite space. And it is that double capacity that we possess as human beings – the capacity to be attracted at one and the same time to the security of what is intimately known and the challenges and entrancements of what is beyond us – it is this double capacity that poetry springs from and addresses. (2002: 48)

The connection of poetry with the desire to remain within our boundaries while at the same time wishing to transcend them, further strengthens his idea of the complexity that is created by poetic writing. The space of literature, in this case, is one wherein there is a lot of border traffic, and where the movement is an index of the doubleness of which he speaks. It is his way of working towards that regulative idea of an 'infinite space' where the bounded interacts with, and is influenced by, the unbounded, and where different traditions can mutually interrelate.

Once again, there is a parallel with Derrida, who also speaks of borderlines, and notes that we:

have to cross the border but not to destroy the border; that is we have to cross the border in order to understand not only their relationship to the Western tradition [he is speaking about Romanian philosophy], but also to understand what they are doing with their own background, language, traditions, we have to travel, to go in their direction. (1993: 33)

In terms of crossing a border or frontier, in terms of locating the self in a relationship with the other, and in terms of seeing identity as, not fixed, but fluid, both writers are very much in concord. We have already noted Heaney's preoccupation with justice, so too Derrida sees justice as intimately connected with notions of responsibility to the 'absolute singularity of the other' (1993: 25).

In a lecture given in his second year in Oxford, Heaney cites a comment of Robert Pinsky's from an aptly entitled essay called 'Responsibilities of the Poet'[12] where Pinsky makes the point that the artist requires, not so much an audience *per se*, as much as the 'need to feel an answer, a promise to respond' (1995a: xiv). This need to respond presupposes the presence of an other, of a form of alterity to which our response is addressed, and it locates poetry as a profoundly ethical discourse. Once again, there is a clear similarity between his thought and that of Derrida, who notes that it is only through the acknowledgement of the other that the self can fully come into being, as it is the ear of the other that 'says me to me and constitutes the *autos* of my autobiography' (1985: 51).

For Derrida, the whole notion of identity is bound up with this dialectical oscillation between self and other, and this movement predicates what Heaney terms a concentration on the self, through the 'need to respond' which can achieve the 'imaginative transformation of human life' (1995a: xv). Derrida sees separation and dissociation as the conditions of any relationship with the other (1997b: 14). He also notes that:

> the identity of a culture is a way of being different from itself; a culture is different from itself; language is different from itself; the person is different from itself. Once you take into account this inner and other difference, then you pay attention to the other and you understand that fighting for your own identity is not exclusive of another identity, is open to another identity. And this prevents totalitarianism, nationalism, egocentrism and so on. (1997b: 13–14)

This notion of self-differentiating identity leaves some form of gap within the self, be that self singular or communal, and it is this very gap (Derrida 1992b: 9–11), analogous I would argue to Heaney's view of poetry as occurring in the space between what 'has to happen and what we would like to happen', that allows for the interaction with the other, and for this interaction to influence our notion of selfhood. It is this dialectic, this field of force, that constitutes our notions of self, and poetry has the ability to influence this. By responding to the other, we are creating the self, and it is to this relationship between the self, poetry and society that our focus, in this chapter, is finally drawn.

In the title essay of *The Redress of Poetry*, Heaney addresses directly how poetry can be 'of present use'.[13] Citing Philip Sidney and Wallace Stephens, he fixes on Plato's world of ideal forms as the 'court of appeal through which poetic imagination seeks to redress whatever is wrong or exacerbating in the prevailing conditions' (1995a: 1). Having used the term 'redress' in this opening paragraph, Heaney explores its etymological complexity at a later stage, and explains his differing usages of the word:

The OED has four entries for 'redress' as a noun, and I began by calling on the first sense which it provides: 'Reparation of, satisfaction or compensation for, a wrong sustained or the loss resulting from this.' For 'redress' as a verb the dictionary gives fifteen separate entries, all of them subdivided two or three times, and almost all of the usages noted as obsolete. I have also taken account of the first of these obsolete meanings, which is given as, 'To set (a person or a thing) upright again; to raise again to an erect position. Also *fig*. To set up again, restore, re-establish.' (1995a: 15)

It is interesting that this etymological examination does not occur until late in the essay. The earlier discussions of the notion of redressal, as 'affirming that which is denied voice', take place under the rubric of poetry being 'of present use', and are seen in terms of being part of a motivated 'field of force'. As he puts it 'engaged parties' will see poetry as an 'applied art' which can be harnessed to their own movements. He explains that they will 'always want the redress of poetry to be an exercise of leverage on behalf of *their* point of view' (1995a: 2). The use of the terms 'field of force', and the notion of a committed poetry, remind us of the earlier definition of the epistemology of poetry in *Preoccupations* (1980), but more importantly of the two initial caveats that preceded that definition, namely that poetry is neither exclusively liberal lamentation nor praise or execration of violent action; that its force is one which provides a symbolic nexus of images which enable the continuing encompassment of reason and atavism, and possible realignments of the relationship between them.

Here too, Heaney will reiterate his epistemology of poetry. Rather than seeing redress as simply a one-sided answering, subsumed within political and ideological movements, he is making a space for poetry *sui generis*, as an independent field of force which will be related to, but not dependent on, politics and ideology. He does not, as he puts it in *North*, see poetry as a 'slingstone [to be] / Whirled for the desperate' (1975: 72). Instead, he follows the advice of Wallace Stevens, who sees poetry as creating the world to which we turn, and as giving life to the 'supreme fictions' without which we would have difficulty in interpreting that world (Heaney 1995a: 2).[14] Heaney's notion of redress as a parallel to the actual is clear in his expansion of these ideas. He notes that if our experience is a labyrinth, then the poet is capable of countering its impassibility by 'imagining some equivalent of the labyrinth and presenting himself and us with a vivid experience of it' (1995a: 2). Here, the redressal is achieved by setting up that oscillation between literature, where 'license is given to the writer to say everything he wants to or everything he can' (Derrida 1992a: 37) and the political and societal world. The 'affirming of that which is denied voice' (Heaney 1995a: 2) takes place in this oscillation, this re-vision of the 'I' through art as a corrective to that of the 'I' involved in politics.

Heaney explains the interstitial connection between these aspects of his field of force by stressing that such an operation 'does not intervene in the actual' but offers consciousness 'a chance to recognise its predicaments, foreknow its capacities and rehearse its comebacks' (1995a: 2). Hence, it redresses what Simone Weil has seen as 'the greatest sin', namely 'obedience to the force of gravity' (Heaney 1995a: 3),[15] with gravity seen as the pull of essentialist and atavistic intensities, what he had termed in *Preoccupations* 'religious' intensities, and which also figured in the already quoted *Kinship* as the 'appetites of gravity' (1975: 43).

Weil sees the intervention of poetry or art in society as a force of counter weighting. This is not to see redress as a political tool *per se*, rather it is to see art as setting up a 'conception of equilibrium' and then being ready to change sides so as to 'add weight to the lighter scale', an ever-changing, dynamic process, like justice which she sees as 'that fugitive from the camp of conquerors' (1995a: 3).[16] The value of this notion of the redress of poetry for Heaney is threefold: it is independent, it is dialectical and transgressive, and it is ethically driven in its mode of action. As he puts it:

> Her whole book is informed by the idea of counter weighting, of balancing out the forces, of redress – tilting the scales of reality towards some transcendent equilibrium. And in the activity of poetry too, there is a tendency to place a counter-reality in the scales – a reality which may be only imagined but which nevertheless has weight because it is imagined within the gravitational pull of the actual and can therefore hold its own and balance out against the historical situation. The redressing effect of poetry comes from its being a glimpsed alternative, a revelation of potential that is denied or constantly threatened by circumstances. (1995a: 3–4)

Here we see another constituent to his field of force, an anastomosis, an interpenetration of the actual and the imagined, which parallels that of the earlier cited text and context. This redress is temporally and spatially fragile; it seems to be constantly under threat from the forces of gravity, of actuality, and those of the political and social spheres. However, as it is imagined within the gravitational pull of the actual, it can achieve a point of balance, which is focused inwardly on the reading or writing consciousness, and which is a powerful agent for change on both. The balance can be a point of stasis, or more accurately, a balance of opposed motions which cross and recross the frontier of writing. This is clear from the final poem in 'Settings' where it is the relational that provides the focus:

> Air and ocean known as antecedents
> Of each other. In opposition with
> Omnipresence, equilibrium, brim. (1991: 80)

As his work develops, it is this complexity and nuanced response to experience that has become one of the defining characteristics of Heaney's writing.

Interestingly, this is not the end of the interstitial field of force, as there is an additional dialectical oscillation in the weave that shapes his view of poetry. As I have already pointed out, Heaney's notion of the frontier of writing is a necessary component of that *Kraftfeldt*, as it is by crossings and transgressions that transformations of relationships and perceptions can take place. As a further complication of the field of force, it also functions as a dividing line between the 'actual conditions of our daily lives' and the 'imaginative representation of those conditions' and, by extension, as a dividing line between the 'world of social speech and the world of poetic language' (1995a: xvi). As well as its ethical force of redress, poetry also sets up a force which is unique to poetry *qua* poetry. Citing Auden's poetic trivium of making, judging and knowing, Heaney notes that the making faculty seems to have a 'free pass' which enables it 'to range beyond the jurisdiction of the other two', and this process, this 'fundamentally self-delighting inventiveness' (1995a: 5) is also a necessary aspect of his epistemology of poetry, and can be seen to involve a neglected meaning of 'redress':

> a meaning which comes in entry four of the verb, subsection (b): '*Hunting*. To bring back (the hounds or deer) to the proper course.' In this redress there is no hint of ethical obligation, it is more a matter of finding a course for the breakaway of innate capacity, a

course where something unhindered, yet directed, can sweep ahead into its full potential. (1995a: 15)

In a manner analogous to his anastomosis of 'text and context', Heaney here allows the different meanings of the weave of the word 'redress' to oscillate and penetrate each other so as to more fully define his epistemological view of the meaning of poetry. The faculty of making (deriving from the Greek '*poieín*', meaning 'to make'), is here adduced to redress the ethical imperative by setting up what we might term an aesthetic imperative which will bring out the 'innate capacity' of thought and language, the 'self-delighting inventiveness', the joy experienced in being a 'process of language' (1995a: 5). These different interactive redressals are not, however, confined to the realms of theory.

Both are part of the constellation which he sees as embodying the functions of poetry. On 12 May 1981 Heaney was a guest at an Oxford college dinner, on the same day that Francis Hughes, an IRA hunger striker, died in prison.[17] Hughes, Heaney tells us, belonged to a neighbour's family, and Heaney felt the contradictory emotions brought about by his place at an Oxford occasion, while imagining the funeral rites that would be taking place in his native County Derry. In this lecture, 'Frontiers of Writing', he discusses the role of poetry with respect to such political problems. He makes the point that the individual consciousness is torn between conflicting demands: feelings of betrayal at enjoying the hospitality of an Establishment college (1995a: 188) while at the same time not wishing to support the hunger strike overtly because this would be taken as an endorsement of the 'violent means and programmes of the Provisional IRA' (1995a: 187). In this very real context, where the weight of the actual is palpable, he again stresses the dialectical functions of poetry, namely to be 'a source of truth and at the same time a vehicle of harmony', to be capable of being both socially responsible and creatively free' (1995a: 193). Once again, in his use of binarisms to undermine the solidity of those binarisms, Heaney is tracing out an argument that is similar to that of Derrida, who, speaking about his early neologism, *différance*, notes that it is 'neither *this* nor *that*; but rather this *and* that (e.g. the act of differing and of deferring) without being reducible to a dialectical logic either' (1981c: 161).[18] Both writers predicate the complex interaction of elements as ultimately destructive of oversimplifications, and Heaney stresses the necessary imbrication of redress as a counterweighting political action and redress as redress of this political involvement by veering towards the aesthetic.

Heaney sees this redress as the 'redress of poetry *as* poetry', as the inception of 'its own category' which exerts an 'eminence' and a 'pressure' through 'distinctly linguistic means' (1995a: 5–6). While cognisant of the necessity for the denial of the normative linguistic or literary standards in any 'movement of liberation', Heaney sees part of the field of force of poetry as being independent of such political gravitational pulls. He feels that there must be a dialectical awareness that, while in some way connected with the enforcement of cultural hegemonic regimes and mindsets, nevertheless poetry cannot be attenuated into a *post factum* political appendage. Such attenuation of the role of poetry in the world is the very antithesis of Heaney's view of its effect. He makes the point that its integrity should not be impugned because 'at any given moment it happens to be a refraction of some discredited cultural or political system' (1995a: 7). It is against such oversimplifications that much of Heaney's writing is directed, arguing again and again for notions of poetry as a working model of 'inclusive consciousness'; a consciousness that is susceptible to the demands of the actual, the ethical and the aesthetic, as is made very clear in his Nobel Prize lecture, *Crediting Poetry*.

In this lecture, Heaney traces his early steps in the acquisition of language, and the manner in which different discourses awakened in him a curiosity about the wider world outside rural County Derry. He discusses his alertness to different night sounds, seeing his reception to these sounds mirrored by the delicate, concentric ripples caused in a bucket of drinking water in the family scullery by the passing of nearby trains (1995b: 11). He goes on to explain the effect of listening to the different radio stations and his 'first encounters with the gutturals and sibilants of European speech', stimuli which had initiated a journey 'into the wideness of the world'. He expands this metaphor into a journey into 'the wideness of language, a journey where each point of arrival – whether in one's poetry or one's life – turned out to be a stepping stone rather than a destination' (1995b: 11). Such a set of stepping stones leads to the space of poetry where different forces can work together; where microcosm and macrocosm intersect and interact, where:

> Poetry can make an order as true to the impact of external reality and as sensitive to the inner laws of the poet's being as the ripples

that rippled in and rippled out across the water in that scullery bucket fifty years ago. An order where we can at last grow up to that which we stored as we grew. An order which satisfies all that is appetitive in the intelligence and prehensile in the affections. I credit poetry, in other words, both for being itself and for being a help, for making possible a fluid and restorative relationship between the mind's centre and its circumference. (1995b: 11–12)

Here, the *Kraftfeldt* is again explained and reinforced. Poetry sets up dialectical relationships between self and other, itself and politics, language and the mind, motion and stasis, all woven together in a textile that calls us back to the earlier images of text being permeated by context, and the differing notions of identity that co-existed and interpenetrated in the field of force that was Catherine Bradley's linen sampler. Once again he is describing the force of writing in the sand, something which creates a reflective space between the music of what happens and that which we would like to happen. The 'fluid relationship' is suggestive of a force which sets up connections which interact, intersect and interpenetrate without ever becoming solidified into foundationalist positions: as Heaney puts it: 'Who ever saw / The limit in the given anyhow?' (1991: 46), a telling phrase in which he encompasses the dialectic between the real and the imagined.

Poetry holds attention in this space, and functions, as we have already noted, 'not as distraction but as pure concentration, a focus where our power to concentrate is concentrated back on ourselves' (Heaney 1988: 108). To concentrate on the self is to develop new notions of the self, and of the role of the self in culture. For Heaney, this focus on the self invokes a responsibility to the other, as his notion of selfhood is defined by an interaction of different forces. He is attempting to find what Derrida has termed 'the other in oneself already' (1997a: 24). Here there is a correlation with the work of Levinas who says that: 'I am defined as a subjectivity, as a singular person, as an "I", precisely because I am exposed to the other' (1981a: 192). For Levinas, the ethical quality of language itself involves this notion of a response to the call of the other. The ability to look from the mind's centre to its circumference and vice versa involves an opening of 'me to the other before saying what is said' (1989: 183).

At this point, we return to the sampler of Catherine Bradley, and the two emblems of the value systems, which explode daily in Northern Ireland, and which are lodged like 'dormant munitions' on the piece of Ulster linen (Heaney 1983a: 6). Heaney's notion of poetry will transform the violence of the term 'munition' into the 'saying of the law' that is implied in the cognate term 'muniment'. A 'saying' of the rights and privileges of the other can have a similarly explosive force on entrenched attitudes and ideologies, and it is such an ethical 'saying' or Derridean 'response to a call' that Heaney has in mind here. The ripple effect may seem small, but it does have a force of its own. As already noted, poetry creates a dialectical questioning of the 'I' by the 'I'; it allows our 'power to concentrate' to be 'concentrated back on ourselves' (Heaney 1988: 108). In a real sense, it presents a community with an option of looking from its own centre to its circumference so as to acknowledge its limits. However, as Derrida notes, it is possible for 'its limit to be its *opening*' (1995: 355), a point implicit in much of Heaney's writing.

Speaking of the difficulty of attempting to demonstrate how a community's limit can also be its opening to the other, Heaney, in *Crediting Poetry*, recalls one of the most savage events in the long history of the violence in Northern Ireland. In 1976, a minibus full of workers was stopped at Kingsmills, near Bessbrook in County Armagh at a bogus checkpoint. The occupants were lined up at the side of the road, and were asked 'any Catholics among you, step out here'. Heaney notes that, since the majority of the group were Protestants, with a single exception, the presumption must have been that 'the masked men were Protestant paramilitaries about to carry out a tit-for-tat sectarian killing' (1995b: 18).[19] He goes on:

It was a terrible moment for him, caught between dread and witness, but he did make a motion to step forward. Then, the story goes, in that split second of decision, and in the relative cover of the winter evening darkness, he felt the hand of the Protestant worker next to him take his hand and squeeze it in a signal that said no, don't move, we'll not betray you, nobody need know what faith or party you belong to. (1995b: 18)

The man did step forward, but was thrown aside to watch the execution of the ten Protestant workers, murdered by 'presumably, the Provisional IRA' (1995b: 18).[20] Heaney notes that, in the face of such atrocity, we are 'rightly suspicious of that which gives too much consolation in these circumstances' (1995b: 19). However, if art is to be of 'present use', then its redress must take account of both the hand that gripped its other, as well as those which murdered their others. Here, in this symbol of a connection between self and other, we see how the very finality of the limit of one community, its total sectarian attack on the other as other, can also function as a tiny symbol of opening, an opening upon which some type of structure of community can be built. Heaney's field of force hopes to credit the 'marvellous' as well as the 'murderous' (1995b: 20). That he enunciates this telling point in an essay as opposed to a poem further underscores my point that his prose writing is a seminal aspect of his overall project. At the level of his own writing, his field of force also consists of an anastomosis between poetry and prose as both genres combine to produce the complexity of response which is the teleological aim of his writing.

He credits poetry both for 'being itself and for being a help' (1995b: 11); as well as redressing the socio-political, Heaney's searches for answers will take into account the restorative relation of poetry to the self. In terms of the dialectic with which we began, he concludes his lecture with some assertions of the nature of the field of force that is his definition of poetry. He sees poetic form as both 'the ship and the anchor. It is at once both a buoyancy and a holding, allowing for the simultaneous gratification of whatever is centrifugal and centripetal in mind and body' (1995b: 29). The sense of movement of opposing forces within an encompassing structure which values both in their different ways is again enunciated and is, I would suggest, at the very core of Heaney's aesthetic.

Ultimately, this aesthetic is an attempt at gratifying the twin demands that pull us in different directions, whether these are violence or humane reason, emblems on an embroidered sampler, different definitions of Ulster, the ethical or the aesthetic in terms of the function of poetry. These binarisms are not, however, over-schematic or specious; instead they are ethical in the sense that self is defined on an ongoing basis against some notion of alterity or otherness. This definition is ephemeral and transitory, and constantly changing and comes from the 'resolution and independence which the entirely realised poem sponsors' (1995b: 28). For Heaney, the achievement of poetry, that which will always be to poetry's credit, is 'the power to persuade that vulnerable part of our consciousness of its own rightness in spite of the evidence of wrongness all around it' (1995b: 29).

Heaney's searches for answers are located in this desire to vindicate the question of consciousness that is central to the formation and ongoing development of the individual as individual. These searches for answers are profoundly ethical in that they prescribe a sense of responsibility on the part of the individual. The activity of persuading the self means that we are constantly opening to changes in that self, changes which are wrought through the form and language and generic singularity of poetry. As Derrida notes: 'it is because I am not one with myself that I can speak with the other and address the other', and he goes on to see such notions of selfhood as the only way to 'take responsibility and make decisions' (1997b: 14). Heaney's epistemology of poetry is similarly ethically informed. It is that which reminds us that we are 'hunters and gatherers of values, that our very solitudes and distresses are creditable, in so far as they, too, are an earnest of our veritable human being' (Heaney 1995b: 29). Here, in a nutshell, we have Heaney's epistemology of poetry. It credits all our emotions, sets them in dialectical oscillation, and attempts, by a process of adjudication which involves aesthetic and ethical standards, to create a space which allows the revelation of the self to the self in a way that increases our humanity, and our response to, and responsibility for, the other.

We can now begin to see the shape of his field of force, a structure which allows different, opposing forces to pass through its interstices, and which, like Brussels lace, acknowledges the gaps which underlie the connections. The series of dialectical oscillations which we have traced demonstrates the fluid relationship of Heaney's continual adjudication between different positions and perspectives that is the essence of his epistemology of poetry. His searches for answers to those preoccupying questions have led him to a threshold, or frontier from where he looks in different directions, and attempts to create a space for their interaction.

For Heaney, this multiple perspective is central to the force of poetry, and his citing of the Czeslaw Milosz poem, appropriately entitled 'Ars Poetica?' underlines this point. Speaking in *The Government of the Tongue* about the necessity for poetry to 'put poetic considerations first – expressive considerations...based upon its own genetic laws', he nevertheless grants the equal need to 'concede the justice' of Milosz's 'rebuke to the autocracy of such romantic presumption' (1988: 166). He goes on to cite the following lines, where the openness of the self to the other is seen as the province of poetry, and I would see these as paradigmatic of his epistemology of poetry:

> The purpose of poetry is to remind us
> How difficult it is to remain just one person,
> For our house is open, there are no keys in the doors,
> And invisible guests come in and out at will. (1988: 167)

This notion of poetry as a way in which selfhood can be transformed through the entrance of new ideas, thoughts and experiences has much in common with Heaney's own poem 'Markings' which, as we have seen, speaks of a similar experience where 'All these things entered you / As if they were both the door and what came through it' (1991: 9). The field of force image has clearly influenced his general concept of the epistemological structure of poetry; in the next chapter, his attitude to the vexed question of the role that poetry can, and should, play in terms of the political sphere will be explored. Given that in politics, especially the polarised political space of Northern Ireland, selfhood can often become attenuated into the imperatives of the tribe, the expansionist aspects of Heaney's notion of poetry could be seen to have an important ameliorative function. However, the interrelationship of the poetic and the political is fraught with dangers, and there is a need for poetry to engage with, but retain a certain distance from, the discourse of politics. Heaney stresses the need for some form of ethical dimension to the poetic, within the individual as opposed to the group consciousness. As he puts it in 'Weighing In', all 'good tidings' amount to:

> This principle of bearing, bearing up,
> And bearing out, just having to
>
> Balance the intolerable in others
> Against our own. (1996: 17)

The notion of balance, of redressal, of counterweighting and of a structure which accommodates selfhood and alterity will underwrite his exploration of the relationship between the poetic and the politic.

4   'Surviving Amphibiously': Poetry and Politics

In terms of the nexus between poetry and politics, perhaps the most opportune place to begin is with the title of his second collection of prose writings, *The Government of the Tongue*.[1] Like much of Heaney's writing, this phrase resounds with a productive ambiguity. He tells us that what he had in mind was the

> aspect of poetry as its own vindicating force. In this dispensation, the tongue (representing both a poet's personal gift of utterance and the common resources of language itself) has been granted the right to govern. The poetic art is credited with an authority of its own. (1988: 93)

This confident assertion of the power of poetry to become operative in the world of language without undue deference to political ideologies is balanced later in the essay, by a more negative interpretation:

> 'Govern your tongue,' it says, compelling me to remember that my title can also imply a *denial* of the tongue's autonomy and permission....This manifests a world where the prevalent values and necessities leave poetry in a relatively underprivileged situation, requiring it to take a position that is secondary to religious truth or state security or public order....In ideal republics, Soviet republics, in the Vatican and Bible-belt, it is a common expectation that the writer will sign over his or her individual, venturesome and potentially disruptive activity into the keeping of an official doctrine, a traditional system, a party line, whatever. In such contexts, no further elaboration or exploration of the language or forms currently in place is permissible. An order has been handed down and the shape of things has been established. (1988: 96)

Under the 'whatever' rubric of this quotation, Heaney might well have added the term 'nationalist ideology' to flag the felt need on his part, and on the part of others, that he should in some way articulate this sense of nationalist identity in Northern Ireland. This sense of a social or tribal duty has been baggage which Heaney has carried for some time during his career.

Much of Heaney's writing probes this nexus of connections between the poetic and the politic. In keeping with the epistemological structure which has already been sketched in the introduction and opening chapter, Heaney is unwilling to completely valorise one perspective over the other: instead, he will attempt to initiate a field of force wherein both senses of the government of the tongue can be teased out to their fullest extent: 'Sea broke on land to full identity' (1966: 47). That this identity comes from the interaction of opposing forces is significant in the light of the argument being advanced in this book. In *Preoccupations*, Heaney has already flagged the problematic nature of his own community: 'if this was the country of community, it was also the realm of division' (1980: 20), and part of his function as a poet is to voice both of these strands of identity. Perhaps the core question is whether he will take on the colourings of the given political divisions or attempt to use poetry to in some way transform these. As in all of Heaney's work, this will not be a simple or overt project; instead, he will initiate an anastomosis between writer and context similar to that between text and context as discussed earlier. As he puts it: 'the curtain was about to rise on the larger drama of our politics and the writers were to find themselves in a play within a play' (1980: 30). Whether this role would be predefined or fluid is the question which this chapter attempts to probe.

As early as *Wintering Out*, Heaney is gesturing towards his own political constituency in the epigraph to the book which introduces the themes 'disorientation, place, history, and the collective fate' and the routes through which those themes are enunciated 'the drive from present to past, past to present, future to past' (Parker 1993: 93). This poem, entitled 'For David Hammond and Michael Longley', sets out the grim reality of what life was like in Northern Ireland in 1972. Internment without trial had been introduced in Northern Ireland in 1971, with some 1,500 people, the vast majority of these nationalists, being interned.[2] Heaney's epigraph to *Wintering Out* is located firmly in this period. Indeed the book's title refers to an Ulster term meaning to 'survive a crisis' (Parker 1993: 90), and it is the lineaments of this crisis that are the subject of the poem.

Heaney describes driving along a 'dewy motorway' and seeing 'the new camp for the internees',[3] with attendant bomb-craters and 'machine-gun posts'. The only comparison that can be made is to Second World War films, 'some film made / of Stalag 17' (1972: 5); the only response that enters his head is graffiti written in a nationalist area: 'Is there life before death? That's chalked up / on a wall downtown' (1972: 5).[4] In the final line of the poem, there is a pronominal swerve, as the 'I' of the initial two quatrains becomes immersed in the 'we' of his community: 'we hug our little destiny again' (1972: 5). In this poem, and in others, Heaney feels the obligation to voice his own group's sense of identity. In an essay entitled 'Christmas, 1971', he describes the contemporary situation and its effect on him as both a person and a writer.[5] In a style reminiscent of the epigraph to *Wintering Out*, Heaney describes the ongoing political context where 'we have to live with the army', where 'we survive explosions and funerals' and where 'soldiers with cocked guns are watching you' (1980: 30). He goes on to describe how if 'it is not the army, it is the vigilantes', and details some of the slogans on the walls: 'Keep Ulster Protestant', 'Keep Blacks and Fenians out of Ulster', 'Six into Twenty-Six won't go'. He also poses the questions on people's minds as to the identity of 'the next target on the Provisional list'[6] or whether the resultant reprisals 'won't strike where you are' (1980: 31). The imagery of the war film in the epigraph is replicated here, with the poet caught in the middle. He also refers to his three-year-old son being brought with him to a police station near the Falls Road, and to his wife's being 'cornered' by a security man in a shop because of an old clock she had in her bag which may have been a 'timing device' for a bomb (1980: 31).

Interestingly, even in the middle of such a situation, Heaney's attitudes attempt to transcend the givens of his ideological positioning. In the fourth paragraph from the end, he probes the 'Ulster Protestant consciousness' as enunciated by Louis MacNeice, W. R. Rodgers and John Hewitt who are all seen as exploring 'in different ways' their relationship to 'the old sow that eats her farrow'. This gesture of an embattled consciousness towards some understanding of the voice of the other is an important node in Heaney's developing understanding of the transformative role of poetry within culture. At an unconscious level, the binaries still structure his grasp of the situation, as he contrasts a reading of Martin Luther King's 'I have a Dream' speech with an actual dream he had himself while in California: 'I was shaving at the mirror of the bathroom when I glimpsed in the mirror a wounded man falling towards me with his bloodied hands lifted to tear at me or to implore' (1980: 33).

I would argue that these dreams symbolise the different meanings of the government of the tongue: on the one hand, the voiced dream attempts to transform the present with a vision of the future which is ameliorative – 'free at last' – whereas on the other, it is an image of present discord which attempts to embrace the poet. This oneiric symbolisation of the binaries could be seen as a negative index of any chance of relating the two. However, in a later essay from *Preoccupations*, entitled 'Feeling into Words', Heaney ponders the imperatives that such bifurcations place on a poet, and reaches conclusions which are potentially liberating for him and his work. Having worked through the concept of the 'field of force', as discussed in the opening chapter, Heaney answers the central question about the role of the poet in this situation: 'the question, as ever, is "How with this rage shall beauty hold a plea?" And my answer is, by offering "befitting emblems of adversity"' (1980: 57). These emblems are predicated neither on one specific meaning of the notion of the government of the tongue, nor do they valorise either specific oneiric vision of the nature of poetry. Instead, they attempt to initiate the differing parameters of that field of force of which we spoke, a structure which will grant the 'religious intensity of the violence' while at the same time encompassing the perspectives of 'a humane reason' (1980: 56–7). Hence, his work will look for symbolic expression of the many facets of the Northern Irish situation, and to see him as espousing one tradition or perspective over others is to seriously attenuate the scope and vision of his work.

Hence I would argue that a critic like Elmer Andrews is only partially correct when he speaks of Heaney being 'the voice of instinct probing the soft mulches of feeling and sensation' (1988: 55), or when he speaks of Heaney's accepting 'a desolating heritage of brutality and defeat' (1988: 97). The same is true of Blake Morrison's assertion that *North* has been seen both as conflating the poetic with the politic and of being politically one-sided: 'it ends up speaking the language of the tribe, brutal though that language may be' (1982: 68). This is true, but only insofar as Heaney is granting the visceral intensity that allows people to kill each other in the name of a sense of identity as one of those adequate symbolic texts which will interact with the social and cultural context. The voicing of a sense of essentialist nationalist Irishness is a necessary aspect of this strand. Before the tongue can be freed to govern the contextual structures that have shaped it, it must first voice the 'appetites of gravity' (Heaney 1975: 43), the pull of those forces on the voice of the poet. In this interaction of text and context, Heaney's thought parallels that of Derrida who sees such a permeation as a seminal aspect of deconstructive thought:

> 'There is no outside-the-text' signifies that one never accedes to a text without some relation to its contextual opening and that a context is not made up of what is so trivially called a text, that is, the words of a book or the more or less biodegradable paper document in a library. (Derrida 1989c: 841)

He goes on to add that if one does not understand this transformation of text and context, then one understands nothing about deconstruction. I would argue that there is a thematically dominant strand of such transformation at work in Heaney's poetry and in his writing about the purpose and function of poetry. The anastomosis that we traced in the opening chapter also applies broadly to issues of culture, language and identity. Heaney is constantly aware of the intersection of different texts and contexts and he is also at pains to tease out this interaction.

Therefore, in 'Fodder', this sense of a personal identity being located within a broader contextual framework is encapsulated in the pronominal shift between 'we' and 'I' and in the use of the image of embracing:

> Fodder
> Or, as we said,
> *fother*, I open
> my arms for it
> again. (1972: 13)

Here, the preconceived notion of language and identity of which he spoke in *The Government of the Tongue* exerts its force as the dialect pronunciation exerts a gravitational pull on the consciousness of the poet. The language of the 'I' in this stanza is predicated on the social language of the group, the 'we'. He is aware of both the need to voice his own group identity and also of the dangers of such a project which could leave him 'snared, swinging / an ear-ring of sharp wire' (1972: 22). To be attenuated by the parameters of one's own tradition is to risk being 'sleeved in' by 'alluvial mud' with 'elvers' tailing his hair (1972: 26). This image of immersion within a culture is echoed throughout the early part of *Wintering Out*, as he sees himself as 'lobe and larynx / of the mossy places' (1972: 28). In these poems, language as a given is a constructive, and constricting, force on the development of identity: the tongue is being governed by social and linguistic constraints, by the handed down and established order of things. Utterance has a political subtext even when the thematic material is not ostensibly political. There is a need to cross the border into the language of the other as opposed to remaining snared in the language of one's own community.

In one of his most famous early poems, 'The Other Side', Heaney speaks of a Protestant neighbour in a language that is very much that of binary opposition. The neighbour's comments that a piece of ground is 'as poor as Lazarus' is seen as metonymic of a different way of speaking: 'his fabulous, biblical dismissal, / that tongue of chosen people...he prophesied' (1972: 34). The identity of the neighbour is similarly couched in the language of an established order, both in terms of his own speech, and also in terms of how Heaney envisions him and his identity:

> His brain was a whitewashed kitchen
> hung with texts, swept tidy
> as the body o' the kirk. (1972: 35)

This identification with the binaries of Northern Ireland becomes more politically overt in *North*, where the identificatory connections of *Wintering Out* become weighed down by political, ideological and racial 'official doctrines'. In this poem, the personal pronoun first person plural 'we' is used in an exclusionary and differentiating manner:

> Then sometimes when the rosary was dragging
> Mournfully on in the kitchen
> We would hear his step round the gable. (1972: 35)

That the discourse invoked in this quotation is that of prayer is significant as culturally and semiotically this precise form of language exercises a defining imperative in terms of what constitutes selfhood and alterity. In the opening section, the Protestant neighbour is described in a similar yet opposite religious discourse: 'his fabulous biblical dismissal, / that tongue of chosen people' (1972: 34), and the binary opposition is voiced from both sides, with the neighbour speaking of 'your side of the house' (1972: 35), referring to his Catholic neighbours.[7]

However, in terms of structuration, the notion of an 'other side' presupposes a figure where there is also a same side: the very title of the poem sees the Protestant neighbour as relationally connected to the 'I' of the poem. What the poem enacts is the difficulty of negotiating the borders and frontiers that block the movement between these two sides of a seminal binary opposition in Northern Ireland of Protestant/Catholic. Rather than attempt to blur these differences, created through language, religion and history, Heaney, in this poem, spells out the limits of the binary opposition which has defined the politics of Northern Ireland since its foundation. Structures which attempt to sanitise these differences are predestined to failure as they can never sufficiently engage with the ideological positions of either side.[8] In this poem the discursive constitution of each side is foregrounded as opposed to being elided, and the final discursive mode of the poem is that of silence as the 'I' of the poem stands behind the Protestant neighbour 'in the dark yard, in the moan of prayers' (1972: 36). The response to the religious discourse which divides the community into two sides is silence, in which a form of connection is posited:

> Should I slip away, I wonder,
> Or go up and touch his shoulder
> And talk about the weather
>
> Or the price of grass-seed? (1972: 36)

It is significant in this context that this conversation is optative: it does not take place. Instead, the vocal discourse of the poem is that of religion, while any real form of communication is predicated in the future. Edna Longley sees this poem as entering into the 'idiom of the other side' and also as spanning 'two languages to create a third' (1986: 201), and while this may be a little premature in terms of the poem itself, which as noted, ends not in a further language but in silence, nevertheless it is a perceptive observation in terms of Heaney's ongoing project. The projected discourse at the end of the poem supplants the religious frame of reference with those of weather and commerce, perhaps indicating the tenor of this 'further language'.

At this juncture it is important to note that in the poem there is no sense of this type of language as having been developed: as Wells-Cole remarks, any attempt at unity here is evaded by the Protestant other (1995: 142).[9] Brewster is undoubtedly correct when he notes that

'The Other Side' stages a 'face-to-face' encounter that, on the face of it, typifies the awkward proximities threaded through Northern Irish culture. Yet the poem is striking for the way it avoids facing up to the face (for Levinas the incarnation of non-violence) or envisaging the difficulties of approaching a cultural and political divide and attempting to find a shared point of access. (Brewster forthcoming 2004)

Brewster's invocation of the work of Emmanuel Levinas as a lens through which aspects of Heaney's work can be analysed is an important dimension in contemporary cultural discourse. For my purposes, it is Levinas's distinction between the 'saying' and the 'said' that will be of most significance. In his study of otherness, published in English in 1981 entitled *Otherwise Than Being Or, Beyond Essence*, Levinas make a distinction between the '*saying*' and the '*said*', and in an interview with Richard Kearney in the same year, he discussed this differentiation. Levinas made the point that '*saying*' is 'ethical sincerity in so far as it is exposition' and as such, is irreducible 'to the ontological definability of the *said*' (1981a: 193–4).[10] In other words, '*saying*' presupposes an 'ethical openness to the other' (1981a: 194). The 'said' is ontologically definable and constitutive of fixed identities by proclaiming and establishing an 'identification of this with that in the *already said*' (1981b: 37). The 'saying', on the other hand, 'states and thematises the said, but signifies it to the other, a neighbour, with a signification that has to be distinguished from that borne by words in the said' (1981b: 46). The use of the term 'neighbour' is especially significant here, in the context of our discussion.

As Simon Critchley summarises, the philosopher's project is the 'reduction of the Said to the Saying', and he goes on to make the point that ethics, far from overcoming or abandoning ontology, actually deconstructs the latter's limits (1992: 8). For Levinas: 'saying makes signs to the other, but in this sign signifies the very giving of signs'. He goes on to stress the primacy of alterity in the saying, noting that it 'opens me to the other before saying what is said' (1989: 183). As he puts it, language as 'saying is ethical sincerity', it is 'an ethical openness to the other' (1981a: 193–4), and this is what

I suggest we will find as Heaney develops his notion of the 'other side' in a later poem where this locution is taken and given a broader contextual framework wherein movement and interaction are more fluent and more positive. Paradoxically, however, the silence at the end of this poem is an index of the development of an ethical position towards the other and towards a form of intersubjective communication.

That 'The Other Side' ends in silence would seem to indicate an inability to broach this 'saying' in terms of a relationship with the other. However, as Brewster correctly points out: silence is not necessarily testimony to an ethical failure (forthcoming 2004) and both Derrida and Levinas, in their explorations of the ethical imperative, foreground this very point. Speaking about the concepts of hope and the promise of a better future, specifically in the context of the Arab-Israeli question, Levinas describes the difference between the reality of a Jewish state, and his own conception of 'longing for Zion', which can be his notion of the 'promised' Jerusalem, of what he terms 'the humanity of the Torah':

> Our text which began with the cities of refuge, reminds us or teaches us that the *longing* for Zion, that Zionism, is not one more nationalism or particularism; nor is it a simple search for a place of refuge. It is the hope of a science of society, and of a society, which are wholly human. (1994: 51–2)

Reading this passage, Derrida notes that the whole concept of this 'promise' is voiced in Levinas's idea of the saying, but he also foregrounds the role of the recipient of this promise in terms of listening and a silence which has parallels with the openness to alterity of the 'saying':

> Can we not hear this promise? We can also receive and listen to it. We can even feel ourselves engaged by it without, however, remaining insensitive to the silence it bears at the heart of the call. This silence can also be a figure of a hiatus, that is, a mouth opened to speak and eat, but a mouth that is still silent. (1999: 113–14)

Derrida goes on to speak of this silence in Levinas's phrase 'a hope beyond refuge', and proceeds to read this silence as a necessary step in the inauguration of a new future:

Silence is kept concerning the rules or schemas...that would procure for us better or less bad mediations: between ethics or the holiness of messianic hospitality on the one hand and the 'peace process', the process of political peace, on the other. (1999: 114)

Derrida is speaking in the context of the Arab-Israeli conflict but interestingly, the term 'peace process' has come to have a discernibly Irish connotation (at least in an Anglocentric context), and one could read the silence at the end of 'The Other Side' precisely in terms of this moment of preparedness for some form of relation to the other, a relation which, because it has no further language, must begin in silence. In this context, the silence at the end of the poem is a necessary ethical step towards a furtherance of a willed connection between self and other.

The 'I' of the poem is at a decisive point in determining whether he should, or should not, touch his neighbour before speaking to him. This is a necessary silence which delimits a space wherein the connection is willed but also where there is not a template or paradigm within which to sustain it. In that moment of decision as to whether he should 'slip away' or 'touch' his neighbour, a personal ethics of self and other is about to be sketched. As Derrida notes, this silence, this:

non-response conditions my responsibility, there where I alone must respond. Without silence, without the hiatus, which is not the absence of rules but the necessity of a leap at the moment of ethical, political or juridical decision, we could simply unfold knowledge into a program or course of action. (1999: 117)

In terms of achieving a form of intersubjective relationship with the other side of the political, religious and ideological divide that is constitutive of identity in Northern Ireland, this silence is fundamental. Indeed, it is through this trope of silence (but a silence that is contextually amplified), that Heaney will develop his appreciation of the need for connection with the 'other side'.

In 'The Pitchfork' in *Seeing Things*, Heaney is writing in the mode of the first two books, *Death of a Naturalist* and *Door into the Dark*. Here, the tools of the artisan take on a connotative signification as they symbolise aspects of the poet's art. One is reminded of the spade in 'Digging'; the jam-pots in 'Death of a Naturalist'; the scythe in 'The Barn'; pea-tins and jam-pots in 'Blackberry-Picking'; the churns in 'Churning Day'; the gaff and net of 'The Salmon Fisher to the Salmon'; the anvil of 'The Forge'; the bag of knives in 'Thatcher', and this is far from an exhaustive list. It is, I would argue, no coincidence that the pitchfork would be part of the discourse of 'weather' and 'the price of grass-seed' that is envisioned at the end of 'The Other Side'. As an object, it is an index of the commonality that is at the heart of rural living: it is an implement used by both sides of the divide, and as such, should be free of ideological and sectarian baggage. Unlike the religious discursive thread which ran through 'The Other Side', this should be an area which stresses connection as opposed to dislocation.

In this poem, the pitchfork is described in terms of both the actual and the imagined: as a descriptor, the pitchfork crosses the frontier of the real and the imagined: 'of all implements, the pitchfork was the one / That came near to an imagined perfection' (1991: 23), and it is this sense of an imagined reality which transcends the given one that resonates through this poem, and which connects it with the previously discussed one:

And then when he thought of probes that reached the farthest,
He would see the shaft of a pitchfork sailing past
Evenly, imperturbably through space,
Its prongs starlit and absolutely soundless –

But has learned at last to follow that simple lead
Past its own aim, out to an other side
Where perfection – or nearness to it – is imagined
Not in the aiming but the opening hand. (1991: 23)

This image of the opening hand is symbolic of the Levinasian notion of the 'saying' as opposed to the 'said', inasmuch as it is a gesture which does not seek closure. Perfection, in this stanza, may never be achieved, but the idea of 'nearness to it' is central in that it provides an open-ended goal in terms of relation with the other. I feel that it is no accident that the same tropes of otherness and silence are revisited in this poem. It allows Heaney to reconceptualise otherness in terms of an imagined connection where a sense of openness will transfigure the relationship just as the pitchfork becomes an imagined type of space probe, which is able to go 'past its own aim', in a process analogous to Levinas's 'saying', a process where a sense of responsibility to and for the other is important: 'In the saying of responsibility, which is an exposure to an obligation for which no one could replace me, I am unique. Peace with the other is first of all my business' (Levinas 1981b: 138–9).

The context of an imaginary pitchfork gliding through a silent space takes the silence at the conclusion of 'The Other Side' and transforms it into an image of peace and hope, both of which are oriented towards the future. The contextual frameworks of both poems enact this development. In the former, the context of Heaney's childhood home, rural County Derry, where the discourse that is operative is differential in that the Protestant neighbour speaks in biblical language and talks about the 'book' (the Bible) as a point of differentiation, while within the house, it is the rosary, a specifically Catholic prayer, that is heard. This sense of contextual closure is further highlighted by the inside–outside binary opposition that delimits the interaction of the protagonists in the poem. In 'The Pitchfork', however, there is a contextual expansion from the farm yard to the realm of space, a realm which is very much beyond that of the narrow farmyard. Here, the other side takes on a new signification: it describes a realm which is transcendent in terms of the immanent sectarian either/or choices that constrain the givens of identity in Northern Ireland. Indeed, this poem, seen in tandem with 'The Other Side' exemplifies Derrida's notion of the interaction of text and context:

> Every sign, linguistic or non-linguistic, spoken or written...in a small or large unit, can be cited, put between quotation marks; in so doing it can break with every given context, engendering an infinity of new contexts in a manner which is absolutely illimitable. This does not imply that the mark is valid outside of a context, but on the contrary that there are only contexts without any centre or absolute anchorage. (Derrida 1988: 12)

One of the shared cognitive attitudes of Heaney and Derrida is this desire to probe the givens, the seeming fixities of anchorage and to destabilise them in order to enlarge the contextual parameters that govern our discursive practices.

Hence 'The Pitchfork' defines a new context for the term the 'other side', a context which is as expansive and transcendent as the initial context was narrow and circumscribed. The sense of perfection here is related to Levinas's sense of an ethics of plurality which derives from this form of transcendence:

Transcendence or goodness is produced as pluralism....Pluralism is accomplished in goodness proceeding from me to the other....The unity of plurality is peace, and not the coherence of the elements that constitute plurality....Peace therefore cannot be identified with the end of combats that cease for want of combatants, by the defeat of some and the victory of others, that is, with cemeteries or future empires. Peace must be my peace, in a relation that starts from an I assured of the convergence of morality and reality. (Levinas 1969: 305)

This sense of peace can be produced by a broadening of the contextual framework, and it is with this in mind that we should examine Heaney's political poetry. He has often been accused of writing from within the logos and mythos of his own side. Certainly parts of *Wintering Out* and *North* have received a fair share of criticism in these terms. I have spoken elsewhere about the misreadings, as I see them, of the so-called 'land and language' poems of *Wintering Out*, specifically 'Broagh' and 'Anahorish'.[11] These poems have been largely read as statements of linguistic and cultural resistance to the encroachment of the British presence in Ireland.

The genesis of such readings can be seen to emanate from Heaney's own explanation of the beginnings of the poems:

Mossbawn was bordered by the townlands of Broagh and Anahorish, townlands that are forgotten Gaelic music in the throat, *bruach* and *anach fhíor uisce,* the riverbank and the place of clear water. The names lead past the literary mists of a Celtic twilight into that civilization whose demise was effected by administrators like Spenser and Davies, whose lifeline was bitten through when the squared-off walls of bawn and demesne dropped on the country like the jaws of a man-trap. (1980: 36)

In the light of this paragraph, the two poems have been read from a broadly anti-colonial perspective. Both poems begin with the first line seemingly translating the title – Anahorish: 'My "place of clear water"' (1972: 16), and Broagh: 'Riverbank, the long rigs / ending in broad docken' (1972: 27), and both proceed to make connections between place and the language and people who formally inhabited those places. 'Anahorish' speaks of the italicised word 'Anahorish' conjuring up visions of the earliest inhabitants 'mound-dwellers' who are imagined as going 'waist-deep in mist' (1972: 16), while

'Broagh' speaks of a fusion of signifier and referent with the mark of a heel in the 'garden mould' being seen as 'the black O // in *Broagh*' (1972: 27), an identification culminating in the very name of the place being seen as an index of identity and difference: a way of dividing people into one's own side and the other side, as the 'shower' of rain:

> ended almost
> suddenly, like that last
> *gh* the strangers found
> difficult to manage. (1972: 27)

These poems would seem to be a repression of the process of contextual openness of which we have been speaking, as placenames are seen as divisive and polarising. There is no Levinasian or Derridean ethical silence at work here: the names seem to speak the 'absolute anchorage' of the centres of nationalist identity. Andrews reads the end of the poem in this light as exploring the 'relationship between landscape, language and people, it ends by alerting us to the nationalistic implications of all this' (1988: 55), while Ronald Tamplin observes that language 'acts as a line of recognition, marking intimate from stranger' and thus is operative 'in political terms' in the poem (1989: 41–2).

However, keeping in mind the anastomosis with which we began this discussion of Heaney's work, and the resultant series of inter-relationships between text and context, these readings become less determined. The prose description of the genesis of these poems from *Preoccupations* has already been noted. However, that paragraph which speaks of the English cultural imperative in the simile of a 'man-trap' is followed by another one which would seem to suggest a different relationship with this 'other side':

> Yet I also looked across our fields to Grove Hill and Back Park, names that fetch the imagination in a different direction. They insist that this familiar locale is a version of pastoral....Grove is a word that I associate with translations from the classics, a sunlit treeline, a tonsured hillock approached by white-robed priests. The literary word and the earthwork sentried by Scotch firs sit ill together. My illiterate ear isn't totally satisfied, as it is by another name, The Dirraghs, from *doire* as in Derry, also usually Englished as 'oak grove'. Grove and park, they do not reach me as a fibre

from a tap-root but remind me of the intricate and various foliage of history and culture that I grew up beneath. (Heaney 1980: 36)

In this paragraph, that contextual exfoliation of which we spoke in terms of 'The Other Side' and 'The Pitchfork' is again foregrounded. Far from lodging the psyche in the names of his home place and in the Irish language, what we see at work here is a *glissement* of Gaelic, English and classical traditions, creating a context within which the communication between selfhood and alterity becomes a 'saying' as opposed to a 'said': there is an openness and an orientation towards a future ethics and politics instead of the closure that critics read in 'Anahorish' and 'Broagh'. This sense of interaction is enunciated in the closing lines from this essay:

If you like, I began as a poet when my roots were crossed with my reading. I think of the personal and Irish pieties as vowels, and the literary awarenesses nourished on English as consonants. My hope is that the poems will be vocables adequate to my whole experience. (1980: 37)

This would indicate that Heaney's conception of language is very much that of Levinas in terms of seeing language in general, and poetic language in particular, as a 'saying' which 'presupposes an 'ethical openness to the other' (Levinas 1981a: 194).

In the light of these contextual placements, if we revisit 'Broagh' and 'Anahorish', a different reading will become clear, one which firmly locates these poems within his broader ethical and aesthetic project. Indeed, I would see these poems as instantiating the 'intricate and various foliage of history and culture' of which he spoke in *Preoccupations*. These two signifiers are neither Gaelic nor English language terms, nor are they direct translations. The Irish word '*bruach*' translates as 'riverbank', and the Irish string '*anach fhíor uisce*' translates as 'place of clear water': however, the signifier 'Broagh' is a new term, related to both but identical with neither; similarly 'Anahorish' has the same structural relationship and non-relationship with both languages. To see these terms as translations in the strict sense, with the Irish-language term antedating the English one, is simply incorrect. Instead, both placenames embody the pluralities, complexities and traces of the complex interaction of Irish and English cultures in a historical context. As I have noted:

Given the difficulty of the Gaelic phonetic system, as we have seen, British cartographers transliterated many such names into the British phonetic and graphological system; hence the transliteration from 'bruach' to 'broagh.' 'Broagh' then, like 'Anahorish,' is *not* a Gaelic word, but rather it is a transliteration of the Gaelic word 'bruach' by the very 'strangers' who are deemed to find it so 'difficult to manage' in the first place. The 'strangers' who found the original pronunciation 'difficult' have altered it, changing the phonetic area of difficulty into another sound that, almost by definition, they *will* be able to manage. (O'Brien 2003: 60)

The signifiers 'Broagh' and 'Anahorish', then, are neologisms, they are vocables, in Heaney's sense of the word, a language of 'saying' wherein self and other interact and intersect in a transformative manner. In this sense, they embody a more complicated concept of translation, a concept which sees it as an index of the interaction and pluralisation of languages as opposed to a simplistic exchange of meaning between one and another. Derrida makes the following connection between deconstruction and this more complex idea of translation. Deconstruction, he says, consists:

only of transference, and of a thinking through of transference, in all the senses that this word acquires in more than one language, and first of all that of the transference between languages. If I had to risk a single definition of deconstruction, one as brief, elliptical and economical as a password, I would say simply and without overstatement: *plus d'une langue* – both more than a language and no more of *a* language. (Derrida 1989b: 14–15)

I would argue that both 'Broagh' and 'Anahorish' enact this transference, underlining the transformative nature of the interaction, and locating themselves as sites wherein self and other may communicate. The difficulty and friction that is necessitated by such communication is in no way elided in these works, nor in the contextual passages from *Preoccupations*. Heaney's sense of the two traditions 'sitting ill together' underlines this but nevertheless the communication is ongoing and both words transgress the borders of the simplistic self and other binary in a way which becomes 'through-other' a term which we will revisit later in this discussion, in Chapter 6.

Ironically, little has been made of Heaney's early efforts at creating a more inclusive and open relationship between selfhood and alterity. Indeed, in much of the criticism of his poetry of this period, the view that Heaney is speaking very much from within his own tradition, that his tongue is being governed by its constitutive ideology, has become a commonplace. Speaking about 'Kinship', Andrews, for example, notes that a 'guttural cacophonous music takes over as the poet accepts his kinship not only with Romantic victim but with barbaric tribe' (1988: 96). James Simmons notes that 'Heaney's affirmations and omissions suggest that he feels absolutely closer to the hopes and actions of the IRA than he does to any sort of British soldier or Ulster policeman' (1992: 57).[12] David Annwn argues that some of the bog poems suggest that 'republican violence is the dark side of Catholicism', it is the destructive aspect 'of the pre-Marian goddess which have not found a "home" in Christian doctrine' (1984: 145). Stephen Wade asserts that in poems such as 'The Tollund Man' and 'Punishment' there is an 'emotional closeness' in the imagery and diction (1993: 42).

In *North*, this argument is developed in both a mythic and political sphere. In the first part of the book, Heaney has been attacked for speaking too much in the voice of the tribe, in poems like 'Punishment' and 'Kinship' where his sense of being the 'lobe and larynx' of his own identity becomes governed by the atavisms of that very identity:

> Who would connive
> in civilised outrage
> yet understand the exact
> and tribal, intimate revenge. (1975: 38)

> ...report us fairly,
> how we slaughter
> for the common good

> and shave the heads
> of the notorious. (1975: 45)

I have argued elsewhere that to see this as the limit of *North*'s thematic concerns is to grossly oversimplify one of Heaney's most complex books. However, there is no doubt that this type of enunciation of visceral sectarianism that has been part of much of the nationalist psyche over the past 30 years, must be addressed in any complex enunciation of identity.[13] David Lloyd's critique of Heaney focuses on precisely this facet of his writing, what might be termed the governed aspect of his voice. The gradual deictic slide from 'I' to 'we' achieves its most basic expression in these mythic poems as Ireland is personified as a mother figure:

> Our mother ground
> is sour with the blood
> of her faithful. (Heaney 1975: 45)

As Lloyd notes, these associations of Ireland with 'Irish ground, linked as the associations are through Cathleen Ni Houlihan, the motherland, together produce the forms in which the aestheticisation of Irish politics is masked' (1993: 17). Heaney has been accused, by many critics, of writing from within his *mythos* in a manner which is widely seen as wrong. Conor Cruise O'Brien calls 'the area where literature and politics overlap' an 'unhealthy intersection'; because, 'suffused with romanticism', it breeds bad politics – fascism and nationalism (1975a, 1975b).[14] But it also breeds 'bad literature, particularly, bad poetry, which in a vicious circle breeds – or inbreeds – bad politics' (Longley 1986: 185).

However, the issue of agency is an important one here: Heaney is not espousing this type of essentialist nationalism as a credo or an ethos. He is not invoking what Derrida has termed the *telos* of nationalism: 'killing the future in the name of the old frontiers' (1994: 169). Instead, what he is doing is giving voice to that visceral aspect of his own community's sense of self which valorises the killing of the other in the name of that very concept of such an ideology. Terry Eagleton's assertion that 'ideology is a function of the relation of an utterance to its social context' (1991: 9) is significant here as the social context of Heaney's utterance is the Northern Irish violence spread over 30 years. However, the context of the utterance of the poetry is mythical as opposed to actual. The bog people, while figures from an archetypal past, are largely from cultures other than that of Northern Ireland. The figure of Tacitus, invoked as an observer in 'Kinship', is fictional in the context that the Romans never came to Ireland. His presence in the poem does not describe any motivated connection between Heaney's *mythos* and the land of Ireland. Similarly, many of the bog poems are set in a European as opposed to an Irish context, with the bog people themselves having no connection with Ireland – the Windeby Girl (Germany), the Tollund Man and the Grauballe Man (Denmark), while the goddess Nerthus was worshipped in Europe as opposed to Ireland.

My point here is that the connection between these bog people and the matter of Northern Ireland is not one which sees Heaney subordinating the freedom of the tongue to the governing imperatives of the nationalist *mythos*, despite the widespread critical consensus to the contrary. These connections are literary and created by Heaney in terms of finding adequate symbols for the situation in Northern Ireland. He is attempting to universalise and distance his imagery. As he told Edward Broadbridge:

> There's a kind of sectarian conflict going on. Something that was repressed and held under, but which has forced itself to the surface again, and I've tried to make a connection lately between things that come to the surface in bogs, in particular in Danish bogs, and the violence that was coming to the surface in the north of Ireland. (Broadbridge 1977a: 11)

The connection between the Iron Age bog victims and the victims of contemporary Northern Irish violence is a willed one, and I would maintain that it is this very connection that exercises a deconstructive force on the received meaning of the governing of the utterance by the gravitational demands of Heaney's own community.

The connections between, for example, the Windeby Girl and the 'betraying sisters / cauled in tar' (Heaney 1975: 38) who were punished by the nationalist community for dating British soldiers are created as opposed to being in some way 'given'; Heaney is choosing to write about material which is aesthetically, temporally and spatially distant from his own political context in order to achieve the symbolic adequation of which he spoke in *Preoccupations*. He is not being forced to inhabit a position inside one of the contextual binary oppositions of nationalist–unionist; republican–loyalist; Catholic–Protestant or, at a broader level, poetry–politics and the tongue being governed as opposed to being self-governing. Instead, in these poems, he is deconstructing the received relationship between the aesthetic and the political by firstly reversing the binary and secondly by reconstituting the whole structure in order to redefine the role of the poetic text within the political context.

This process is emblematic of how Derrida describes the act of deconstruction. This reversal of prevailing hierarchical binary oppositions is a necessary step in a deconstructive reading. As Derrida himself notes: 'to deconstruct the opposition, first of all, is to overturn the hierarchy at a given moment' (1981a: 41). But this reversal is only the first step in the deconstructive project. Making the point that an opposition of metaphysical concepts is never the face-to-face of two terms, but a hierarchy and an order of subordination, Derrida goes on to say:

> Deconstruction cannot limit itself or proceed immediately to a neutralization: it must, by means of a double gesture, a double science, a double writing, practice an *overturning* of the classical opposition *and* a general *displacement* of the system. It is only on this condition that deconstruction will provide itself the means with which to *intervene* in the field of oppositions that it criticises, which is also a field of non-discursive forces. Each concept, moreover, belongs to a systematic chain, and itself constitutes a system of predicates. There is no metaphysical concept in and of itself. There is a work – metaphysical or not – on conceptual systems. Deconstruction does not consist in passing from one concept to another, but in overturning and displacing a conceptual order, as well as the nonconceptual order with which the conceptual order is articulated. (1982: 329)

Heaney is setting up links in this systematic chain, this field of force, in order to provide for a change in the meaning of the idea of the government of the tongue. He is creating a broader contextual framework within which he can locate different aspects of his discussion of his themes. So, what is at work in the bog poems is not an atavistic expression of some form of essentialist identity; instead, it is a reformulation of experience within the generic structure of poetry. He is involved in the process of overturning the conceptual order of the received relationship between poetry and politics through this dialectical interaction of differing perspectives and symbolic structures. We have already noted his statement in 'Squarings', that a place can mean 'A state of mind. Or different states of mind // At different times' (1991: 97), and it is this sense of difference or plurality that is his most important step in overturning the binaries.

The epigraph to *Wintering Out* has already been discussed, but it appears again, in recontextualised form, in *North*. In a poem which is located in modern-day Northern Ireland, 'Whatever You Say Say

Nothing', he speaks in a contemporary voice about the situatedness of his position as a Catholic nationalist poet who is attempting to locate his art within this circumscribed political and ideological space: 'I sit here with a pestering / Drouth for words at once both gaff and bait' (1975: 59). In this poem he has 'levelled his voice to the conversational, turned his anthropomorphic gaze to the ordinary ways life is lived' (Vendler 1998: 74), and is asking questions of himself that are the core of this chapter, namely, the correct relationship between poetry and politics.

He examines his desire to 'draw the line through bigotry and sham' (1975: 59) while at the same time feeling that 'the liberal papist note sounds hollow // When amplified and mixed in with the bangs' of the ongoing explosions (1975: 58). He goes on to ponder the contradiction that despite his linguistic gifts, he is 'incapable' of finding that 'right line':

> The famous
> Northern reticence, the tight gag of place
> And times: yes, yes. Of the 'wee six' I sing
> Where to be saved you only must save face
> And whatever you say, you say nothing. (1975: 59)

The penultimate section of the poem compares the nationalist community to the Greeks in the wooden horse of Troy, besieged 'within the siege, whispering morse' (1975: 60). The final image of this section again gestures towards that silence which is a prerequisite for ethical action.

Any attempt to use poetry as a direct mode of address to in some way salve the wounds of division will be patently ineffective. Heaney's reaction in both *Wintering Out* and *North* has been far more nuanced: he has broadened the contextual framework in order to reimagine the contemporary situation. Through such a process of recontextualisation, and in essence, this is what the mythopoeic swerve in Heaney's poetry entails, the current political and sectarian situation is complicated and thickened in order to destabilise the fixities of meaning and create a new field of force wherein differences can be discussed. This impulse, which can be traced through other works such as his translations: *Sweeney Astray, Beowulf, The Midnight Verdict, The Cure at Troy* and 'Mycenae Lookout' in *The Spirit Level*, is a parallel enunciation of one of the many definitions that Derrida has given of the epistemological thrust of deconstruction:

One of the definitions of what is called deconstruction would be the effort to take this limitless context into account, to pay the sharpest and broadest attention possible to context and thus to an incessant movement of recontextualisation. (Derrida 1988: 136)

Thus, when operating in the more contemporary and more declarative world of 'the Irish thing', and when using the jargon that has been established by 'politicians and newspapermen' who have 'scribbled down' the situation in their own terms:

Who proved upon their pulses 'escalate',
'Backlash' and 'crack down', 'the provisional wing',
'Polarization' and 'long-standing hate', (Heaney 1975: 57)

Heaney is contextually circumscribed. He is forced to operate within the given linguistic context and all transformative attempts are frustrated by a language which is locked within the conflictual paradigm, and which has no opening to alterity through which to usher in some form of dialogue. Hence, the Levinasian silence of which we have already spoken comes into play in both the title and in the conclusion of the above quotation.

Interestingly, it is after this injunction to silence that another recontextualisation occurs, the repetition of the epigraph to *Wintering Out*. Vendler makes the point that the conversational tone of this poem stresses the lack of power of conversational discourse to encompass the sheer complexity of the situation in which Heaney finds himself. It is in this context that the epigraph beginning 'This morning from a dewy motorway' is repeated, and the altered perspective underlines the act that such descriptions can only give one impression of the reality that is Belfast 'where bad news is no longer news' (1975: 57). Desmond Fennell has taken the title of this poem as the title of a pamphlet in which he offers Heaney's poetry and reputation to a form of interrogation. He stresses Heaney's lack of overt statement about matters political: 'his [Heaney's] poetry says nothing, plainly or figuratively, about the war, about any of the three main parties to it, or about the issues at stake' (1991: 16). However, this is to miss the point that is at issue in terms of Heaney's developing epistemological approach to the relationship between the aesthetic and the political.

Writing in *The Redress of Poetry*, Heaney makes a core point in relation to this relationship:

Poetry, let us say, whether it belongs to an old political dispensation or aspires to express a new one, has to be a working model of inclusive consciousness. It should not simplify. Its projections and inventions should be a match for the complex reality which surrounds it and out of which it is generated....As long as the co-ordinates of the imagined thing correspond to those of the world that we live in and endure, poetry is fulfilling its counterweighting function. (1995a: 8)

Heaney is at pains not to adopt a simplistic response to 'the Troubles'; in the conversational discourse of 'Whatever You Say Say Nothing', he tells us that when so asked, he is 'incapable', and the recontextualised appearance of the epigraph underlines this point. The dreamlike aura and oneiric description of the camp at Long Kesh in terms of its similarity to a silent war film underline the difficulty of responding to the specific situation without falling into a simplistic and clichéd frame of reference. The anastomosis of text and context discussed earlier is at work again here as the repetition of the twelve lines (the only such repetition in the Heaney canon) stresses the problematic nature of the demand to write for the group or community. The parergonal framework traced by the repetition of these lines describes a specific facet of Heaney's writings on poetry and politics.

The epigraph introduces two books that were broadly similar in terms of structure and theme. Indeed, Heaney has told John Haffenden that he was certain that 'up to *North* that that was one book' (1981: 64). Both books offer overt and allusive responses to the political situation in Northern Ireland, and can be seen as his attempt to address this vexed issue from a broadly communitarian perspective. On seeing a volume entitled *North*, the horizon of expectations at the time, given that the poet himself came from County Derry, would have anticipated a book about the contemporary situation in Northern Ireland in 1975. Blake Morrison makes the point that there was a certain demand for 'war poets' (Morrison 1982: 55). However, I would argue that the repeated epigraph stylistically makes the point that Heaney's probings have not really developed any further from the beginning of *Wintering Out* to the close of *North*, hence the circularity and closure of the oneiric epigraph. In this sense the framing circularity voices one connotation of the phrase the 'government of the tongue' which we have already discussed, namely the 'denial of the tongue's autonomy and permission', with the poet having to take up a position that is 'secondary to religious truth or state security or public order' (Heaney 1988: 96).

However, having traced some strands of the governing of the tongue in terms of the denial of the tongue's autonomy and permission, the other strand of this particular field of force must also be investigated and, significantly, this investigation can also begin with that epigraph from *Wintering Out*. In 'The Interesting Case of Nero, Chekhov's Cognac and a Knocker', Heaney tells that in 1972, he and David Hammond were on their way to a recording studio to assemble 'a tape of songs and poems' for a friend in Michigan:

> The tape was to be sent in memory of a party which the man from Michigan had attended some months beforehand, when tunes and staves had been uttered with great conviction. The occasion had been immensely enjoyable and the whole point of the tape was to promote that happiness and expansiveness which song, meaning both poetry and music, exists to promote in the first place. (1988: xi)

However, on the way to the studio, a number of explosions occurred in Belfast, and the sound of ambulances rang through the city. These explosions were part of a campaign of terror waged by the Provisional IRA, and as such, by members of Heaney's own Catholic, nationalist community, a point clear from his description of the 'certain half-directed fury' directed at them by the loyalist BBC security man when they arrived at the studio. In the face of the explosions and the sound of ambulance sirens, both Heaney and Hammond felt that 'the music of the guitar' could make 'little impression', that the 'very notion of beginning to sing at that moment when others were beginning to suffer seemed like an offence against their suffering'. So both men drove off 'into the destroyed evening' (1988: xi). Here, song is definitely seen as 'secondary' to the prevailing orthodoxies of sectarian identity, the tongue is definitely governed by political and ideological imperatives. The silence of the performance is an eloquent one as the sounds of discord prevail. In ways, this is the nadir of the relationship as politics silences the voice of imagination.

However, the very fact that he can write about the experience is an aporetic swerve away from this position, allowing him to acknowledge the governing power of the violence and political action but at the same time, to voice a regret at allowing utterance and poetic freedom to be so governed. At the end of 'Nero, Chekhov's

Cognac and a Knocker', he tells us of a poem he wrote for David Hammond 'after the event described at the beginning of this introduction', citing its concluding stanzas as 'a point of repose and a point of departure' (1988: xxiii):

> When I came here first you were always singing,
> a hint of the clip of the pick
> in your winnowing climb and attack.
> Raise it again, man. We still believe what we hear. (1979: 27)

In this poem, another strand of the *Kraftfeldt* (force-field) is set up as the imperative to sing in the face of suffering is declared. Rather than being governed by the context of the violence, poetry here is attempting to create its own contextual framework: the song here represents that 'aspect of poetry as its own vindicating force'; the tongue now has been 'granted the right to govern'; the poetic art is 'credited with an authority of its own' (1988: 93).

From an ethical perspective, the concept of singing in the face of suffering is indicative of a less violent and more dialogic response to the other. It is a response that attempts to break out of the dreamlike trance of the 'bad dream with no sound' (1975: 60) and instead to recreate the self through an exposure to the voice, and face, of alterity. This, in a manner redolent of Derrida, is achieved through a process of recontextualisation. It is after this closing of the oneiric framework that a perceptible shift occurs in his poetic search for answers as in 'Exposure', he finds a further context within which to frame his ongoing search for answers.

The 'I' of this poem is located within a very broad contextual framework, staring at 'a comet that was lost', from a standpoint for once physically outside Northern Ireland, in 'December in Wicklow' (1975: 72), and seeing itself in terms of Ovid's 'responsible *tristia*'. The opening of a spatial, temporal and classical structure of possible contexts allows the speaker of the poem to relocate himself in terms of the politics which has hitherto circumscribed his development. That he should describe himself as an 'inner émigré' is a further recontextualisation, as the term, with its connotations of internal exile within the Soviet union (a connotation which opens what will prove to be a strong contextual connection with eastern European writers in general, and Osip and Nadezhda Mandelstam in particular), will allow him to reconfigure the relationship between the aesthetic and the political, in other contexts. Of course the title of the poem,

'Exposure' is highly significant in terms of the developing idea of ethics that Levinas has been tracing as the idea of exposure presupposes an other to whom one is exposed.

The increasingly open contextual framework will allow Heaney to espouse a sense of 'saying' in terms of the political as opposed to the strictures of the 'said', strictures which were clearly felt in 'Whatever You Say Say Nothing'. In this context, Critchley's conspectus of the difference between the 'saying and the 'said' is noteworthy at the level of the signifier:

> The Saying is my exposure – corporeal, sensible – to the Other, my inability to refuse the Other's approach. It is the performative stating, proposing, or expressive position of myself facing the Other. It is the verbal or non-verbal ethical performance, whose essence cannot be caught in constative propositions....By contrast, the Said is a statement, assertion, or proposition (of the form S is P), concerning which the truth or falsity can be ascertained. (Critchley 1992: 7)

That Critchley should use the term 'exposure' is hardly coincidental, given the associations of otherness that it connotes. The recontextualisations of which we have spoken are predicated on this notion of exposure of text to context and by extension, of self to other. Levinas, too, sees his own work predicated on similar notions of exposure:

> Responsibility for the other, in its antecedence to my freedom, its antecedence to the present and to representation, is a passivity more passive than all passivity, an exposure to the other without this exposure being assumed, and exposure without holding back, exposure of exposedness, expression, saying. This exposure is the frankness, sincerity, veracity of saying. (1981b: 15)

Heaney's work is also predicated on such exposure and by broadening his contextual framework, he exposes his own problematic of the aesthetic and the poetic to the example of other cultures which experienced a similar dilemma. Explaining why he has turned to the writers of communist Eastern Europe, he stresses their ability to address the terms of a political crisis on their own terms while remaining faithful to the dictates of the aesthetic. As he says: 'one of the challenges which they face is to survive amphibiously in the realm

of "the times" and the realm of their moral and artistic self-respect'
a challenge which he goes on to equate with the parallel Irish situation
(1988: xx). His purpose in citing such writing is to stress that poetry
is its own form of wisdom; that it must be creative of a complex sense
of personhood and while taking account of the political context, must
nevertheless attempt to transcend that context.

In his poetry, this is brought about by a series of poems in which
the balance of selfhood and alterity is open in the sense that there
is a fluidity of response. Thus, in 'Markings', he speaks of passing
'some limit' and of remembering past events, the marking of a pitch
with 'four jackets for four goalposts' in a game of football, or the
marking of 'the outline of a house foundation' with 'tight white
string' (1991: 8). The passing of the limit, however, involves
remembering the transforming power of these events, so that the
football game transcends its context by becoming a game that the
'youngsters' were 'playing in their heads', while the marked lines of
the house foundation becomes an 'imaginary line straight down'
(1991: 9). Perhaps the ultimate symbol of such transformations
echoes the lines already quoted from Squarings, where the imaginary
ship floated over the heads of the 'monks of Clonmacnoise' (1991:
62), as the poem ends with an image of transformation of the
element of the poem itself, an image redolent of the responsibility
of poetry to alter the terms of the actual:

> Two men with a cross-cut kept it swimming
> Into a felled beech backwards and forwards
> So that they seemed to row the steady earth. (1991: 9)

This image of rowing on land is a paradigm of the altered response
to reality that Heaney endorses. It embodies his responsibility to
develop a more complex sense of selfhood through the aesthetic.
Here, relationships are the result of interaction, an interaction that
can be transformative, as the beech is recontextualised into a boat,
and land becomes sea.

In 'The Flight Path', the whole issue of the relationship between
poetry and politics, and between the self as complex individual consciousness and the self as contextually belonging to a tribe or group
is finally played out. In this poem, the self describes the ongoing
process of recontextualisation that has been his life. It is a type of
poetic *Bildungsroman*, from the images of his father making a 'paper
boat' which, despite its promise, would 'go soggy once you launched

it' to an image of looking up at a 'late jet out of Dublin' (1996: 22),
to a moment where self and other fuse. He is standing in a doorway:

> early in the night,
> Standing-in in myself for all of those
> The stance perpetuates: the stay-at-homes
> Who leant against the jamb and watched and waited....
> ....Who never once forgot
> A name or a face, nor looked down suddenly
> As the plane was reaching cruising altitude
> To realize that the house they'd just past over –
> Too far back to see – was the same house
> They'd left an hour before. (1996: 23)

In this image, the 'I' of the poem exposes himself to the other in that
he 'stands in' for those who stayed at home and imaginatively puts
himself in their position watching him leave on one of his many
journeys. He then undertakes a chiasmatic reversal as he images
them, in litotes, never having had that feeling of spatial defamiliar-
isation as he looks down at a house made tiny and unfamiliar by
distance and perspective, while at the same time remembering that
it was the familiar house which had just been left behind. In this
sense, the relation to the other is seen as transcendent in terms of the
self: as Derrida notes, 'dissociation, separation, is the condition of
my relation to the other' (1997b: 14). This movement between self
and other sets the tone for the ethical movement of this poem as the
'I', through processes of recontextualisation and travel – 'Manhattan',
'California' – has become more assured and more aware of the value
of the individual. Having waited until he was 'nearly fifty / To credit
marvels' (Heaney 1991: 50), he has gradually begun to accept that the
duty to the group is redressed by the duty to the self.

   In the fourth section of the poem, he describes how he was
approached by a friend, presumably a member of the IRA, who, in a
dream, had asked him to take part in setting an explosion at a
'customs post / At Pettigo' (1996: 24). This section epitomises that
complexity of response of which we have been speaking. One of the
strengths of Heaney's writing with respect to the relationship between
poetry and politics lies in his inhabiting a constellation whose
components include both the desire to transcend the actual as well
as the gravitational pull of the actual. Hence, as we saw earlier in this
chapter, he has been much criticised for writing, in *North*, about those

very appetites of gravity which cause people to murder others in the name of an ideology, creed or belief. He has spoken of how 'we' (and the pronoun is used advisedly) 'slaughter / for the common good' (1975: 45) and also of understanding the 'the exact / and tribal, intimate revenge' (1975: 38).

To contextualise this section of 'The Flight Path', we need to focus on a section of *Crediting Poetry*, where he tells of his own near surrender to the appetites of gravity as he recalls:

> Shocking myself with a thought I had about that friend who was imprisoned in the seventies upon suspicion of having been involved with a political murder: I shocked myself by thinking that even if he were guilty, he might still perhaps be helping the future to be born, breaking the repressive forms and liberating new potential in the only way that worked, that is to say the violent way – which therefore became, by extension, the right way. (1995a: 18)

He goes on to describe this as a moment of 'exposure to interstellar cold' (1995a: 19), and also to see it as a turning point in his own view of the relationship between self and other. This moment of exposure (and again, in terms of his own work and that of Levinas, this word is significant) brings him to an epiphany in terms of the interaction between communities of selfhood and alterity. In a telling point, he adds that what would best point towards 'helping the future to be born' would be the image of the 'contraction which that terrified Catholic felt on the roadside when another hand gripped his hand' (1995a: 19). Here, the sense of responsibility to the 'other side' becomes palpable and the 'I' that is capable of such a gesture reminds us of Levinas's idea of exposure to the other as 'the frankness, sincerity, veracity of saying' (1981b: 15). He is unwilling to have his responses pre-programmed by aspects of his tradition.

Thus the oneiric image of his being asked to join in this communally sanctioned violence in 'The Flight Path', harks back to feelings of doubt as to whether his art should be, in some respects 'a slingstone / whirled for the desperate' (Heaney 1975: 72), or whether he should attempt to transcend such 'attenuations' and 'entrapments'. This culturally unconscious dimension of identity with which Heaney has long struggled, is finally consigned to the past in the following interchange:

So he enters and sits down
Opposite and goes for me head on.
'When, for fuck's sake, are you going to write
Something for us?' 'If I do write something,
Whatever it is, I'll be writing for myself.'
And that was that. Or words to that effect. (1996: 25)

Here, the 'I' is decentred from its position as belonging to the 'we',
he is transforming the givens of his situation in order to focus
attention on the self. The 'I' is open to a saying, to a sense of selfhood
that is predicated on the future as opposed to the past. Rather than
take his bearings from within his own mythos, Heaney here is
expressing a desire to recreate himself, keeping that mythos as part,
but not the defining part, of his sense of self. In this sense, he echoes
one of Derrida's many gnomic definitions of deconstruction.
Speaking of the inauguration of a new programme in philosophy in
Villanova University, Derrida makes the point that deconstruction
has never been in favour of 'repeating an institution' (1997b: 5).
Instead, he suggests that if an institution is to be an institution: 'it
must to some extent break with the past, keep the memory of the
past, while inaugurating something absolutely new' (1997b: 6).
Heaney's sense of writing for himself implies that such writing will
play a large part in the defining of the field of force that is the self
in this context. In a Levinasian sense, he is now taking responsibility for the creation of his own complex consciousness. He is
furthering that process of continuous adjudication of which we
spoke, and attempting to survive amphibiously through the
redressing effect of poetry. He sees this effect as coming from its being
'a glimpsed alternative, a revelation of potential that is denied or
constantly threatened by circumstances' (1995a: 4). This furthers his
definition of poetry as 'pure concentration, a focus where our power
to concentrate is concentrated back on ourselves' (1988: 108), as well
as instantiating the idea that poetry can bring 'human existence into
a fuller life' (1995a: xvii).

His view of the epistemology of poetry, I would argue, is informed
by this notion of redressal, or what he also terms 'counterweighting':

of balancing out the forces, of redress – tilting the scales of reality
towards some transcendent equilibrium. And in the activity of
poetry too, there is a tendency to place a counter-reality in the
scales – a reality which may be only imagined but which neverthe-

less has weight because it is imagined within the gravitational pull of the actual and can therefore hold its own and balance out against the historical situation. (1995b: 4–5)

In the next chapter, this balance of opposites, this creation of a counter-reality will be examined with specific reference to Heaney's notion of place.

5 'A Bright Nowhere':
The Deconstruction of Place

Keeping in mind Heaney's notion of counterweighting reality, and also his view that the relationship between poetry and actuality needs to be transformative, the section from 'The Flight Path', cited in the previous chapter, is followed by an interrogation of the speaker of the poem 'at a roadblock', who, on being asked where he came from, answers 'I came from "far away"', and he goes on to speak of notions of home and belonging in very defamiliarising terms:

> And now it is – both where I have been living
> And where I left – a distance still to go
> Like starlight that is light years on the go
> From far away and takes light years arriving. (Heaney 1996: 25)

The mood of this stanza illustrates the transforming of place that has become central to Heaney's aesthetic throughout his work. I have dealt with the issue of Heaney and place at some length elsewhere.[1] However, in this section I hope to focus on some specific places that are important in Heaney's work, and by an examination of the transformation of these places to develop a further strand in Heaney's ongoing search for answers to the question of how the individual can develop within such a society. Heaney makes it clear that the enculturation of a sense of place in Northern Ireland is riven by ideological fissures: 'the Irish political leader operating between two systems of loyalty, the Irish writer responsive to two cultural *milieux*, the Irish place invoked under two different systems of naming' (1995b: 188). To name one's home as 'Derry' for example is to trace a cultural and etymological heritage back to the Irish language name '*Doire Colmcille*', where the signifier '*doire*' means an oak tree, and Colmcille was a saint who lived in early Christian Ireland. It is to enunciate a nationalist ideological position. On the other hand, to name one's home as 'Londonderry' is to espouse a British and colonial heritage, as it was common practice to name places in the new colony after places in the colonial centre, to cement the bonds between the two. It is to espouse a unionist ideological position.

In terms of history then, Irish places became ideologically dense signifiers of cultural and political association: one's place of origin determined much of one's political identity. Heaney's process of continuous adjudication, and his attempt to create a field of force wherein such fissured notions of identity could in some way cohere, is a project that has connections with one of Heaney's early avatars, William Wordsworth. Heaney recalls how Wordsworth, torn between admiration for the revolutionary ideals of France and a sense of patriotism towards his English home, was caught on the 'horns of a dilemma'. This was specifically dramatised, and this point is certainly pertinent to a Northern Irish context, in a church service where Wordsworth experienced feelings of 'alienation and treacherous disaffection' during prayers 'for the English armies' who were fighting the French. Heaney goes on to see *The Prelude* as being about 'a consciousness coming together through the effort of articulating its conflict and crisis' (1995b: 189), and his own sense of a developing consciousness is similarly expressed.

Taking his cue from the explicit idea that poetry is that force which can redress the balance of the actual weight of history with another discourse which can tilt 'the scales of reality towards some transcendent equilibrium' (1995b: 3), Heaney proceeds to balance ideas of place as ideologically predefined, and which accordingly ideologically load those who live in that place with another, less weighty conception of place. Here, the redressal of poetry comes from 'its being a glimpsed alternative, a revelation of potential that is denied or constantly threatened by circumstances' (1995a: 4). In this sense, place becomes more of a space wherein there is potential for development as opposed to a predictive, historically driven imperative from the past. He goes on to describe poetry as 'more a threshold than a path' and sees it as one which is 'constantly approached and constantly departed from', and which affects the reader in terms of the experience of being 'at the same time summoned and released' (1988: 108).

This view of poetry as the creation of an ideational place is expressed in 'The Placeless Heaven: Another Look at Kavanagh'. In this essay, he recalls that his aunt, who held him in great affection, planted a chestnut tree which was associated with the young Heaney from that time onward. However, when new owners arrived, they cut down the tree. Heaney's association with the tree gradually became replaced by an association with the 'space where the tree had been or would have been', and he goes on to note that he saw this space as a kind of 'luminous emptiness' (1988: 13). In a paragraph which has implications for any reading of Heaney's poems which relate to place, he avers that:

> It was not so much a matter of attaching oneself to a living symbol of being rooted in the native ground; it was more a matter of preparing to be unrooted, to be spirited away into some transparent, yet indigenous afterlife. The new place was all idea, if you like; it was generated out of my experience of the old place but it was not a topographical location. It was and remains an imagined realm, even if it can be located at an earthly spot. (1988: 4)

It is this progression, from a clearly defined 'somewhere' to a creative space which can be oriented towards the future, that will be traced in this chapter. In 'The Wishing Tree', he further dislocates the place of the tree by seeing the tree 'lifted root and branch to heaven' (1987: 36). The connection can again be made with some of Derrida's thinking, as he speaks of the site of philosophy as a 'non-site' (*non-lieu*) (Derrida 1981c: 159),[2] meaning that philosophy can become a creative space for thinking in ways which are outside normal parameters or borders.

In the eighth poem from 'Clearances', again speaking of this chestnut tree, Heaney specifically voids place and sees this voiding as the creation of a space which becomes a source:

> I thought of walking round and round a space
> Utterly empty, utterly a source
> Where the decked chestnut tree had lost its place. (1987: 32)

The idea of absence as a source is crucial to Heaney's decentring and recontextualisation of place: it is as if he wishes to create a space wherein the contradictions and oppositional forces with which writing is concerned (those 'made of uneasiness', which are 'made of contradictions' and which are 'not very stable or secure' (Blanchot 1981: 44)), can be contained: in other words, in the space of literature. In such a space, 'when everything seems put into question' (Blanchot 1981: 38), the true function of writing can become operative. In the space created by the absence of the chestnut tree 'my coeval' (Heaney 1987: 32), part of Heaney's selfhood has an existence:

> Its heft and hush become a bright nowhere
> A soul ramifying and forever
> Silent, beyond silence listened for. (1987: 32)

Such emptiness allows for that concentration on the self that has been an *a priori* aspect of Heaney's view of the epistemological structure of poetry. Once again, Blanchot describes the process of self-concentration, making the point that in writing, the poet hears: 'himself, hears the eternally reverberating echo of his own progress, a progress towards silence' (1982a: 16). In this sense, the nullness of the space of literature deracinates the predesignations of ideology, culture and history and instead provides a space (*non-lieu*) wherein contradictions can possibly be recontextualised in a more productive encounter. Derrida has also made the point that literature is, in a real sense, connected to 'a juridical institution, to acquired rights', and, in the context of his discussion of Roman civilisation, to the concept of '*civitas*' (2000a: 24). For him, 'foundational to *litteratura* is the freedom to say, accept, receive, suffer and simulate anything' (Rapaport 2003: 33). This is precisely the claim that Heaney's episte-mological position makes for literature, and it is a position that is intrinsically similar to that of Maurice Blanchot.

In his book entitled *The Space of Literature*, Blanchot time and again sees literature as a point of nullity: 'if literature coincides with nothing, for just an instant, it is immediately everything, and this everything begins to exist' (1982a: 22). The similarity between this position and that of Heaney in 'The Disappearing Island' is clear. In this poem, the island with its 'blue hills and those sandless shores' becomes an image of nullity and absence as:

> The island broke beneath us like a wave.
>
> The land sustaining us seemed to hold firm
> Only when we embraced it *in extremis*.
> All I believed that happened there was vision. (1987: 50)

This idea that vision can only occur when the seeming solidity of place disappears is a metaphorical parallel with Blanchot's view of literature as a space from where things can be re-envisaged. It is a location, or space, wherein the speaker 'treads the tightrope of his uncertainty in a line that stretches between two opposing truths' (Heaney 1989: 54). This is because, speaking of 'each thing and each being' (the components of all binary oppositions), and starting from a sense of space, literature is now 'seeing and naming them from the starting point of everything, from the starting point of the absence of everything, that is, from nothing' (Blanchot 1981: 36). It is this process of voiding place that validates the literary aim of sifting 'the sense of things from what's imagined' (Heaney 1987: 51).

The poem which offers a paradigm of this process is 'The Stone Grinder' in *The Haw Lantern*. In this poem the process at work is that of the creation of an absence by the grinding away of stones: 'I ground the same stones for fifty years / and what I undid was never the thing I had done.' This absence will prepare the way for new processes of signification: 'I prepared my surfaces to survive what came over it' (1987: 8), highlighting, as Peter McDonald puts it, Heaney's interest in a 'future of absences as well as presences' (McDonald 1997: 13). The same point is made in the next poem 'A Daylight Art' when he speaks of 'daylight through the rod's eye or the nib's eye' (Heaney 1987: 9), once again valorising space as opposed to place, absence as opposed to presence. Like the grinding away of the stone, transformation can only occur when there is a space cleared, and Heaney's overt reconceptualisation of such places is certainly predicated on this notion of transformation:

> The space we stood around had been emptied
> into us to keep, it penetrated
> Clearances that suddenly stood open.
> High cries were felled and a pure change happened. (1987: 31)

Perhaps it is this orientation towards change that is the key in Heaney's ongoing recontextualisation of place in his work, the imperative towards change and transformation. Derrida, in an interview entitled 'This Strange Institution Called Literature',[3] speaks about literature as that 'institution which allows one to *say everything*, in *every way*' (1992a: 36),[4] and this places a responsibility on literature to enhance transformations as much as possible. Derrida stresses the responsibility of literature to a notion of democracy in this interview, stressing that he means:

> Not the democracy of tomorrow, not a future democracy which will be present tomorrow but one whose concept is linked to the to-come [*à-venir*, cf. *avenir*, future], to the experience of a promise engaged, that is always an endless promise. (1992a: 38)

The grinding of stones in Heaney's poem embodies the necessary friction and space that will bring about such a change. By preparing surfaces for new writings and new markings, the stone grinder is oriented towards the future. By preparing his 'surface to survive what came over it' (Heaney 1987: 8) the stone grinder is practising a form of prophecy, a point underlined by the use of 'haruspicated' in the poem, a word deriving from the idea of soothsaying by reading the entrails of a sacrificial victim, but ultimately deriving from the Latin '*specere*', meaning 'to look at'. Etymologically, then, the grinding down of the material is a way of seeing the imaginary or immaterial: it is a way of seeing the space that is created when place is voided. This form of wearing away the actual in order to create a space for the imagined is paralleled by Blanchot's notion of reading which 'makes of the book what the sea and the wind make of objects fashioned by men: a smoother stone, a fragment fallen from the sky' (1982a: 193). Heaney too is engaging in a process wherein the certitudes and ideological baggage that have accrued to place and placename in Irish culture can become etiolated through a conceptual recontextualisation.

Thus, in *Wintering Out*, he speaks of the name '*Toome*', which derives from the Irish language word '*Tuaim*', meaning 'a burial mound', and makes what seems to be a motivated connection between the sound of the place and its physical history. This is achieved by a rhetorical swerve which transposes the 'dislodged / slab of the tongue' (1972: 26) into a souterrain, a subterranean chamber in which items were often stored. He then prospects in this psychic burial mound, finding shards of the lost tradition until he becomes imaginatively engulfed by the rising waters of his tradition:

> till I am sleeved in
>
> alluvial mud that shelves
> suddenly under
> bogwater and tributaries
> and elvers tail my hair. (1972: 26)

This attenuation of the speaker in the poem is enacted in the present tense, a fact that is indicative of the ease with which one can become fused with the givens of one's tradition. In this context, the place, with its linguistic and historical accretions, has entrapped the 'I' of the poem, symbolising how one's sense of home and community can become predictive of one's conceptual and emotional development. He has become a Medusa figure, with the difference between self and home blurred as his body takes on aspects of the place. The mythological connotations of the Medusa figure, the turning to stone of any who look at her, is an important aspect of my reading of the dimension of place in this poem, as positions of fixity in terms of place are written into the history of Ireland in general and Northern Ireland in particular. Symbolically, to be mired in the attachments of place, the appetites of gravity, is to become ossified in terms of one's development and political allegiances. We are looking at the very antithesis of a poetry of an inclusive consciousness, which must not simplify in this type of imagery: here there is no sense of the Derridean promise, or of any sense of an openness to the other. In terms of Blanchot's notion of literature as a null point, as a structure predicated on absence, we need to look at another poetic enunciation of this place, and this is to be found in *Electric Light*.

The first poem, 'At Toomebridge', again refers to this place, but in a completely altered manner. The stress on the bridge in the title is important as it signifies a connection between places, and by extension, ideological positions, as opposed to a fixed location. The use of the preposition 'at' further underscores the sense of movement in this poem as the presentness of the poem is foregrounded: to be 'at Toomebridge' is to stress the fact that one had to come from somewhere and that one will be progressing elsewhere: the rootedness of 'Toome' is definitely absent and the image of water is used in a totally different context. In a manner redolent of the rhetorical structure of two of his other placename poems, 'Broagh' and Anahorish', the title becomes part of the opening sentence of the poem, as we begin in mid-sentence 'At Toomebridge' where the 'flat water' came 'pouring' over the weir:

> As if it had reached an edge of the flat earth
> And fallen shining to the continuous
> Present of the Bann. (2001: 3)

The idea of the 'continuous present' of the water would seem to elide the burial mound of history that is etymologically contained within the placename of 'Toome' itself. Water, which in the former poem was symbolic of the tidal pull of the past, with its 'alluvial mud' and 'bogwater' (1972: 26), is now pictured as 'shining' and 'flat'. Both of these images signify a horizontal plane at work in the poem, whereas there was an artesian imperative in the previous poem, as the image of the souterrain indicated. In this poem, the surfaces are both flat and reflective – a further indication of absence as opposed to place with reflection and refraction playing with the 'shining' light as opposed to probing the depths beneath the water.

The fact that the signifier 'present' is used overtly in the poem, is significant, and this significance is further enhanced by the direct use of the past tense in the second half of the same line, detailing where the checkpoint '*used* to be'[5] and in the next line, which tells where the 'rebel boy *was* hanged' [*my italics*] (2001: 3).[6] Thus, the place is signified in terms of the 'continuous present' of the water and denied in oppositional terms with respect to the historical and political associations of the past. These incidents from the past, these associations of historical action and place are exactly what were being excavated mythologically in 'Toome'; they are the lodged, ossified gravitational aspects of place which turn the 'I' of the poem into a Medusa figure. In this poem, they are seen as part of the past of the place: they have no minatory force in the poem, or in the worldview of the poem. Instead, the description of the place is very much predicated on the absence of such ideological memories of the past. In this sense, 'At Toomebridge' empties the previous significations of that place of all such ideological associations and instead, valorises a different source of poetry.

In the previous poem, the 'I' is embracing the underground depths of imagery and symbol: 'I push into a souterrain' (1972: 26) whereas in this poem, there is a valuing of the negative as opposed to the positive, of absence as opposed to presence: 'Where negative ions in the open air / Are poetry to me' (2001: 3). In this context, it is the negative other that is valued as a source of poetry as opposed to the prospected positive relics of sameness; it is the open air that is valued as opposed to the underground storehouse of memory; and perhaps, most importantly, and symbolically, it is the influences of the present that 'are poetry to me' as opposed to those items buried for 'a hundred centuries' in 'Toome'. A further symbolic opposition between the poems is that the action in 'Toome' is enclosed, underground and takes place in darkness, while that of 'At Toomebridge' is expansive, located in the open, and soaked in light. The closing lines of the poem make explicit this development from a poetry of enclosure to one of openness.

The use of the term 'ion' is interesting as these are atoms that have a positive or negative electrical charge as the result of the addition or subtraction of an electron. In other words, they are atoms which are capable of change, which are open to transformation and difference. That these should be placed in apposition to the 'flints, musket-balls' and 'fragmented ware' of 'Toome' signifies that it is the transformational, as opposed to the enduring, that has become a source of interest to Heaney: 'as once before / The slime and sliver of the fattened eel' was of interest (2001: 3). While this is obviously a reference to the 'elvers' in 'Toome', there is a submerged reference to a previous poem in *Door into the Dark*, entitled 'A Lough Neagh Sequence', where he discusses the eel fishermen of Lough Neagh. While the whole poem is devoted to this topic, the final section of the seven-poem sequence, 'Vision', deals with eels in a manner redolent of the closing stanza of 'Toome'. Here, the eels are seen as symbolic of a more malign form of transformation:

> ...when eels
> Moved through the grass like hatched fears
>
> Towards the water....
> To watch the eels crossing land
>
> Re-wound his world's live girdle.
> Phosphorescent, sinewed slime
> Continued at his feet. Time
> Confirmed the horrid cable. (1969: 45)

The image of the eels as encircling both poet and place within their orbit is a chilling reminder of the appetites of gravity with which Heaney has been struggling in many of his writings about place, home and notions of belonging. That all of this occurs 'at night' further reinforces the connection with the dark world of 'Toome', and further reinforces the sense of transformation that is flagged in 'At Toomebridge' as Heaney looks for a more 'open' experience of place as opposed to a 're-wound' cable.

From the perspective of the speaking 'I' of the poem, such a sense of the present, and of openness allows for an engagement with the plurality of the 'now' as opposed to the singularity of the traditional narration of selfhood. In terms of the vastly different enunciations of place that we find in 'Toome' and 'At Toomebridge', the Derridean dictum that '*Il n'y a pas de hors-texte*' (there is nothing outside the text) (Derrida 1976: 158) can be rewritten as '*Il n'y a pas de hors contexte*' (there is nothing outside of context) (Derrida 1988: 136).[7] By recontextualising the same place in two different poems, Heaney is taking on the need to see literature as valuing that notion of an 'endless promise' to the future (Derrida 1992a: 38). The emptying of the ideological associations of 'Toome' is paradigmatic of the 'luminous absence' of the chestnut tree, a place which was now 'a bright nowhere', and which will be 'utterly a source' (Heaney 1987: 32).

At a further meta-level of context, the titles of the volumes in which these poems appear also serve to recontextualise notions of place and space, presence and absence. 'A Lough Neagh Sequence' is to be found in *Door into the Dark*, a thematically significant title for Heaney's early work. 'Toome' appears in *Wintering Out*, a volume which focuses, at both the mythical and discursive level, on the nationalist tradition of exclusion and colonisation, while 'At Toomebridge' is the opening poem of *Electric Light*, a volume where technological advances are seen as a significant aspect of the place of the book. It is my contention that this process of gradual decentring of place is a significant aspect of Heaney's ongoing progression in terms of defining the 'I' and the 'we' of community and ideology. It is a project which is especially visible in the ongoing spatial transformation of his own 'first place', Mossbawn (Heaney 1980: 18).

In both poetry and prose, Heaney has located himself, symbolically, within this particular point of reference. The first essay in *Preoccupations* is entitled 'Mossbawn', and the passage has become a *locus classsicus* in terms of readings of Heaney as a poet who is very much rooted in tradition and a concrete notion of place: it might almost be seen as an index of the provenance of those elvers in 'Toome':

> I would begin with the Greek word, *omphalos*, meaning the navel, and hence the stone that marked the centre of the world, and repeat it, *omphalos, omphalos, omphalos*, until its blunt and falling music becomes the music of somebody pumping water at the pump outside our back door. (1980: 17)

This has been read as almost typical 'Heaney-speak' and it has also been seen as an index of a very solid and concrete notion of place. However, the other, in terms of language and culture, is already present in this placename, with the Greek signifier '*omphalos*' acting as the initial point of reference, and standing for the call of the other within Heaney's notion of home. In fact, this signifier indicates an absence at the heart of his sense of home that will be repeated through different aspects of his work.[8] In this context, he is at one with Derrida who also sees identity as being shot through with traces of alterity. Later in the same essay, he traces further strands of alterity, further absences, in the name of Mossbawn:

> Our farm was called Mossbawn. *Moss*, a Scots word probably carried to Ulster by the Planters, and *bawn*, the name the English colonists gave to their fortified farmhouses. Mossbawn, the planter's house on the bog. Yet in spite of this Ordinance Survey spelling, we pronounced it Moss bann, and *Bán* is the Gaelic word for white. So might not the thing mean the white moss, the moss of bog-cotton? In the syllables of my home I see a metaphor of the split culture of Ulster. (1980: 35)

In a poem from *North*, 'Belderg', Heaney seems to be inhabiting the same territory that he prospected in 'Toome', speaking of a 'landscape fossilised' (1975: 13), before going on to make the same point as the essay in *Preoccupations*, by speaking of 'bawn' as an 'English fort' and also of the 'persistent if outworn' Irish-language root of the word, but here, a further absence is accounted for as he poses the question: 'But the Norse ring on your tree?' (1975: 14). His point here is that there are many linguistic sources from which seemingly Irish, nationalist or Gaelic placenames derive: in these poems, it is the voice of the other, the sense of absence at the heart of literature, that is being adduced here. Any form of identitarian politics which takes a given notion of place as its starting point is deconstructed by the unveiling of the linguistic traces that inhere in the signifiers as they now exist. Mossbawn, as home, is now implicated with the trace of four languages: Greek, Irish, English and Norse:

> The dissimulation of the woven texture can in any case take centuries to undo its web: a web that envelops a web, undoing the web for centuries; reconstructing it too as an organism, indefinitely regenerating its own tissue behind the cutting trace, the decision of each reading. (Derrida 1981b: 63)

Any politics based on a supposed intimate or Cratylistic connection between land and language must take account of such pluralistic and polyglossic frames of reference. The pluralistic etymologies of place feature as a deconstructive lever in the essentialist conflation of place with a particular political, ideological or linguistic tradition. One is reminded of Derrida's remarks on language in terms of its differential structure:

> Textuality is being constituted by difference and by differences from differences, it is by nature absolutely heterogeneous and is constantly composing with the forces that tend to annihilate it. (1981b: 98)

Heaney's decentring of place is akin to a textualisation in that he is stressing the complexity of the connections that are made between tradition and place through the medium of language. At this juncture, there is no sense of oversimplification: instead, the connections between place and ideology are, on a micro-level, what Colin Graham sees on a macro-level in terms of Ireland, as being: 'everywhere and nowhere, "broken in pieces"', enveloped in a story in which 'its particularity and therefore its definitions will never be resolved' (2001: 23).[9]

Heaney's probing of the linguistic plurality of place is entirely in keeping with his searches for answers in connection with issues of belonging. He probes the nexus of intersections that are constitutive of how place becomes enculturated into a particular ideological position. He then deconstructs the hegemonic strand by stressing that it is merely one strand, chosen for specific reasons, with no more 'motivated' connection to the place than any of the others. In fact, he is transforming location into locution by substituting the notion of space for place, in a manner which draws assurance from the chestnut tree of his youth, which has now become the 'bright nowhere' of his imagination. As Derrida puts it: dissociation, 'separation, is the condition of my relation to the other' (1997b: 14), and indeed, of the identity of a culture, person, nation, and language. In all cases, he sees such identity as self-differentiating, as having a gap or opening within it (1992b: 9–11). For Derrida then, as for Heaney, it follows that this gap in personal identity allows the address and speech towards the other; such identificatory tensions allow a space for alterity, and so, far from being 'a way of avoiding responsibility', instead it is the only way to 'take responsibility and to make decisions'

(Derrida 1997b: 14). Heaney is making these decisions by probing the relationship between poetry and place, and by taking responsibility for the creation of plural enunciations of place and tradition, as opposed to accepting those that are cultural and ideological default positions for him. Instead of accepting the preconditions of the actual, instead of being governed by the actual, poetry allows the tongue to govern in its turn, to become 'another truth to which we can have recourse' (Heaney 1995a: 8). He is complicating the binary opposition, validated by history, of Irish versus British, and instead offering what he terms 'two-mindedness' (1995a: 202). He is attempting to define the culture of Irishness in a way which is 'to be not identical to itself' but rather to be 'different *with itself*' (Derrida 1992b: 9–10). In short, he is attempting to define Irishness *otherwise*.

In this context, Heaney is participating in the postcolonial project, as defined by Graham, who stresses the deconstructive aspect of this theoretical position with particular reference to an Irish context:

> Rethinking concepts such as irony, hybridity, mimicry, the 'contact zone' and transculturation in the Irish context will produce readings of Irish culture which arise out of a recognition of the claustrophobic intensity of the relationship between Ireland and Britain. It can also allow for the fractured range of complex cross-colonial affiliations which have existed within the British/Irish cultural axis....It is these abilities to read culture as ideological, while criticising the homogeneity of ideology, and to prioritise cultural interchange within a colonial structure, which makes post-colonial theory an essential critical tool for understanding Irish culture. (2001: 93)

It is this level of reinterpretation and unpacking of previously axiomatic and hegemonic concepts that makes Heaney's work so important in the renegotiation of the relationship between ideology and place.

Working at a microcosmic level, Heaney recontextualises placenames which are relevant to him, and his work, leaving the reader to extrapolate the macrocosmic political ramifications of his procedures. The relevance of this image to a discussion of his views on poetry and politics will become clear shortly. In the sequence 'Glanmore Revisited', the issue of recontextualisation, echoing that epigraph from *Wintering Out* which appeared again in *North*, is raised. Heaney's 'Glanmore Sonnets' were a seminal part of his collection

Field Work. Here, he described his life in the present tense in terms of a period which he saw as 'fundamental to securing my sense of myself as a poet' (Murphy 2000b: 87), using Glanmore as a place which provided him a form of respite from the actuality of the violence in Northern Ireland. I have discussed the importance of Glanmore as a new context for his writing elsewhere:

> Poetry as a form of communication between self and other is enunciated in the opening line: 'Vowels ploughed into other: opened ground'. Seeing Glanmore as a "hedge-school", Heaney finds time to write about himself and his rural surroundings. (O'Brien 2002a: 65)

He also finds time to write a number of elegies for victims of the Northern Irish conflict, 'The Strand at Lough Beg' refers to Colum McCartney, a second cousin of Heaney's who was 'shot arbitrarily' as he was 'coming home from a football match in Dublin' (Randall 1979: 21). 'A Postcard from North Antrim' concerns a man named Sean Armstrong whom Heaney had known at Queens, and who had been part of the 'commune pot-smoking generation' in Sausalito, before coming back to Belfast 'to get involved in social work' by working 'at children's playgrounds'. He was 'shot by some unknown youth' (Randall 1979: 21). The third elegy, 'Casualty', describes a fisherman, Louis O'Neill, who used to come to Heaney's father-in-law's public house in County Tyrone, and who was 'blown to bits' by the IRA in the aftermath of Bloody Sunday:

> He was blown to bits
> Out drinking in a curfew
> Others obeyed, three nights
> After they shot dead
> The thirteen men in Derry. (Heaney 1979: 22)

Perhaps the most important aspect of Glanmore was its connectedness with the actuality of life in Ireland in the late 1970s, and with Heaney's own early life. The sequence is shot through with references to the *Lebenswelt* of Mossbawn: the 'small ripples' which shook across the 'drinking water' (Heaney 1979: 36) call to mind 'the ripples in the ripples that rippled in and rippled out across the water in that scullery bucket fifty years ago' (Heaney 1995a: 3). The 'boortree's trunk' in Sonnet V recalls 'our bower as children' (Heaney 1979: 37); in Sonnet

VI, the 'Moyola river' is cited as a point of reference, and in Sonnet VII, the litany of names from the shipping forecast on the radio: 'Dogger, Rockall, Malin, Irish Sea' call to mind a similar litany in his Nobel lecture, *Crediting Poetry*, which is cited in recollection of his early childhood home, where he 'grew familiar with the names of foreign stations, with Leipzig and Oslo and Stuttgart and Warsaw and, of course, with Stockholm' (1995b: 3).

In 'Glanmore Revisited', a sequence from *Seeing Things*, such connectedness is fractured and dissipated as the governing image here is that of Scrabble – the word game wherein letters are combined in different games to create different words. In this context, no tradition is taken as hegemonic:

> Taken for granted like any other word
> That was chanced on and allowed within the rules.
> So 'scrabble' let it be. (1991: 31)

This gnomic definition of the necessity of recontextualisation in terms of the signifying of language is precisely the tool that both Heaney and Derrida avail of in their ongoing process of recontextualisation of meaning. Formally, these six poems are also sonnets, but whereas the 'Glanmore Sonnets' were broadly Shakespearean in structure, with three quatrains and a rhyming couplet, those of 'Glanmore Revisited' are more Petrarchan, with an octave and a sestet, allowing for greater development of an idea through the interlaced rhyme scheme of the sestet, especially.

Thus, in 'The Cot', a poem about a remembered item from the childhood of his daughter Catherine, who 'woke in the dawn' and answered '*doodle doo*' to the rooster 'in the farm across the road', one might expect sentimental reification of the item. One might expect that the cot itself would be reified into a signifier of a golden past, frozen in time, and unchanging, and this expectation is furthered by the phrase that the cot is 'back in place.' However, in this revisitation of Glanmore, it is difference as opposed to sameness that is the defining trope:

> The old activity starts up again
> But starts up differently. We're on our own
> Years later in the same *locus amoenus*. (1991: 32)

The point of this reference is that while the place may still be pleasant (the original meaning of *locus amoenus* was a 'pleasant place'), nevertheless, it is not the same pleasant place: it is, and must be, different as temporally and spatially, events have moved on. The cot is now empty, his daughter has grown up, and the cot is further othered in that it is now described as 'the same cot' in which the speaker of the poem had slept while young. Hence, there is an oblique connection with Mossbawn, but it is a connection of difference as opposed to one of sameness. Thus the perceived cot is also connected with, but different from, the cot in which his daughter slept, and the cot in which he slept as a child, because the temporal and spatial contexts were different. In Derrida's words the 'presence of the perceived present can appear as such only inasmuch as it is *continuously compounded* with a nonpresence and nonperception, with primary memory and expectation (retention and protention)' (Derrida 1973: 64). Far from being a symbol of continuance and solidity, the cot becomes a symbol of difference, and a symbol of how contextual change can alter the signification of the same object.

The title of the next poem in the sequence – 'Scene Shifts' – is mimetic of this trend in the revisitation of Glanmore. In this poem, the key act is the inscribing of a name on the bark of an ash tree by 'a friend', and the resultant anger of the 'I' of the poem when 'our kids stripped off the bark' (Heaney 1991: 33). The irony of this absence bringing forth anger, when the original act of cutting down the chestnut tree in Mossbawn brought forth a sense of reconceptualisation of place, is not lost on the reader, and one suspects, on the writer. For, in the sestet of the sonnet, the play of presence and absence that we have noted in the image of the absent tree, and the absent linguistic and etymological origins of words, is again foregrounded:

> Where it shone like bone exposed is healed up now.
> The bark's thick-eared and welted with a scar. (1991: 33)

Once again, the tropes of presence and absence interact, and the simplicities of place and identification are again deconstructed. Given the image-chains which we have looked at in this chapter, I think this particular poem, located at the structural centre of the sequence, can be seen to bear a weight of meaning in terms of the deconstruction of place. The erosion of the marks of a friend on the place brings immediate anger on behalf of the 'I' of the poem: 'I was flailing round the house like a man berserk' (1991: 33). The term 'berserk' has a resonance of its own within the Heaney canon, as in 'Summer 1969', it is the term he uses to describe, following his viewing of a painting by Goya, the two communities at war in Northern Ireland:

> Also, that holmgang
> Where two berserks club each other to death
> For honour's sake, greaved in a bog, and sinking. (1975: 70)

The effects of the expunging of the marks of familial and communal identity on place were severe: we note the image-chain of 'friend...name...house...blood-brother', as well as the oblique reference to customs of tribal bonding:

> It brought back those blood-brother scenes where two
> Braves nick wrists and cross them for a sign. (1991: 33)

However, the structure of the poem enacts the very process of transformation from place to space, and from location to locution of which we have been speaking. The octave is spoken in the past tense, and the emotion that resulted from the erasure of the name from the tree is firmly located in that past, as 'the business had moved me at the time'. The sestet, set in the present, is far calmer, and the more complex relationship between the place and the space of literature is captured in the allusion to an unnamed 'recognition scene' in a book or a film. This allusion is a further complication of the relationship between name and place, adding a further dimension to the scene, and making the point that, without an identifying mark, place can be open to plural significations, a point which once again, relates to his ongoing deconstruction of the simplicities associated with a tribal sense of ownership and territoriality. The closing image, of a 'veteran of the war' stresses the pastness of the conflict in this altered dispensation.

The image of the erased name reappearing as a scar on the bark in the present is a further example of the dialectic of presence and absence that has become central to Heaney's recontextualisation of place. The mark of the friend's name, like the space wherein the chestnut tree had its existence, has neither disappeared nor remained the same. It has been placed '*sous rature*' – 'under erasure' – (Derrida 1976: xiv), in that it is both absent and present, its trace has made a change to the original. Hence, for Derrida, it is 'neither *this* nor *that*; but rather this *and* that (e.g. the act of differing and of deferring) without being reducible to a dialectical logic either' (1981c: 161).[10] His *locus amoenus* has been altered by the revisitation of the subject of the poem, older, wiser, more distanced from the initial sense of emotion that was central to the whole Glanmore experience of *Field Work*. This process continues through the sequence.

In '1973', the year is remembered in terms of his being 'dissociated' from 'things seasonal' in the octave, while in the sestet, the rhyme of 'body' with 'study' revisits the central importance of the Glanmore period as one wherein he was able to place the practice of poetry very much at the centre of his life (Heaney 1991: 34). In 'Bedside Reading' a further dissociation of the realities of the place is verified in the line:

> I swim in Homer. In Book Twenty-three.
> At last Odysseus and Penelope
> Waken together. (1991: 36)

The recontextualisation of Glanmore is complete, with the poet's bed, with its view of 'little shoots of ivy' being compared to the bedpost of Odysseus and Penelope which is 'the living trunk of an old olive tree' (1991: 36). Place has become deconstructed into literary reference and Glanmore takes on new resonances. These are furthered in the final sonnet from the sequence 'The Skylight', where the cutting of a skylight into the roof of the building was at first resisted by the 'I' of the poem 'I liked the snuff-dry feeling', which was all 'hutch and hatch'. However, once the 'slates came off', there was a sense of liberation:

> Sky entered and held surprise wide open,
> For days I felt like an inhabitant
> Of that house where the man sick of the palsy
> Was lowered through the roof, had his sins forgiven,
> Was healed, took up his bed and walked away. (1991: 37)

This image, of an opening to the sky, of an expansion of the ambit of the place itself, is one which is proleptic of his sense of the importance of Terminus, the Roman god of boundaries, which we will discuss in the next chapter. What is actually at work here is the deconstruction of the notion of place as enclosure, as a womblike locus of protection and insulation. Instead, there is an opening, a sense of scope as place becomes space, the space of literature where rural County Wicklow can be equated with the classical Greece of Homer, without any sense of self-consciousness or inappropriateness.

This deconstruction, or recontextualisation of the original place is developed in *Electric Light*. Having played with notions of presence and absence, he now, in the classically entitled 'Glanmore Eclogue', effects a further recontextualisation. The term 'eclogue' is usually associated with pastoral poetry by Virgil, but etymologically is interesting in that it derives from the Greek '*eklegein*', meaning 'to select', and it is this process of selection that allows for a development of the signification of the placename itself. Here, the dialogue is between a character called 'Myles' and a 'poet', presumably a voicing of Heaney's own concerns. Myles seems to be autochthonous to the place while the poet is a more recent inhabitant of Glanmore (with both of them standing in synecdoche for larger paradigms of colonisation and conquest):

> Outsiders own
> The country nowadays, but even so
> I don't begrudge you. You're Augusta's tenant
> And that's enough. (2001: 35)

Another character in the poem, Meliboeus, who originates in Virgil's seventh eclogue, is constantly mentioned throughout the poem, being pictured as a former denizen of the place in a process of ongoing transformation: 'First it was Meliboeus' people / Went to the wall, now it will be us' (2001: 36). This picture of an altered range of inhabitants is underscored by the changed languages of the place. Myles speaks of 'our old language' that Meliboeus had learned, and he in turn asks the poet to translate one of the songs of this language so that 'the rest of us / Can understand' before offering a simple nature poem, very similar to those nature lyrics that we see in *Sweeney Astray*. This pluralisation of dialogue, language and cultural references, with a figure from a Latin poem appearing in an Irish location, a *locus amoenus* of Glanmore, speaking English and translating a poem with strong resonances of Old Irish and Middle English nature lyrics, demonstrates the process of recontextualisation that Heaney has undertaken with respect to the signification of this placename.[11] Once again, we are reminded of Derrida's point that one of the possible definitions of deconstruction is 'the effort to take this limitless context into account, to pay the sharpest and broadest attention possible to context and thus to an incessant movement of recontextualisation' (Derrida 1988: 136).

This process of translating location into complex and plural forms of locution proceeds apace in the later poems of *Electric Light*. In the 'Sonnets from Hellas' which follow the 'Glanmore Eclogue', the voiding of the certainties of place through recontextualisation is developed as the sights, sounds and smells of Greece 'from Argos into Arcadia' (Heaney 2001: 38) are refracted through the familiar sights, sounds and smells of home. Hence, as he looked at his 'favourite bas-relief':

> ...there in Olympia, down among the green willows,
> the lustral wash and run of river shallows
> That we heard of Sean Browne's murder in the grounds
> Of Bellaghy GAA Club. And imagined
> Hose-water smashing hard back off the asphalt
> In the car park where his athlete's blood ran cold. (2001: 41)

The conflation of the Greek location with the equally vivid description of the Irish location of the murder underscores the voiding of place as a single signifier of anything. In future, any thoughts of that day on Olympia, examining and appreciating the image of Athene showing Heracles where 'to broach the river bank' will be forever shadowed by the image of the dead body in Bellaghy. Ireland and Greece are connected by this recontextualisation of place.

The same is true of the sonnet 'Desfina', where that *locus amoenus* of poetic inspiration, Mount Parnassus, is recontextualised in a similar manner:

> Mount Parnassus placid on the skyline:
> Slieve na mBard, Knock Filiocht, Ben Duan.
> We gaelicised new names for Poetry Hill. (2001: 43)

In this case, the place of literature has become the space of literature in the sense used by Blanchot. Here, the idea of literature as having a specific originary place is deconstructed as recontextualisation allows for the interaction of three languages and cultures in the (literally) name of poetic inspiration. Here we inhabit Blanchot's space of literature, as different traditions are placed in a structure which sees them 'quitting themselves and detaining each other together outside themselves in the restless unity of their common belonging' (Blanchot 1982a: 200).

This sense of the voiding of any essentialist connections with place is an ongoing trope in *Electric Light*. In 'The Gaeltacht', a poem about a specifically Irish language-speaking area of Ireland, one would expect the connection between place and ideology to be fixed and stable, but instead we find a field of force in which four languages interact and intersect: English, the language of the poem; Irish, the language of the title signifier; French, the locative '*mon vieux*' of the first line; and Italian, in the frame of reference and allusion of the last three lines:

> ...and if this sonnet
> In imitation of Dante's, where he's set free
> In a boat with Lapo and Guido, with their girlfriends in it,
> Could be the wildtrack of our gabble above the sea.
>
> (Heaney 2001: 44)

This 'wildtrack' of 'gabble' indicates a linguistic frame of reference which can become a vehicle of transformation in terms of the actual. His recontextualisations involve a posited answer to a question he posed of himself in 'Known World': 'How does the real get into the made up?' (2001: 21). Here it is the second meaning of the phrase the government of the tongue, the idea of the tongue being 'suddenly ungoverned' and 'unconstrained' (Heaney 1988: xxii), that is operative as it suggests an aspect of 'poetry as its own vindicating force' (1988: 93). Place can only be expressed through language, and in the voiding of any motivated connections between location and locution, a space is created for a pluralistic enculturation of place and language, a relation with largely transformative implications for any study of Irishness. In the next chapter, some of these implications will be traced.

6 'Through-Otherness': The Deconstruction of Language

In keeping with his view of poetry as encouraging complex and dialectical transformations of the actual, this chapter will discuss how Heaney grants both the effectiveness and plurality of notions of Irishness. In *North*, he writes in a manner which grants the strength of atavism, myth and visceral notions of Irishness. In the poems of the opening section, coming to a climax in 'Kinship', Heaney enunciates the strength and power of the *mythos* which causes people to kill for the good of the *Volk*. The phrase 'how we slaughter for the common good' (1975: 45) has become something of a *cause célèbre* in Heaney studies, and in this chapter I will argue that what he is doing here is granting the efficacy and strength of this notion, as opposed to either celebrating it or giving it some form of moral or ethical validation. Heaney's ethical project in his writing involves, as we saw in the last chapter, foregrounding what might be termed the eclogic factor, the notion of choice in terms of the narrative strands that achieve hegemonic status in the construction of identity. Thus *North* has been offered to reductive readings which focused on two particular quotations which seemed to give a certain ratification to a visceral sense of nationalist aggression.

These quotations, from 'Punishment' and 'Kinship' respectively, have been used to point a finger at Heaney as a writer, and to accuse him of partiality at the very least, and at worst of voicing the aims of the Provisional IRA:

> I who have stood dumb...
> who would connive
> in civilised outrage
> yet understand the exact
> and tribal, intimate revenge. (1975: 38)

> ...report us fairly,
> how we slaughter
> for the common good

> and shave the heads
> of the notorious,
> how the goddess swallows
> our love and terror. (1975: 45)

Critics have focused on these lines as signifying that Heaney is locating his voice very much within his *mythos*. In a word, he is being accused of the very epistemological flaw which he has warned against when he said that poetry has to be 'a working model of inclusive consciousness. It should not simplify' (1995a: 8). Different critics have isolated these points, and have extrapolated from this a pro-republican, pro-nationalist and pro-violence stance: 'it is as if there never were and never will be any political consequences of such acts' (Carson 1975: 184). Edna Longley accuses Heaney of being '"outrageously honest" about his own reactions' (1986: 154), while Blake Morrison maintains that these poems give an 'historical respectability' to the 'sectarian killing' (1982: 68).

Heaney here is being seen as locating himself within the givens of his culture; it seems as if he is having these poems 'written for him' by his nationalist, Catholic psyche (Morrison 1982: 67). And if all of the poems in this book were to expand on this trope, perhaps this criticism would have some value. However, the connections between place, ideology and language are in fact much more plural and complex than it would originally seem, and this is especially true with relation to his use of language in this, and other books. The connections between land and language, as we have seen in the last chapter, are hegemonically foregrounded in terms of the choices that are made in our naming of places. Just as he has recontextualised placenames to underscore the complexity and nuanced nature of the connections between land and language, so too, he recontextualises the language aspect of that couplet in order to complicate the levels of response. Thus, for example, in *Viking Dublin: Trial Pieces* a Viking ship and the signifier 'Dublin' are joined by simile:

> its clinker-built hull
> spined and plosive
> as *Dublin*. (Heaney 1975: 22)

This would seem to deconstruct the tribal readings of *North*, as Dublin traces its etymology from two Irish language words '*dubh*', meaning 'black', and '*linn*' meaning 'pool'. This name was clearly a descriptor of the place as it was when first inhabited. However, in the poem, the word is being posited in some sort of motivated relationship with the 'clinker-built hull' of the Viking ship.[1] This is precisely the opposite of the aesthetic ideological perspective for which the book has been attacked: namely, the fusion of lands with a sense of Irishness as expressed through language. Instead, what is happening is that signifier and signified are being recontextualised in order to gesture towards that complexity of which Heaney has been speaking. Here, history is viewed as a field of force wherein different languages, ideologies and cultures interacted and intersected.

Clearly for Heaney, the connection between language and reality is plural and in no way confined to the nationalist republican paradigm. In 'Bone Dreams', for example, there is a constant interchange between the realms of phenomena and cognition, as a piece of 'white bone' becomes blended with 'Bone-house' which in turn leads to the Anglo-Saxon '*ban-hus*'. Then, there is an ideological progression from language: 'come back past / philology and kennings' to the sensuous phenomena of memory:

> where the bone's lair
> is a love-nest
> in the grass.
> I hold my lady's head
> like a crystal
>
> and ossify myself
> by gazing: I am screes
> on her escarpments. (1975: 29)

The kenning '*ban-hus*' is transformed into its physical referent by appeal to the senses: 'brain...cauldron of generation...love-den, blood-holt...love nest', and through prosopopeia, the land is given face, and becomes the personified 'my lady'. Of course, the irony here is that the personified 'lady' represents England as opposed to Ireland: here is the very complexity which we have been discussing. Once again, it is the plurality of the signifier that is at work as Heaney probes the language in all of its different aspects. It is in the interstices of the linguistic interchange that he is interested. Far from evoking a binary-oppositional confrontation between the Irish and English languages, as synecdoches of political confrontations, he is, I would argue, far more interested in the new structures that can be seen as emerging from the connections between the different discourses. In *Among Schoolchildren*, there is a significant example of this process.

Heaney tells of seeing the word '*lachtar*' in Dineen's Irish-language dictionary, and realising that this word was part of the Irish-language dialect of his own county Derry. The word means 'a flock of young chickens', and for Heaney it caused a cultural frisson, as up to then, he had thought that this commonly used word was English in origin, but now, he realised that it 'lived upon our tongues like a capillary stretching back to a time when Irish was the *lingua franca* of the whole place'. He goes on to describe the effect that this realisation had on him, the animation 'with the fact of loss', and it is an important point for our discussion:

> Suddenly the resentful nationalism of my Catholic minority experience was fused with a concept of identity that was enlarging and releasing and would eventually help me to relate my literary education with the heritage of the home ground. (1983a: 9)

That such a broadened perspective can be brought about by language is an important aspect of my argument: just as language can endorse forms of essentialism, so also, in particular in terms of the aesthetic, can it deconstruct such essentialisms. This interaction of the English and Irish languages can open a space which is salubrious to forms of interchange and discussion. It can help to progress the relationship between selfhood and alterity. It can also, in Gerry Smyth's words, help to produce

> cognitive maps which enable Irish people to locate themselves in relation to their own local environment and to the series of increasingly larger networks of power which bear upon these environments. (2001: 19)

It is this very relationship that is being created in Heaney's attitude to languages and their contextual interaction.

Heaney's moment of linguistic anagnorisis is deconstructive of any sense of oppositional logic. Immediately prior to this quotation, he locates his discussion within the ambit of the work of Daniel Corkery:[2]

> What came to fill the gap between the parish and the academy, between the culture of the GAA hall and the culture of Shakespeare...was, first of all, Daniel Corkery and his potent

monocular vision of *The Hidden Ireland*. Corkery's message was succinct and potent. 'We were robbed', he said. We lost what made us what we are. We had lost the indigenous Gaelic civilization and he evoked that civilization in its decline with elegiac nostalgia as he wrote lovingly and romantically about the poets of Munster in the seventeenth century, poets of a people whom the parliament in Dublin regarded as 'the common enemy'. (1983a: 8)

So, it is within this nationalistic paradigm that his '*lachtar*' epiphany takes place, and the common enemy is transformed into a shared history. As he puts it later in the same essay, what had seemed 'disabling and provincial is suddenly found to be corroborating and fundamental and potentially universal' (1983a: 11).

Taking issue with Corkery's notion of Irish as the original language being supplanted by English, Heaney recontextualises the historical point being made. Instead of seeing the progression as an indigenous Irishness being supplanted, and eradicated by an imposed Englishness, a classic binary opposition with one side achieving dominance, he now sees the interaction as exemplifying what Derrida has described as supplementary logic. For Derrida, '*supplement* has a double signification'. Firstly, it 'adds itself, it is a surplus, a plenitude enriching another plenitude, the *fullest measure* of presence' (1976: 144). Secondly, however, the supplement adds only to replace, to insinuate itself '*in-the-place-of*; if it fills it is as if one fills a void' (1976: 145).

This is not to postulate any relationship of superiority or inferiority in terms of Irish and English; rather does it point to the dialectical economy of the interlinguistic relationship, an economy which deconstructs the hierarchical structure that is posited in the passage in favour of a differential process: 'each of the two significations is by turns effaced or becomes discreetly vague in the presence of the other' (Derrida 1976: 145). Here is the very complexity of expression that we saw traced in the signification of place in the last chapter.

A further implication of the signifier '*lachtar*' seems to be that, despite the political and linguistic colonisation, the ancient tongue has still survived, and in fact has exercised a reversal by becoming part of the distinct dialect form of English which is spoken in a particular part of Ireland. The metaphoric use of 'capillary' deconstructs the 'we were robbed' trope as a capillary is one of the minute blood vessels that connect arterioles and venules. These blood vessels form an intricate network throughout the body for the interchange of various substances, such as oxygen and carbon dioxide, between blood and tissue cells. Capillarity then, metaphorically, is a symbol of interchange and growth: it gestures towards an almost organic interaction of the languages over time. It does not symbolise the victory, in a political and cultural sense, of one side over the other; rather does it underline and reinforce the complexity of the field of force which is the language as it is spoken in the space of Irish discourse.

The use of *'lingua franca'* in the same sentence acts as a metaphorical post modifier, in this case as the term 'lingua franca' (literally, Frankish language), is defined as a:

> hybrid language, consisting largely of Italian, used by the Latin races in dealing with Arabs, Turks, Greeks. Any hybrid language similarly used, as any jargon. Any language used internationally as a trade or communications medium. (Bernhart 1972: 1206)

Hence, hybridity and interchange, the very points being symbolised by the use of the capillary metaphor, are reinforced by this internationalisation of language. Heaney is foregrounding the hybridity that is a fact of all language, and which deconstructs the aesthetic ideology that attempts to locate an originary Adamic (Ashcroft *et al.* 1989: 34) relationship between place and the Irish language. Indeed, hybridity can be seen as the very condition of language, specifically in the case of recontextualisation. In this perspective on the plurality of language, Heaney again echoes the thought of Derrida who has made a similar point with respect to the plurality of language:

> We only ever speak one language...
> (yes, but)
> We never speak only one language. (1998: 10)

Heaney's discussion of the plurality and contradiction that is the signifier *'lachtar'* follows this epistemology of language in recognising the paradox that inheres in a developed language wherein historical conflicts are often subsumed in the new structures of signification that result from cultural and ideological interaction. The 'one language' which we speak is shot through with traces of other languages, and specifically in the context of literature, the contradiction between the 'oneness' of language and the plurality of interchange, influence and intersection with other languages becomes foregrounded. Herman Rapaport, in an incisive reading of Derrida's later work, makes the point that in Derrida's work, binary oppositions are found to be an inadequate metaphor for the sheer complexity of the synchronic structures of language, and instead, Derrida probes the 'interplay of implicative differences' that inhere in literary language (Rapaport 2003: 27).

In 'Something to Write Home About', Heaney speaks of a similar signifier which exerts a similar effect on his consciousness. Speaking of the different linguistic and political dimensions of his childhood, and exploring the diversity of these influences, Heaney notes that some words, which come from that world 'between times and languages' have a strong effect on him:

> A word like 'hoke', for example. When I hear somebody say *hoke*, I'm returned to the very first place in myself. It's not a standard English word and it's not an Irish-language word either, but it's undislodgeably there, buried in the very foundations of my own speech. (2002: 50)

The term means 'to root about and delve into and forage and root around' (2002: 50), and given what has been seen as Heaney's artesian imagination, one could be forgiven for expecting that he would use this word to dig back and down into his own tradition. However, this reaction would be oversimplistic and, as we have seen, simplicity and partisanship are far from being *desiderata* in Heaney's epistemology of poetry. His use of the image of 'the very first place in myself' instantly parallels the early essay in *Preoccupations* where his childhood home, Mossbawn, is referred to in a similar manner: 'Mossbawn, the first place' (1980: 18). However, this first place is far from being either essentialist or autochthonous: as we have seen in Chapter 5, it is defined in terms of the Greek word for the centre of the earth, in other words, it is already being seen in terms of complex association and recontextualisation. His conception of a first place is already redolent with his concept of the field of force: there are two different centres in dialogue here: 'the stone that marked the centre of the world....the pump stands...marking the centre of another world' (1980: 17), just as there are different versions of the 'I' who is placed within this skein of memory. The 'I' who first saw the pump in the yard is not the same 'I' who can unselfconsciously conflate a rural part of County Derry with Delphi in classical Greece.

Interestingly, the word 'hoked' is similarly foregrounded in his poem 'Terminus' from *The Haw Lantern*:

> When I hoked there, I would find
> An acorn and a rusted bolt.
>
> If I lifted my eyes, a factory chimney
> And a dormant mountain.
>
> If I listened, an engine shunting
> And a trotting horse.
>
> Is it any wonder when I thought
> I would have second thoughts? (1987: 4)

Like '*lachtar*', this word gestures towards the plurality of language and to the hybrid nature of the development of different aspects of signification. Whereas the poem foregrounds the strict binaries that are operative across the board in Northern Ireland in terms of the agrarian (acorn, mountain, horse) versus the industrial (bolt, chimney, engine), every time that the 'I' is mentioned, there is a crossing of those borders and mutuality of influences, which I will cite seriatim:

> when I thought
> I would have second thoughts?....
> I was the march drain and the march drain's banks
> Suffering the limits of each claim....
> I grew up in between...
> Baronies, parishes met where I was born....
> When I stood on the central stepping stone. (1987: 4–5)

In this context, it is the crossing of borders and boundaries, or the place where they intersect that is important in the poem. The 'I', far from being driven by the signifier 'hoked' to stake a claim for his nationalist heritage, consciously situates itself 'in between' the two.

Language, specifically poetic language, is a central conduit for this process, as exemplified by his play on the meaning of the word 'march'. In a Northern Irish context, this word would generally be associated with parades of either tradition, but more usually the unionist one, where various dates connected with the victory of

William of Orange over James II are celebrated during the summer 'marching season'. The word has become associated with the division of the two communities as violence often flares up during these marches, and the right of various parades to march through areas which are predominantly Catholic has become an ongoing source of conflict each summer, as encapsulated in the Garvaghy Road area of Portadown. In this poem, however Heaney is using the word in a more inclusive context as he explains: 'the verb meant to meet at the boundary, to be bordered by, to be matched up to and yet marked off from' (2002: 51). He goes on:

> The word did not mean 'walk in a military manner', but to be close, to lie alongside, to border upon and be bordered upon. It was a word that acknowledged division but it contained a definite suggestion of solidarity as well. If my land marched your land, we were bound by that boundary as well as separated by it. If the whole of the liberating sky was over the head of the god terminus, the whole of the solid earth was under what he stood for, the march hedge and the march drain. (2002: 52)

Once again, it is the plurality of language that allows for this sense of connectedness between self and other: the boundary or border can be both a point of limitation as well as being a point of connection. In this sense, what is at work here is a paradigm of hybridity. Robert Young makes the point that the term hybridity was used originally to refer to a physiological phenomenon but has now been reactivated to describe a cultural one. He tells us that hybrid-isation consists of the 'forcing of a single entity into two or more parts, a severing of a single object into two, turning sameness into difference'. Hybridity thus 'makes difference into sameness and sameness into difference, but in a way which makes the same no longer the same, the different no longer simply different' (Young 1995: 26). Employing Derrida's term 'brisure', Young discusses how 'hybridity thus consists of a bizarre binate operation, in which each impulse is qualified against the other, forcing momentary forms of dislocation and displacement into complex economies of agonistic reticulation' (1995: 26–7).[3]

Homi K. Bhabha has discussed this whole notion of hybridity and borders in his influential book *The Location of Culture*, where the notion of being 'in-between', a form of interstitial identity, is viewed as a positive, indeed, a necessary position to take in an increasingly multicultural society. It is precisely such an 'interstitial passage' between 'fixed identifications' that, in the words of Bhabha, 'opens up the possibility of a cultural hybridity that entertains difference without an assumed or imposed hierarchy' (1994: 4). Such a politics would attempt to:

> think beyond narratives of originary and initial subjectivities and to focus on those moments or processes that are produced in the articulation of cultural differences. These 'in-between' spaces provide the terrain for elaborating strategies of selfhood – singular or communal – that initiate new signs of identity, and innovative sites of collaboration, and contestation, in the act of defining the idea of society itself. (Bhabha 1994: 1–2)

This notion of cultural hybridity, which is based on difference rather than on similarity or some form of oppositional hierarchy, would seem to posit some hope of a political discourse which would be relevant to Northern Ireland. Significantly however, Heaney is not over-concerned with the macro-political import of his work; instead, his focus is on the individual mind which can be altered by such a strand of thinking.

'Terminus' participates in this process as the 'I' is influenced by both sides of the divide, while the felicitous ambiguity of the word 'march' also allows for an interaction between selfhood and alterity: 'I grew up in between.' Indeed, the image of the 'I' standing on a stepping stone in the third section of the poem is redolent of a border in itself as he is between the two sides of the river as well as merging land and water. As such the stepping stone is a polysemic symbol of an interstitial position, and one which embodies the complexity of which we have been speaking, a point made in Poem XXXII of *Lightenings*:

> Running water never disappointed.
> Crossing water always furthered something.
> Stepping stones were stations of the soul.
>
> A kesh could mean the track some called a causey
> Raised above the wetness of the bog,
> Or the causey where it bridged old drains and streams.
> (Heaney 1991: 90)[4]

As interstitial, liminal points, these stones enact his idea that borders, points of connection, the notion of the 'in-between' are all central to his field of force, and to that sense of space that is the provenance of literature and poetry. He reiterates that point, again availing of the image of a stepping stone, in his Nobel lecture *Crediting Poetry*:

> I grew familiar with the names of foreign stations, with Leipzig and Oslo and Stuttgart and Warsaw and, of course, with Stockholm. I also got used to hearing short bursts of foreign languages as the dial hand swept round from BBC to Radio Eireann, from the intonations of London to those of Dublin, and even though I did not understand what was being said in those first encounters with the gutturals and sibilants of European speech, I had already begun a journey into the wideness of the world beyond. This in turn became a journey into the wideness of language, a journey where each point of arrival – whether in one's poetry or one's life turned out to be a stepping stone rather than a destination, and it is that journey which has brought me now to this honoured spot. And yet the platform here feels more like a space station than a stepping stone, so that is why, for once in my life, I am permitting myself the luxury of walking on air. (1995b: 11)

Here again, it is the sense of hybridity and recontextualisation that is being foregrounded with respect to the different languages and cultures which acted as influences on his developing consciousness. Language provided the space for that progression, and the image of the stepping stone, itself balanced between the two different banks of a river, as well as between land and water and sky, is a *terminus a quo* from which such a progression can be developed. Indeed, the whole notion of recontextualisation can be seen as a changing of borders and a redrawing of limits and contexts.

In his essay 'Signature Event Context', Derrida speaks of the iterability of every sign or phrase which is part of the structure of every mark, spoken or written, and which posits the possibility of the mark being repeated outside of contextual or hermeneutic parameters, and cut off from 'its "original" meaning and from its belonging to a saturable and constraining context' (Derrida 1982: 320). In this case, the 'saturable and constraining context' of the word '*lachtar*' is the Irish language, the context and source of the signifier's 'original' meaning. The 'citational grafting' of this word into the English that is the 'natural speech' of Heaney is part of the condition of language, and of the very ontology of the sign. As Geoffrey Bennington notes, 'every signifier functions by referring to other signifiers, without one ever arriving at a signified' (Bennington 1993: 33). This is because of the iterability of the sign. Every sign, linguistic or non-linguistic can be '*cited*, put between quotation marks; thereby it can break with every given context, and engender infinitely new contexts in an absolutely nonsaturatable fashion' (Derrida 1982: 320–1).[5] In other words, this is the condition of Heaney's idea of complexity and of his field of force, where single, motivated meanings are continually deconstructed by the altered significatory contexts.

The iteribility of '*lachtar*', the trace of the Irish language that has been cited and located within a new linguistic context, is not, therefore, a paradigm for the survival of an originary language, with its metonymic connection to an ur-culture with a privileged relationship to the land. Rather is it a paradigm of the *différance* that is a motive force of all language: one can always extract a syntagma from its context without losing the 'meaning' of the syntagma; indeed, by inserting it into other contexts, different and plural aspects of 'meaning' may be foregrounded. As Derrida notes, 'no context can enclose it. Nor can any code' (Derrida 1982: 317).[6] Hence, in his use of '*lachtar*', what Heaney is actually describing is not the survival of a Gaelic word, with the implied metonymic connection to the possible survival of some ideological aspects of an ur-Irish world *à la* Corkery, or some form of the return of the Gaelic repressed, but rather the process of the grafting of the signifier across a code or contextual barrier. This process is emblematic of his view of writing as complicating our response to culture and ideology, a view that also informs Heaney's notions of borderlines and their names.

In the beginning of this discussion, we spoke of the trope of anastomosis, and of how Heaney used this idea to set up an interaction between text and context in his work. This same process is operative in the connection between the essay 'Something to Write Home About', and 'Terminus'. The poem ends as follows:

> Baronies, parishes met where I was born.
> When I stood on the central stepping stone
>
> I was the last earl on horseback in midstream
> Still parleying, in earshot of his peers. (1987: 5)

The reference to the 'last earl' is a historical one, as Hugh O'Neill, Earl of Tyrone, was one of the last great leaders of Gaelic Ireland. His forces were defeated by the English at the Battle of Kinsale in 1601, and with the departure of O'Neill and his ally Hugh O'Donnell from Ireland, an event that is iconically referred to as 'the flight of the earls', in 1607, the death knell of that Gaelic culture was signalled. O'Neill is one of the great figures in the Irish historical pantheon and as such would seem to be an unusual icon for Heaney to use in a poem and an essay which deal with notions of liminality and hybridity.

However, O'Neill's historical situation is a little more complicated than it might at first seem:

> By English law, O'Neill was the Earl of Tyrone, and therefore, in the understanding of Queen Elizabeth, the English queen's loyal representative in the kingdom of Ireland. But by Irish birth and genealogy, O'Neill was descended from the mythic Irish leader, Niall of the Nine Hostages, and to the Irish he therefore appeared as the hereditary leader of the Gaelic O'Neills, with a destined role. (2002: 54–5)

In this light, O'Neill is a personification of those stepping stones of which we have been speaking. He is a liminal figure, educated in England while loyal to a sense of Irishness. Just as Heaney could have chosen to write about '*lachtar*' and 'hoked' in terms of a return of an Irish repressed, but instead chose to see both words as part of a hybrid, and by extension, inclusive transformation of identity, so here, in the case of O'Neill, he sees his position as essentially liminal, and, iconically and metaphorically, imagines O'Neill as a type of stepping stone in one particular historical situation.

In 1599, in the throes of O'Neill's nine years' war against the armies of Elizabethan England, he was faced by the Earl of Essex, a strong favourite of Queen Elizabeth, across the banks of the River Glyde, in County Louth, in Ireland. O'Neill, given his education in the English tradition, with Essex's father, Walter Devereux, acting as his patron, was in a position where the binary opposition of Irishness-Englishness was not quite so well-defined, and, given his historical association with the Devereux family, he was able to arrange a parley with Essex in the middle of the river (obviously an iconic image for Heaney, given the significance he attaches to stepping stones):[7]

O'Neill was on horseback, out in midstream, with the water up to his horse's belly and his Irish-speaking soldiers behind him, speaking English to Essex, who was standing facing him on the other bank....So, for each of them, this meeting by the river was a mysterious turn, a hiatus, a frozen frame in the violent action...the balance trembled and held, the water ran and the sky moved silently above them. (2002: 55)

The significance of this dialogue for Heaney, and indeed, for the thrust of our discussion, is that of liminal dialogue, in the midst of political confrontation. Here, while perhaps not an example of room to rhyme, both men found room to talk and this discussion served to avert a battle at that point in time.[8] What fascinates Heaney about this scene is that very notion of a liminal dialogue, of a space where the human relationship deconstructs the demands of the political one. The notion of two conflictual figures in dialogue is very much emblematic of his concepts of complexity, anastomosis and the field of force. As he puts it elsewhere, poetry 'floats adjacent to, parallel to, the historical moment' (1988: 121) and as such this is a moment where the space of literature becomes operative in that imagined realm contiguous to, but apart from, the real historical moment, and he describes this in terms of the ambiguity already discussed in terms of 'march':

There was no way, given their historical circumstances, that O'Neill and Essex could cross to each other's side. Their march had turned into something irrevocably military. They were at the terminus in an extreme sense of that word. There was no room for two truths. The brutality of power would have to decide the issue not the play of mind. And yet as we think about the scene, we want each of them to be released from the entrapment of history. We want the sky to open above them and grant them release from their earthbound fates. And even if we know that such a release is impossible, we still desire conditions where the longed-for and the actual might be allowed to coincide. A condition where borders are there to be crossed rather than contested. (2002: 56)

This is as clear a statement of Heaney's epistemology of poetry as we will see. It also echoes some comments Heaney has made about the idea of borders elsewhere. Borders, says Heaney, are made to be crossed, and poetry may provide the mode of such a crossing. In political terms, Heaney has expressed the hope that the frontier which partitions Ireland into north and south could become 'a little bit more like the net on a tennis court, a demarcation allowing for agile give-and-take' (1995b: 23). Yet again, there are echoes of Derrida who says that we 'have to cross the border but not to destroy the border' (Derrida 1993: 33). Instead, the border, as a limit point of one community, becomes an opening to the other community. We are in the symbolic constellation of the stepping stones here as these both form a border, a point of limitation, but also form a point of interaction between different types of identity. Linguistically the terms '*lachtar*' and 'hoked', as well as the placenames discussed earlier: 'Toome'; 'Glanmore'; 'Broagh'; 'Anahorish' and 'Mossbawn' also participate in this paradigm of the border, as the deconstructions of language exfoliate from the deconstruction of land in such a way as to create a sense of plurality and hybridity. It is not that one should choose one language, ideology, political position over the other: for both Heaney and Derrida, while the imperatives of *Realpolitik* may force such oppositional choices in the real world, the space of literature provides an opportunity where 'the longed-for and the actual may coincide', and where the 'play of mind' can create conditions where the choice no longer has to be '*neither* the one *nor* the other' (Derrida 2000a: 89). The stepping stone is dry land in water, inhabiting both elements and yet also marking their line of demarcation. This is how the deconstruction of language works in Heaney's writing: the signifier becomes a liminal point, open to different forms of influence.

For Heaney, the aesthetic should not merely reflect actuality: instead, it should critique actuality by offering a parallel vision of possibility which is sufficiently grounded in the actual to retain some purchase on real events, but which provides a form of extension which allows these events to be transformed. Like the shrine of Terminus on the Capitol, poetry while grounded, remains open to the sky. If we recall Heaney's account of Vaclav Havel's definition of 'hope', that we discussed in Chapter 2, this becomes clear. Hope, for Havel, 'is a state of the soul rather than a response to the evidence. It is not the expectation that things will turn out successfully but the conviction that something is worth working for, however it turns out. Its deepest roots are in the transcendental, beyond the horizon' (Heaney 2002: 47). The image of roots being located in the transcendental is both deconstructive and very much at variance with what we might term the consensual critical position on Heaney's writing.

It is, however, very much the *telos* towards which our discussion has been leading. The recontextualisation of the notion of the border in language has been ongoing, with the revisiting of placenames in different books contributing to a more pluralistic and hybrid form of signification. The stressing of the 'border' trope allows Heaney to gesture towards his view of poetry as being of value both in itself and in the cultural debate in Ireland. He concludes 'Something to Write Home About' with a *summa* of his thoughts on the poem 'Terminus', the idea of the border, and the value of poetry in cultural terms. Hardly surprisingly, he focuses on the emblematic trope of the liminal, one might say, terminal point, which he sees as representing the possibility of:

> ...going out on the stepping stone in order to remove yourself from the hardness and fastness of your home ground. The stepping stone invites you to change the terms and the *tearmann* of your understanding; it does not ask you to take your feet off the ground but it refreshes your vision by keeping your head in the air and by bringing you alive to the open sky of possibility that is within you. (2002: 58)

This open sky of possibility has been represented by the deconstruction of language in this chapter as words which seemed to be the possession of a particular identity were seen to embrace alterity as well. The final example that I will adduce in this chapter looks at borders in a broader context. Instead of focusing on the play of the individual mind, Heaney will now open up the political borders and attempt to cite a form of language which deconstructs the exigencies of history and instead offers a new form of identity which can be voiced under a new nominal dispensation.

In his essay 'Through-Other Places, Through-Other Times: The Irish Poet and Britain',[9] Heaney takes the opposition between self and other, a synecdoche of what we have been discussing in this chapter where the different meanings of a word were seen as being ideologically oppositional, and deconstructs it. The notion of 'through-otherness' is a coinage which echoes Derrida's decisional paradigm of 'neither *this* nor *that*; but rather this *and* that' (Derrida 1981c: 161), and also Heaney's own comments in the introduction to his translation of *Beowulf*, where he spoke about his own efforts to transcend the cultural predispositions that urged him to think of

English and Irish as 'adversarial tongues, as either/or conditions rather than both/and' (Heaney 1999: xxiv).

He begins by quoting some lines of the Northern Irish poet W. R. Rodgers, from a poem entitled 'Armagh':

> There is a through-otherness about Armagh
> Of tower and steeple,
> Up on the hill are the arguing graves of the kings
> And below are the people. (2002: 364)

Rodgers is seen as valuable in Heaney's terms because of his sketching of a field of force between the different instances of ideological determination that were operative on the individual consciousness in Northern Ireland in his own time, a project which resonates with much of Heaney's own thinking:

> I am trying to suggest that in the triangulation of Rodgers's understanding of himself between London, Loughgall and the Lowlands, in that three-sided map of his inner-being that he provided with its three cardinal points, in all of that there is something analogous to the triple heritage of Irish, Scottish and English traditions that compound and complicate the cultural and political life of contemporary Ulster. For Rodgers, it wasn't a question of the otherness of any one part of his inheritance, more a recognition of the through-otherness of all of them. (2002: 366)

Once again, we see instantiated the notions of hybridity, of constellation, of anastomosis, of the field of force as Heaney attempts to probe the interstices of the different cultural influences on the individual, and he clearly sees poetry as the ideal space within which this probing should take place.

Rodgers's work serves as an ideal template for Heaney's own stance on these issues, as Rodgers himself becomes the border, or frontier, at which different influences are transformed by being brought into a dialectical interaction. Heaney's sense of dealing with binaries is deconstructive in essence as he refuses to see each term as in any way either mutually exclusive or hermetically sealed within its own borders. Instead, he speaks of influences, confluences and a general sense of penetration and permeation which is constructive of those paradigms of complexity which have been so central to our discussion. For Heaney, the provenance of poetry is this sense of through-otherness, a complexity of structure which deconstructs any essentialist or simplistic structures which refuse to take account of changes in context.

The terms we have examined, from '*lachtar*' and 'hoked' through the different placenames, all participate in this sense of through-otherness: it is a further element in his process of continuous adjudication wherein the relationship between selfhood and alterity is constantly being transformed, with numerous recontextualisations needing to be kept in view. The triangulation that he speaks of in Rodgers's formulation presages his own notion of the quincunx, an imaginative structure where Irish literature is imagined as a field of force with five nodal points, arranged in a diamond formation, which illustrates the complexity of Irish literary history and tradition.

In *The Redress of Poetry*, he outlines this structure in terms of 'a bringing of the frontiers of the country into alignment with the frontiers of writing', and an attempt to sketch an 'integrated literary tradition'. This structure is imagined as five different towers facing each other in a diamond shape, with the fifth point located at the centre. This central tower, 'the tower of prior Irelandness, the round tower of original insular dwelling, located perhaps upon what Louis MacNeice called "the pre-natal mountain"'. This tower stands for the essentialist, autochthonous, ur-Ireland which has so often been seen as the reality of Irish cultural experience. It is important to note, at this juncture, that Heaney is in no way attempting to elide this strand of Irishness: we recall the 'appetites of gravity' referred to in *North*. However, what he is doing is avoiding the complete adequation of Irishness with this single hypertrophied strand. Instead, while granting the status and constituence of any definition of Irishness, he is placing it within a structure which grants the more complex interactions that in fact comprise what we term 'Irishness'. Thus, the other cardinal points, surrounding this central locus are associated with other important figures, themselves emblematic of movements and ideologies, who together comprise what Heaney sees as 'the shape of an integrated literary tradition'.[10]

At the south of the diamond is Edmund Spenser's Kilcolman Castle, symbolic of the English conquest and the Anglicisation of Ireland 'linguistically, culturally, institutionally'. At the west is Yeats's Thoor Ballylee, itself an actual Norman tower, but which in Heaney's construct symbolises Yeats's efforts to restore the 'spiritual values and magical world-view that Spenser's armies and language had destroyed', while on the eastern face of the quincunx is the Martello tower of James Joyce,[11] which appears in the first chapter of *Ulysses* and is symbolic of Joyce's attempt to:

> 'Hellenise the island' his attempt to marginalise the imperium which had marginalised him by replacing the Anglocentric Protestant tradition with a newly forged apparatus of Homeric correspondences, Dantesque scholasticism and a more or less Mediterranean, European, classically endorsed world-view. (1995a: 199)

At the northern point of the diamond is Carrickfergus Castle, associated with William of Orange's landing in Ireland to secure 'the Protestant Settlement and where the British army was garrisoned for generations' (1995a: 200). Heaney also associates this traditionally Protestant icon with a sense of MacNeice's through-otherness, noting that this tower 'once it is sponsored by MacNeice's vision', no longer 'only looks' to the Glorious Revolution and the Mother of Parliaments, but also towards a concept of a 'visionary Ireland' (1995a: 200).

To see this structure as static is to completely misread the imperative that has driven Heaney's discussion of poetic epistemology thus far. What is at work in this structure is the deconstruction of a linguistic and literary essentialism which sees a particular strand of linguistic use as hegemonically 'Irish' to the exclusion or demotion of more complicated interactions. Each of the figures who are constitutive of the quincunx are proto-deconstructers of any simplistic adequation between language, tradition and place. In the work of Spenser, Yeats, Joyce and MacNeice, notions of culture, language, politics and place are interrogated and offered to ongoing critique.

Spenser is seen as a colonising presence in Ireland and yet is also seen as a literary forebear of Heaney's own. Ironically, it is the Spenserian language and literary tradition that have had the most direct effect on succeeding generations of Irish people. Part of the complex association with Spenser embodies the through-otherness of which we are speaking as Heaney can feel a sense of political distance from Spenser the coloniser when the latter watches 'from his castle in Cork' a campaign 'designed to settle the Irish question' through starvation, and at that point Heaney feels 'closer to the natives' (1980: 34). However 'these incidental facts do not interfere with [his] responses to their poetry' (1980: 35). Spenser is an example of through-otherness in that he evokes complex emotions as he crosses and recrosses that border between selfhood and alterity for Heaney:

> One half of one's sensibility is in a cast of mind that comes from belonging to a place, an ancestry, a history, a culture, whatever one wants to call it. But consciousness and quarrels with the self are the result of what Lawrence calls 'the voices of my education'. (1980: 35)

Spenser, as poetic figure crosses that political barrier and Heaney, through his immersion in that tradition endorsed and progressed by Spenser's writing, finds himself crossing that border in a similar manner.

Joyce, as an Irish writer, further complicates issues of Irishness by cross-fertilising his characters with those from other cultures. In *Ulysses*, he creates the great Irish novel with:

> Leopold Bloom, a Hungarian Jewish hero, Molly Bloom, a British heroine born in Gibraltar, and Stephen Dedalus, Irish, but whose name certainly betokens a pluralist vision of identity in itself, as we have seen. The organising myth is Greek, and Bloom's comments on Irish Catholic rituals, themselves synecdoches of centripetal identity, are certainly those of a *spectator ab extra*;[12] while the structural parallel with Homer's classical *Odyssey* foregrounds the identificatory perspective of Joyce. His book is paralleled with one of the first great books of Western civilization; he is placing Ireland, and the subject matter of Ireland squarely in the ambit of European culture, against which Irishness will be defined negatively. The troped name of 'Patrick W. Shakespeare' brings this ethical definition of identity as an openness to alterity into focus, but I would argue that this is not confined to this passage in *Ulysses*. In fact, the Shakespearean spectre is to be found haunting many different portions of Joyce's writings, and this imbrication of Shakespeare and Joyce will have the effect of transforming them both. (O'Brien 1998: 244)

In his creation of the name 'Patrick W. Shakespeare', Joyce is creating the through-other *avant la lettre*, as this character stands in synecdoche for the anastomosis between language, ideology and history by enunciating the influence of the Irish tradition on the English language and literary tradition.

Yeats, too, embodies the through-other in that he has embraced both the Irish and English traditions and conflated them in his own work. In the introduction, we noted his comment that 'I think we should accept the whole past of this nation and not pick and choose.' Throughout his writing career, Yeats attempted to voice what he saw as the complexity of the Irish tradition: a stated aim to help Gaelic Ireland and Anglo-Ireland to unite so that 'neither shall shed its pride' (Yeats 1962: 337). He goes on to contextualise his comments by referring to unionists and nationalists who were 'too busy keeping one or two simple beliefs at their fullest intensity for any complexity of thought or emotion' to develop (Yeats 1975: 184). Throughout his work, with the constant recontextualisation of Ireland as part of a pan-European literature, Yeats is attempting to voice this complex sense of Irishness.

Louis MacNeice, the final figure in the quincunx, is another liminal figure, and given the prominence of cultural hybridity in the other chosen figures, this should hardly be surprising. Heaney advocates these qualities of MacNeice – definitely the least known of the chosen figures – in the essay immediately prior to his outlining of the quincunx and his points are well taken. He sees MacNeice as the sponsor of a notion of Northern Ireland which is 'struggling to be born, one in which the allowances for the priority of some of its citizens' Irishness would not prejudice the rights of others' Britishness' (1995a: 198). He goes on to see MacNeice exploring his 'bilocated extraterritorial fidelities' in his poem 'Carrick Revisited', and explores his sense of the complex inheritance of being Irish in a passage which immediately precedes the outlining of the quincunx and which is the embodiment of the through-other:

> he did not allow the border to enter into his subsequent imaginings: his sense of cultural diversity and historical consequence within the country never congealed into a red and green map. In MacNeice's mind, the colours ran – or bled – into each other. His ancestry in Mayo gave him a native dream-place in the south which complemented his actual birthplace in the north, while his dwelling in England gave him a critical perspective on the peculiar Britishness of that first northern environment. (1995a: 198–9)

In the image of the colours running, or bleeding, into each other, we see an iconographic picture of the through-other, as the elements of a binary opposition merge into each other, creating a new, diverse entity.[13]

To see these figures at different corners of the diamond of towers, with a further tower at the centre as a static structure is to miss the point about Heaney's notion of the field of force. It is in the structures of dynamic interaction that this quincunx becomes an adequate emblem of the complex structure that Heaney's epistemology of literature brings to bear on Irishness. It is through the interaction of these figures, just as it was in the interaction of text and context in Catherine Bradley's sampler, that the complexity of the poetic structure is revealed.

Heaney stresses that it is, first and foremost, a literary and linguistic structure that is at work here, what he calls an 'integrated literary tradition' (1995a: 199). The deconstructive trend that we have traced through the last two chapters finds its apotheosis in Heaney's deconstruction of the signifiers traditionally associated with colonisation: Britain and Britishness. We have already seen Heaney accused of *echt*-nationalist writing in some of his earlier poetry, and he has certainly given voice to that aspect of his tradition. However, in his 'Frontiers of Writing' essay, he makes an interesting point in terms of Ireland as a colony of the British empire. Speaking of John Hewitt, he notes that until 1921:

> Diversity was the norm within the union. From Belfast to Brandon, everybody, whether Gaelic speakers from Ballyferriter or Scots speakers from Braid, everybody had the one home under the crown; if they were not quite at ease within an old dispensation, they were at any rate held equally in place by it. (1995a: 198)

For a poet from the nationalist tradition, this sense of openness to the traditional political and ideological 'other' is an example of the complexity and continuous adjudication which we have been tracing. Rather than see the signifier 'Britain', or 'union' as being predetermined and locked in to a fixed oppressive signification, Heaney deconstructs them to unveil a more expansive meaning.

This point is furthered in his essay from *Finders Keepers*, 'Through-Other Places, Through-Other Times'. In this essay we see a further deconstruction of language as he takes a signifier which is ideologically shot through with the residue of colonisation and conflict, and instead replaces it with a cognate term which, to use the vocabulary of 'Terminus', would open some sky above the horizon of expectations of the signifier in question, along with its attendant signifieds. Comparing a recent history of the British isles by Hugh Kearney[14] with his own co-editorship of *The School Bag*, with Ted Hughes,[15] Heaney notes that both books apply similar editorial guidelines. These guidelines were motivated by a conviction which is expressed at the beginning of the paragraph where the two books are compared: 'I have a dread of pious words like diversity but I believe in what they stand for', going on to add that both Hughes and himself were determined that their editorship of this anthology would 'insist on the diverse and deep traditions that operate through and sustain for good the poetry written in Ireland, England, Scotland and in Wales' (2002: 378). It is with this version of diversity in mind that Heaney approvingly cites Kearney's view that it is only by adopting what he calls 'a Britannic approach' that any possible sense can be made of the histories of England, Ireland, Scotland, Wales, Cornwall or the Isle of Man. Taking this approach, and pondering its ideological aspects, Heaney suggests that:

> In a context where the word 'British' might function like a political reminder, a mnemonic for past invasions and coercions, there is a wonderful originality, in all sense, about employing instead the word 'Britannic', 'Britannic' works more like a cultural wake-up call and gestures not only towards the cultural past but also towards an imaginable future. (2002: 378–9)

That such a perspective enunciates Heaney's idea of the through-other is obvious; that this perspective can exercise a deconstructive force on the prevailing modes of signification should become equally obvious.

While the binary opposition between Ireland and England, so graphically captured by the encounter of Hugh O'Neill and Essex in 'Terminus', may attenuate the political interactions of the two traditions, nevertheless, language as used in poetry has the affirmative ability to suggest other possible interactions. Towards the end of this essay, Heaney talks about the value of imaginative fiction in dealing with the differences between the two islands 'linked and separated' by history and geography, language and culture, and concludes the essay by suggesting that such a practice prefigures work that will be done by Irish poets 'in the coming times' (2002: 382), and this Yeatsian allusion leads us to the final chapter of this discussion, where the relationship between Yeats and Heaney will be discussed.

7   Nobel Causes: Heaney and Yeats

On the inside front cover of *Wintering Out*, a portion of a review of that book by Clive James is printed. James, in a laudatory review, makes the point that soon 'people are going to start comparing him [*Heaney*] with Yeats: the packed forms, that unmistakable combination of clarity with argumentative density – it's all there, robust and abundant'. As Heaney's writing has developed, these comparisons have become more overt as the influence of Yeats becomes stronger on Heaney's work. I would argue that, over the years as Heaney's career has developed, the practice of poetry as embodied by Yeats has been perhaps the most importance influence, from the Irish tradition, on Heaney's writing.

Our discussion began on this theme, with Heaney's review of Roy Foster's biography of Yeats. What interested Heaney in this book was the coherence of biographer and biographee in terms of their shared commitment to an imagining of Irelands of the future as opposed to the narrow narratives of the past. Both writers share an essentially postmodern project of unravelling the monological nationalist narrative of history and instead foregrounding the aporias, antinomies and fault lines that have been glossed over by the sweep of historical narrative. Yeats, as a figure of influence on Heaney's career, is a writer who, as we have discussed in the introduction, has reminded his readership that he 'took the strain of both the major ideologies that were exacerbating Irish political life in that critically important year' (Heaney 1997: 159). Yeats, we remember, wished to commemorate the 'whole past' of Ireland as opposed to a form of selective memory. This type of poetic imperative as espoused by Yeats presents a growing symphysis with Heaney who feels that, above all else, poetry should be a 'working model of inclusive consciousness' which 'should not simplify' (1995a: 8). That both writers should be standing at the same podium in Stockholm, separated by some 70 years, but connected by a strong strand of agreement, would indicate points of connection between their work, but, as we will see, those strands, when examined, prove to be considerably stronger.

It is certainly no accident that at the beginning of Heaney's first collection of prose, *Preoccupations*, there is an epigraph from Yeats, whose own prose runs to a large number of volumes, as well as the two-volume edition of his *Uncollected Prose*.[1] This piece, from 'Samhain: 1905', deals with Yeats's response to being asked whether his play *Cathleen Ni Houlihan* was written to 'affect public opinion'. Yeats emphatically denies this, adding that the inspiration for the play came to him in a dream, and goes on to explain his own views on the relationship between the aesthetic and the politic:

> If we understand our own minds, and the things that are striving to utter themselves through our minds, we move others, not because we have understood or thought about these others, but because all life has the same root. Coventry Patmore has said 'The end of art is peace,' and the following of art is little different from the following of religion in the intense preoccupation it demands. (Heaney 1980: 7)

That Heaney should choose this particular piece to be an epigraph to his first collection of prose is particularly significant, especially in terms of the question and answer motif contained therein. I have taken this motif as central to Heaney's aesthetic epistemology, and the Yeatsian epigraph would seem to reinforce both the importance of the theme itself, and by extension the importance of Yeats as an exemplar. The very title of Heaney's book, *Preoccupations*, comes from Yeats's quotation, and the contextual frame surrounding it is furthered by Heaney's ongoing preoccupations and interrogations of the whole notion of art itself. That Yeats managed to create 'a heroic role for the poet in the modern world' (Heaney 2000b: xii) is an important point of connection with Heaney, especially in view of Heaney's ongoing questioning of the role of art in that very modern, or postmodern, world.

Perhaps one of the seminal interactions of the poetry of Yeats and Heaney is to be found in *Among Schoolchildren*. Towards the end of this lecture, speaking about the value of writing in general and poetry in particular, Heaney offers a reading of W. B. Yeats's late poem, 'Among School Children', from his collection entitled *The Tower*. This reading focuses on the final stanza of the poem:

> Labour is blossoming or dancing where
> The body is not bruised to pleasure soul,

Nor beauty born out of its own despair,
Nor blear-eyed wisdom out of midnight oil.
O chestnut-tree, great-rooted blossomer,
Are you the leaf, the blossom or the bole?
O body swayed to music, O brightening glance,
How can we know the dancer from the dance?
(Yeats 1979: 244–5)

Heaney chose this version of the Yeatsian title, *Among Schoolchildren*, to highlight his interest in the educational process, an interest foregrounded by the occasion of a public lecture which was given in commemoration of the educator John Malone. The opening stanza of the poem places Yeats, a Senator in the Irish Free State, in a school in Waterford in 1926, and is told in the first person for the most part:

I walk through the long schoolroom questioning.
A kind old nun in a white hood replies;
The children learn to cipher and to sing,
To study reading books and histories,
To cut and sew, be neat in everything
In the best modern way – the children's eyes
In momentary wonder stare upon
A sixty-year-old smiling public man. (Yeats 1979: 244)

Heaney sees this stanza as positing a 'world of routine', a world where we are 'our official routine selves' (1983a: 4). However, given his educational train of thought, he goes on to discuss the motivation behind such quotidian classroom routines in the following manner:

Yet any routine world, whether it be primary school classroom or college of education lecture hall, has based its routines upon some vision. The mechanics and humdrum of its operations are evolved to further or realise some end, some ideal result posited upon a vision of what the pupil or the student teacher should become…Yeats himself was much in sympathy with this idea of education as a natural blossoming. (1983a: 4–5)

Heaney himself has long had a participative interest in education across the different institutional and operational levels:

I have spent much of my life teaching, at very different levels. I began in the early 1960s in Saint Thomas's Secondary Intermediate School in the Ballymurphy area of Belfast, in front of a class of deprived and disaffected adolescent boys, many of whom would end up a decade later as active members of the Provisional IRA. I proceeded from there to work in a teacher training college, also in Belfast, and to spend time trying to persuade student teachers of the value of imaginative literature and other kinds of creative play in the educational process; I went on to lecture on poetry in Queen's University, and ended up in more recent years as a poet in residence at Harvard. (Heaney 2002: 67)

In discussing Yeats's poem, Heaney goes on to examine further educational and linguistic issues which have a bearing on what he calls the 'cement of society, these shared conceptions, loyalties and ideals' (1983a: 5) without which society can become unstable. He feels this to be important as in Ireland, 'north and south, this social cement of a common culture and shared national attitudes is not strong or shared or common' (1983a: 6). Having discussed the interaction of traditions in his own life, Heaney brings his discussion back to the notion of 'vision' with which he began, and goes on to read the final Yeatsian stanza as an apotheosis of what education can, ideally, achieve:

So I would end where I began with Yeats's poem. Its final stanza is a guarantee of our human capacity to outstrip the routine world, the borders of ideology and the conditionings of history. It is a vision of harmony and fulfilment, of a natural and effortless richness of being, a vision, in fact, of the paradisal place...where the earthly conflicts between flesh and spirit, beauty, truth, effort and ease, will and temperament, are all elided and assumed into harmony and unity. The images which Yeats uses here are drawn from art and nature, from human order and elemental cycles, and they are couched in a rhythm and a language that is full of summer lushness, full of delight in earthly sensuousness, with words like 'chestnut tree,' 'rooted blossomer,' 'leaf and bole.' But there are also other words like 'swayed to music' and 'brightening glance,' which are radiant with unearthly expectation: *[final stanza quoted in full]*. This is one of the high watermarks of poetry. It has all the energy and physical presence of a green breaking wave, deep and on the move, rising with thrilling self-propelling force, solid and mysterious at once, gone just as it reveals its full crest of power, never fully apprehended but alluring with its suggestions. And what it suggests is the necessity of an idea of transcendence, an impatience with the limitations of systems, a yearning to be completely fulfilled at all levels of our being, to strike beyond the ordinary daily levels of achievement where one goal is won at the expense of another, to arrive at a final place which is not the absence of activity but is, on the contrary, the continuous realisation of all the activities of which we are capable. (1983a: 15–16)

The opening sentence intertextually locates this reading of Yeats within the Modernist paradigm embodied by T. S. Eliot, with its implied invocation of a line from Eliot's *East Coker*: 'In my end is my beginning' (1963: 204). This imbrication of Heaney's writing with that of Eliot is appropriate, given the New Critical aesthetic ideology that permeates this passage. The language of poetry is seen as transcendent with respect to the contrary nature of experience. Poetry embodies this transcendence, this 'impatience with the limitations of systems', it is that field of force, that border which allows for cross-border traffic. In Yeats's stanza, Heaney sees a vision of poetry which is akin to his own: perhaps Yeats is more optimistic and more assured as to the lastingness of the poetic art than is Heaney, who has lived through times where the value of art has become more problematic. Perhaps the importance of the stanza for Heaney is that it gestures towards the 'idea' of transcendence – the notion of a regulative idea towards which we can direct our gaze, and focus our attempts at writing. It is this idea which allows for the second meaning of the government of the tongue, and for the effect of poetry as being akin to the writing in the sand of which we have already spoken. The 'paradisal place' resonates with Heaney's own idea of the 'placeless heaven', both seeing the literary as a space wherein the conflicts of actuality can be in some imaginative way brought into less violent interaction.

The stanza addresses for Heaney what has been at the centre of his own pedagogical imperative throughout his life: 'what was at stake was the credibility of this honoured but hard to define category of human achievement called poetry' (Heaney 2002: 67). The fact that Yeats's stanza concludes with two rhetorical questions underscores Heaney's own guarded view about the performative nature of poetry as an activity.[2] While he is certain of its societal, and moreover, individual value, Heaney's descriptions of this value are highly nuanced and indefatigably complex and plural. As he puts it in 'The Placeless Heaven': poetry is 'a spurt of abundance from a source within and it spills over to irrigate the world beyond the self' (1988: 13); or again, as he notes in the essay 'Sounding Auden':

> on the one hand poetry could be regarded as magical incantation, fundamentally a matter of sound and the power of sound to bind our minds' and bodies' apprehensions within an acoustic complex; on the other hand, poetry is a matter of making wise and true meanings, of commanding our emotional assent by the intelligent disposition and inquisition of human experience. (1988: 109)

Or again, one could cite his commentary on Robert Lowell: 'Lowell succeeded in uniting the aesthetic instinct with the obligation to witness morally and significantly in the realm of public action' (1988: 233).

Certainly, the simile which Heaney uses to describe the force of this stanza seems to postulate a value and a force to both questions, and their extended metaphors of tree and dancer that places them at the core of his sense of the epistemological structure and the ontological status of poetry. The stanza is seen as a 'green breaking wave' (1983a: 16). A wave, synecdochal of the power of the sea, suggests 'an idea of transcendence'; the point seeming to be that, just as the wave is synecdochic of the sea, so the stanza is synecdochic of a location wherein different strands of experience and ideology can co-exist in a dynamic form of being. The organic metaphors of the stanza suggest the possibility, or as Heaney would have it, the 'necessity', of an ideological movement towards a form of complete fulfilment 'at all levels of our being'. Heaney admires the holistic aesthetic embodied by Yeats: 'true poetry, Yeats would declare, had to be the speech of the whole man' (Heaney 2000b: xiv). The rhetoric of the passage, with its gesture towards location and locution, embodies the thrust of what I take to be one of Heaney's most pivotal aims: 'to arrive at a final place which is not the absence of activity but is, on the contrary, the continuous realisation of all the activities of which we are capable' (1983a: 16). This final place is very much akin to Blanchot's 'space of literature' and to Derrida's 'non-lieu', not to mention Heaney's own field of force and Catherine Bradley's sampler, itself an image taken from the beginning of this pamphlet: all embody the power of literature to define ideas which, while lodged in reality, nevertheless offer a vision, or alternative place, which satisfies the 'human capacity to outstrip the routine world'.

Stylistically, and symbolically, there are other reasons which attract Heaney to this stanza, an attraction that is important for a poet. As he puts it in 'Through-Other Places, Through-Other Times':

> A précis of the content, for example, takes no account of the literary echoes and allusions which can be fundamental to its poetic energy. In a poem, words, phrases, cadences and images are linked in to systems of affect and signification which elide the précis-maker. These under-ear activities…may well constitute the most important business which the poem is up to and are more a matter of the erotics of language than the politics and polemics of the argument. (2002: 373)

In this respect, he is in agreement with Derrida who also speaks of the 'précis-making' school of criticism, albeit in different terms: he makes the point that 'literary writing has, almost always and almost everywhere…lent itself to this *transcendent* reading, in that search for the signified' (Derrida 1976: 160). It is in the interaction of signifier with signified that repressed aspects of language and meaning can become revealed: 'polysemy is infinite' (1981b: 253). Both writers feel that the signifying chains of language, especially those of literary language, are subject to much broader ranges of interpretation than have been hitherto achieved through just thematic readings. As we have seen, for Heaney the signifier 'British' entails a completely different range of meanings to the seemingly cognate 'Britannic', as contextually they are very different. Hence, for Heaney, the fact that the image which is central to the Yeatsian stanza is a 'chestnut tree' is hugely significant, echoing as it does the seminal image which we discussed in Chapter 5. The further instance that this tree is envisioned as almost a 'paradisal place', or a 'placeless heaven', to use Heaney's own cognate terminology, with its questioning of the location of the tree: 'are you the leaf, the blossom or the bole?' underscores its influence on Heaney's aesthetic. The 'unearthly expectation' engendered by these images is again redolent of Heaney's own view of the transcendent power of some poetic writing.

The fact that this final place comes at the end of a pamphlet where subjective fracture has been a main topic of discussion is no accident. Earlier in *Among Schoolchildren*, as we remember, Heaney describes a time when the different cultural tensions seemed to be pulling him in different, and opposite directions:

> Was I two persons or one? Was I extending myself or breaking myself apart? Was I being led out or led away? Was I failing to live up to the aspiring literary intellectual effort when I was at home, was I betraying the culture of the parish when I was at the university? (1983a: 8)

In terms of Heaney's reading, which sees parts of the stanza as being 'radiant with unearthly expectation', this poem can be seen as embodying the complex and plural notion of 'place' which is central to his search for answers. At the beginning of *Preoccupations*, Heaney spoke of his childhood home, beginning with the 'Greek word, *omphalos*, meaning the navel, and hence the stone that marked the centre of the world' (1980: 17). He went on to equate this word with the sound made by the pump outside the family home, and saw the pump as 'marking the centre of another world'. Already, his 'first place' was shot through with the through-other.

Consequently, the poem is being read in terms of its offering of a symbolic icon of an idealised synthesis of the 'earthly conflicts between flesh and spirit'. The place of art is to allow such harmony and unity to exist; the aesthetic here subsumes ideological conflict in a Hegelian *Aufhebung*, where all differences, be they political, linguistic or cultural, are synthesised into harmony and unity. Here, the linguistic and cultural contraries that he sees in the signifier 'Mossbawn' will be resolved in 'the final place' of poetry, under the synthesising power of the aesthetic to reveal the 'idea of transcendence.' Just as many of the placenames and signifiers we have examined can be read as indices of opposition, and the different components that comprise them can be seen as conflictual, in art, a parallel sense of meaning is offered, where self and other can become, even in an idealised sense, through-other, and this offers a possibility of a more inclusive and diverse range of meanings. It is as if, on reading the Yeatsian stanza, Heaney is coming home, finding a 'final place,' as Yeats has very much sponsored such a reading of culture.

Writing in 'John Clare's Prog',[3] Heaney is speaking of the type of poetry being written by Clare, a poetry which is located in the 'here-and-nowness, or there-and-thenness, of what happened' (1995a: 66), and he describes this in terms of a dialectic between the 'deep-lodged, hydraulic locatedness within the district' and a 'totally receptive adjustment to the light and heat of solar distances' (1995a: 67). He goes on to describe the latter aspect of Clare's writing in terms of the idea of a world-culture and again, significantly, in terms of a 'final place or state':

> He never heard Mandelstam's famous phrase about Acmeism being a 'nostalgia for world culture', but oddly enough, it makes sense to think of Clare in relation to the arrival of poetry in that longed-for place or state....The dream of a world culture, after all, is a dream of a world where no language will be relegated, a world where the ancient rural province of Boeotia (which Les Murray has made an image for all the outback and dialect cultures of history) will be on an equal footing with the city-state of Athens; where not just Homer but Hesiod will have his due honour. Clare's poetry underwrites a vision like this, where one will never have to think twice about the cultural and linguistic expression of one's world on its own terms since nobody else's terms will be imposed as normative and official. (1995a: 82)

Here the Yeatsian idea of a final place, and Heaney's own notions of the space of literature, achieve an echo in terms of the world culture which he sees as the ultimate goal of so archaic and dialect a poet as Clare. All see literature as a glimpse of that 'longed-for place or state' wherein tensions can co-exist and interact. It is a place, space or state wherein our humanity is both explored and extended through the medium of language at the level of both signifier and signified. For Heaney, Yeats is a *locus classicus* of this process.

'Yeats as an Example', the title of an essay from *Preoccupations* (and a title which would seem to underline my argument in this chapter), makes the point that Yeats's value lies in no small way in the worth he attaches to art as he grows older. It is hard not to detect a note of admiration as Heaney, describing the poem 'Long-legged Fly', notes the theme that art can 'outface history, the imagination can disdain happenings once it has incubated and mastered the secret behind happenings' (1980: 99). In this essay, the question and answer motif is the *modus operandi* for Heaney to explain the value of Yeats as an example, both to himself and to culture in general.

At the purely professional level, Heaney's admiration for Yeats is clear. He sees Yeats as 'an ideal example for a poet approaching middle age' as he is a prescient reminder that 'revision and slog-work' will be necessary if one seeks 'the satisfaction of finish' (1980: 110).

He is also impressed by the vatic certainty that he detects in Yeats with respect to the lasting cultural value of art: 'above all, he reminds you that art is intended, that it is part of the creative push of civilization itself' (1980: 110). I would argue that this is perhaps one of the strongest points of connection between the two writers, the sense of the value of writing in the face of the actual and the political. In Heaney's quincunx, the place of Yeats as part of the frontiers of writing is assured for this very reason. Indeed, the notion of using towers as symbols of different aspects of a pluralistic and hybrid conception of Irish literary identity could well be drawn from Yeats himself, with Thoor Ballylee, and Joyce, with his Martello tower which figures in the opening chapter of *Ulysses*.

In a series of lectures entitled *The Place of Writing*, Heaney discusses the actual and imaginary towers that were central to Yeats's imagination.[4] For Yeats, the notion of place was far from simplistic, and one can sense a resonance in Heaney's discussion of the relationship between place and poetry, a relationship that is directly addressed in Heaney's quincunx. Heaney makes this very point:

the poetic imagination in its strongest manifestation imposes its vision upon a place rather than accepts a vision from it; and that this visionary imposition is never exempt from the imagination's antithetical ability to subvert its own creation. (1989: 20)

The Derridean thrust of this piece is by now unmistakable, as the conceptual movement and constant autocritique mirror Derrida's own descriptions of the nature of the deconstructive impulse. Indeed, one could see this vision of place as deconstructionist *avant la lettre*. However, on the present context, it is the Yeatsian strand of influence that is being traced and here, Yeats, indeed, is an example.

The buying of a Norman keep in the Barony of Kiltartan, dating from the thirteenth century, and registered in *The Booke of Connaught* for £35 was an act which, for Yeats, was both pragmatic and symbolic. For Yeats, the tower became part of his work. By the time he had ceased living in Thoor Ballylee, the tower had become the place, or space, of writing; it was his room to rhyme which became enunciated in the rhyme; it is a paradigm of the actual made into the imaginary. For Heaney, this physical tower is the source of two volumes, *The Tower* (1928) and its sequel *The Winding Stair* (1933). As he puts it, speaking of Yeats who was by then in ill health and no longer living in the tower itself: it had 'entered so deeply into the prophetic strains of the voice that it could be invoked without being inhabited. He no longer needed to live in it since he had attained a state in which he lived by it' (1989: 24).

In an overview of Yeats's work, Heaney stresses the interconnectedness of thought and place for Yeats, and also goes on to define the older poet in terms of the very complexity of response which Heaney himself has made an essential part of his ongoing searches for answers:

> Yeats's radical devotion to the potential and otherness of a specifically Irish reality should never be underestimated....In his early conjuration of Neo-Platonic tradition with the deposits of Irish folklore, and in the mature symbolism of his dwelling in a Norman tower conjoined with a thatched cabin, Yeats intended to open and complicate the meaning of Irishness. In fact, his imagined Ireland represented not only a regenerative breakaway from the imperium of Britain but also from the magisterium of orthodox Christianity. (2000b: xv)

This sense of an ongoing process of complicating the identificatory discourse of Irishness, this sense of an imagined Ireland is an important *point de repère* between the work of Yeats and that of Heaney. Both writers are attempting to enculturate more complex definitions of Irishness through the creation of a 'further language' which will allow for that sense of the 'through-other' of which we have been speaking. Yeats's specific symbolisation of place, of a tower and a cabin, would be an important aspect of this further language.

For Heaney, the tower as symbol has a twofold importance. Firstly, by taking a Norman tower and using it as a symbol of his own contemporary Irishness, Yeats is being true to that complexity of response which we have found to be a touchstone for Heaney's view of poetry: he is acknowledging the complex history that is imbricated in any attempt to enunciate a sense of 'Irishness'. That the great sequence 'Meditations in Time of Civil War' was written there is further demonstration of the complexity of Irishness as envisioned by Yeats. That a Norman tower, built as a fortification to progress the colonisation of the area of Connacht by the Norman family the de Burgos, should then be witness to a civil war wherein Irish people killed each other, is a demonstration of the complexity of the whole situation.

Secondly, Heaney is stressing the ability of poetry to subsume the actual into the symbolic, and, speaking about the 'My House' section in 'Meditations in Time of Civil War', he makes the telling point that:

> nevertheless, the poem does proceed to concentrate its focus inward so that the fortress of stone passing into the fortress of words becomes finally a manifestation of the fortified mind, besieged yet ablaze, exalted and incontrovertible. (1989: 27)

Proceeding to offer a close reading of section four of that sequence, 'My Descendents', Heaney goes on to completely internalise the place of writing, stressing that in this poem the 'place of writing is essentially the stanza form itself' (1989: 29), and it is here, I would suggest, that we see the germ of the quincunx, as Heaney comes to the telling conclusion that it is in the space of literature, the room to rhyme, that place becomes enculturated and enunciated. If that writing is simplistic and ideologically monological, then the enculturation of place will be essentialist and open to sectarian associations; if, on the other hand, that writing is complex, then the enculturation of place will be equally complex, and here again, Yeats serves as an example.

Speaking of Thoor Ballylee, Heaney maintains that it is no longer merely a symbol of a 'particular cultural heritage' but has now become a podium 'from which the spirit's voice can best be projected' (1989: 30), and here, again, we see echoes of Derrida's *non-lieu* and Blanchot's space of literature:

> I had thought of proposing as a title for this book *'Literature's Remove'*. I hoped thereby to capture not only literature's distance from the world, and not only this distance as literature's preserve, but also that when 'space' is literature's, it is space opened by that opening's absence: by the removal of that very interval, which is kept, as if for some other time, in reserve. (Blanchot 1982a: 11)

For Heaney, Yeats's tower embodies that sense of place wherein 'the place of writing shifts its *locus* into psychic space' (1989: 68). While taking up the matter of the givens of its culture, literature as genre, allows for the reconfiguration of that matter through a revisioning of it: 'a dialectic is set in motion in which the new writing does not so much displace the old as strive to displace itself to an enabling distance away from it' (1989: 55). It is this enabling distance which is achieved in the quincunx, and it is also the cause of a conflation of images of place later in this essay on Yeats.

At this juncture, Heaney brings together Yeats, the Gaelic poet of nineteenth-century Ireland, Anthony Raftery,[5] and the German poet Rainer Maria Rilke. In an argument which is based on connectedness between poetic, as opposed to nationalistic, traditions, Heaney sees Raftery and Yeats as being in similar 'extreme positions', as Raftery sees himself with his 'back to the wall', playing his music to 'empty pockets' (1989: 31). Looking at the work of Rilke, Heaney sees a similar situation as, into a world of 'humble, un-self-trusting creaturely life, shabby huts full of common speech and unpoetic desultoriness' the Orphic creation brought forth a transformation:

A tree ascended there. Oh pure transcendence!
Oh Orpheus sings! Oh tall tree in the ear!
And all things hushed. Yet even in that silence
a new beginning, beckoning, change appeared. (Heaney 1989: 32)

This view of silence as essentially creative harks back to our earlier discussion of Levinas in 'The Other Side', but it also allows Heaney to bring the discussion back to Yeats, and specifically to the Yeatsian articulation of the relationship between the aesthetic and the material, between writing and place:

That sense of a temple inside the hearing, of an undeniable acoustic architecture, of a written vaulting, of the firmness and in-placeness and undislodgeableness of poetic form, that is one of Yeats's great gifts to our century; and his power to achieve it was due in no small measure to the 'beckoning' the 'new beginning', the 'pure transcendence' of an old Norman castle in Ballylee, a place that was nowhere until it was a written place. (1989: 32)

Here the Yeatsian influence is clear for all to see: it is an influence which dictates that the role of art with respect to ideology and culture is, of necessity, to be true to its own laws, while simultaneously operating at a distance from the actual, a process which can, in effect, be transformative of that actuality.

Such a transformative role for the aesthetic is brought about by that very fluidity of thought which we have been tracing through Heaney's work and which, I would maintain, is influenced in no small way by Yeats. In a comparative essay on Yeats and Philip Larkin,

Heaney refers to Richard Ellmann's point that Yeats's later poetry enacted the aporia of life being seen as a cornucopia while at the same time, being seen as something of an empty shell.[6] For Heaney, there is no need for the reader, or for Yeats, to make a definite choice between these two perspectives. In fact, quite the opposite is true: 'it is because of Yeats's fidelity to both perceptions and his refusal to foreclose on either that we recognise in him a poet of the highest attainment' (1995a: 151). It is this role of a poet who is of 'the highest attainment' that is the core influence on Heaney who also aspires that literature and poetry should strive to be at the centre of the life of the 'spiritual intellect's great work' (1995a: 158). Indeed, it is in this essay on the work of Yeats that we find Heaney's affirmation of the role of poetry as he would see it, with relation to the social and the cultural spheres. Speaking about the late Yeatsian poem 'Man and Echo', Heaney stresses the transformative quality of literature which he finds enunciated there, noting that it is 'essential' that the 'vision of reality that poetry offers should be transformative' and more than 'just a print out of the given circumstances of its time and place' (1995a: 159):

> The poet who would be most the poet has to attempt an act of writing that outstrips the conditions even as it observes them. The truly creative writer, by interposing his or her perception and expression, will transfigure the conditions and thereby effect what I have been calling 'the redress of poetry'. (1995a: 159)

Such transformational qualities come close to becoming one of the answers which much of his work searches for, a point he makes in an interview with John Brown: 'what I was making up was making a difference in the real' (2002: 75). If the structures of reality are seen as structures, then, by definition, they are prone to the deconstructive force of language which, as we have seen, does not try to lessen or trivialise them but instead attempts to find a space wherein different traditions can be brought together in a new relationship. As Heaney puts it in his preface to the translation of *Beowulf*, such writing attempts to set up, in some 'unpartitioned country of the mind', a language which 'would not be simply a badge of ethnicity or a matter of cultural preference or an official imposition, but an entry into further language' (1999: xxv).[7]

It is the room to rhyme, or the space of literature, that allows for this development of a further language, and his final sections of this essay, which further discuss 'The Man and the Echo' develop this notion to its fullest extent. Citing the lines:

> Up there some hawk or owl has struck
> Dropping out of the sky or rock,
> A stricken rabbit is crying out.
> And its cry distracts my thought (Yeats 1979: 395)

Heaney proceeds to comment on the final rhyme which conflates 'crying out' with 'thought'. He makes the point that it is not a perfect rhyme, and proceeds to explain the signification of this imperfection, enacting as it does the sense that there is at best an imperfect fit between 'the project of civilisation' represented by thought and the facts of pain and death represented by the rabbit's 'crying out' (1995a: 162). For Heaney, this sense of balance between the actual and the possible, between reality and the aesthetic apperception of that reality is crucial, and in Yeats he finds an avatar of his own thinking. As he puts it, what holds the 'thought' and the suffering together is the consciousness which tries to make sense of it all, which, despite the acknowledgement of reality, still asks that we should 'in that great night rejoice' (Yeats 1979: 394). For Heaney, the value of this poem, and by extension, of Yeats's project in general, is its attempt to pit 'human resources against the recalcitrant and the inhuman' and also by pitting 'the positive effort of mind against the desolations of natural and historical violence' (Heaney 1995a: 163).[8]

It is this imperative in Yeats's work that is so attractive to Heaney, who, as we have seen, stresses the point that poetry which aims to be its best, must both address the actual while at the same time outstripping it in some way. His work testifies to the value of the aesthetic, and as such is an important plank in those answers for which Heaney has been searching. As Heaney asserts, there is no doubting Yeats's 'immense contribution' to our 'general intellectual and imaginative resource', nor is there any doubting his 'fundamental importance as the creator of a cultural idea in and for Ireland'. He goes on to discuss further qualities which he finds to be of value in Yeats and, not surprisingly, the Yeatsian imperative towards a fusion of disparate positions is seen as seminal. Heaney speaks admiringly of his 'extreme exploration of the possibilities of reconciling the human impulse to transcendence with the antithetical project of consolidation' and argues that this project is 'universally and inexhaustibly relevant' (Heaney 2000b: xxiv). Given his own drive towards hybridity and complexity of response, towards the 'through-other' and towards that anastomosis of text and context, we should hardly be surprised that Yeats has, indeed, served as an example to Heaney in both poetry and prose, and it is to prose that our discussion now turns.

Perhaps the most overt connection between these two poets is their winning of the Nobel Prize for literature. In terms of their respective Nobel lectures, Yeats's *The Irish Dramatic Movement*, and Heaney's *Crediting Poetry*, there is a symphysis of thought in connection with the role that is played by the aesthetic in the realm of the political. Both writers stress the political circumstances within which their art was created. Yeats outlines the strains of the 'Anglo-Irish war' (1964: 195), and goes on to delineate a gradual brutalisation of the national psyche brought about by the ongoing war, beginning with Lady Gregory:

> The house where she was born was burned down by incendiaries some few months ago, and there has been like disorder over the greater part of Ireland. A trumpery dispute about an acre of land can rouse our people to monstrous savagery, and if in their war with the English auxiliary police they were shown no mercy, they showed none: murder answered murder. (1964: 196)

Heaney, similarly, outlines the contemporary political violence that formed part of the context of his own writing, speaking of living with his own family, in Glanmore, County Wicklow, and listening to the 'news of bombings closer to home – not only those by the Provisional IRA in Belfast but equally atrocious assaults in Dublin by loyalist paramilitaries from the north' (1995b: 14).[9]

Indeed, there is a strong Yeatsian parallel later in the essay as Heaney, in a manner that will recall Yeats's 'murder answered murder', muses on the destructive and repetitive cycle of violence that has marked that era of political engagement in Northern Irish politics, as the 'violence from below was then productive of nothing but a retaliatory violence from above', and 'the dream of justice became subsumed into the callousness of reality' (1995b: 17). Both writers are stressing the weight of the actual in terms of their sense of communal selfhood. For Yeats, Irishness was being defined in terms of an ongoing war against the British, while for Heaney, the same antagonists were still fighting some 70 years later.

For both writers, any notion of literature must take into account the ideological and visceral appetites that have driven aspects of nationalist consciousness, while at the same time, attempting to transcend these. One is reminded of the already discussed Derridean idea that the limit point of a community can be seen as its opening, as opposed to its point of closure. Speaking about this very point, Heaney says that he does not believe in 'ditching attachments' but he is also wary about being 'mired in them', and he goes on to add that 'being dragged down into soul-destroying solidarity' is a major problem for people brought up in Northern Ireland (Brown 2002: 83). He goes on to discuss his own comment, made in an interview with Seamus Deane in 1977, concerning his own writing being a 'slow, obstinate papish burn emanating from the ground I was brought up on' (Deane 1977: 67), adding that in retrospect, this term 'caves into that same old clichéd idiom. It doesn't help. It's not a further language' (Brown 2002: 83).[10] Yeats too has made a similar point, noting that some of the female actors in his theatre movement were from a 'little political society' whose object, according to its enemies, consisted of teaching the poor children in its care a catechism that began: 'What is the origin of evil?' and proceeded to give the monosyllabic answer 'England' (Yeats 1964: 199).

Clearly for both writers, there is a need both to grant the validity of these 'attachments' but concomitantly to avoid becoming enmired in them. In other words, they faced a choice between the either/or paradigm or the both/and one which might lead to that 'further language' of which Heaney spoke. It is Heaney who is the most overt in his readings of the dangers of these attachments, remembering an occasion when, on hearing that a friend had been imprisoned on suspicion of committing a political murder, he shocked himself by thinking that 'even if he were guilty, he might still perhaps be helping the future to be born, breaking the repressive forms and liberating new potential in the only way that worked, that is to say the violent way – which therefore became, by extension, the right way' (1995b: 18).

In the aforementioned 'The Man and the Echo', Yeats utters a similar sense of anxiety about the relationship between creative language and the actual, as he ponders the effects of his political plays, specifically *Cathleen Ni Houlihan*:

> Did that play of mine send out
> Certain men the English shot? (1979: 393)

In this context, he is pondering the relationship between poetry and politics in a manner analogous to that of Heaney in his Nobel lecture. Both writers are probing the need for modes of identity through language which will be capable of transforming, as opposed to replicating, the surge of nationalistic feeling that has been a contextual framework for both of their respective bodies of work. There is a need for Heaney's notion of a 'further language' here, one which is paralleled by Derrida's advocation of an 'experience of language that would be as respectful as possible of linguistic difference' (1993: 31). Here, he means that language must always attempt to create that sense of difference and distance between the actuality of violence and the potentiality of writing. To paraphrase the idiom of 'The Man and the Echo', while the pain of the stricken animal must be recorded, the overarching effort at making sense of such pain and suffering, through some form of aesthetic experience, is a necessary function of Heaney's aesthetic epistemology:

> O Rocky Voice,
> Shall we in that great night rejoice?
> What do we know but that we face
> One another in this place? (Yeats 1979: 394)

In this respect, there is a further parallel in the Nobel lectures, as Yeats proceeds to delineate the gradual birth of the Irish Dramatic Movement as a redressive function to a society where, increasingly 'murder answered murder' (1964: 196).

Yeats, in some detail, discussed the practical and aesthetic development of the movement, a movement which attempted to bring a new vision, a further language, to the expression of an Irish aesthetic. The themes and topics became highly controversial – being denounced by unionists and nationalists alike for complicating the responses of those seemingly essentialist positions, while the church also took issue with some of the dramas that were produced: 'we were from the first a recognised public danger' (1964: 201). What his Nobel lecture traces is a process whereby another avenue for the enunciation of a sense of Irishness was gradually and painstakingly created. That Yeats should foreground his dramatic, as opposed to poetic career, is an interesting point, but given the imperative he clearly felt, of creating a form of anastomosis between the political context and his own work, possibly drama was seen as a more pertinent option.

In an era when levels of literacy would have been quite low, any attempt to influence a large number of people would be far more likely to succeed in the dramatic, as opposed to the poetic, genre. However, it was aesthetic considerations that finally gave the movement success as that 'strange man of genius' John Millington Synge, was to become the synecdochal figure of the Irish Dramatic Movement. Yeats interestingly likens Synge's effect on Irish culture to that of Robert Burns on that of Scotland: 'when Scotland thought herself gloomy and religious, providence restored her imaginative spontaneity by raising up Robert Burns to commend drink and the Devil' (1964: 202), and this is perhaps the most interesting aspect of Yeats's lecture, for the purposes of this discussion.[11]

While focusing on the political context, he foregrounds the transformations wrought in that context by specific textual encounters – by that gesture towards a 'further language', so to speak. Synge's art, standing as the apotheosis of what the Irish Dramatic Movement was capable of achieving, created a different vision of selfhood to that espoused by what Yeats terms 'the mob'. It is also significantly different from the three repressive strands that are woven through his Nobel lecture when speaking of the obstacles faced by the theatre: nationalist opinion, unionist opinion and the Catholic Church. These ideological positions were all espousing culture-specific definitions of Irishness, and were valuing the aesthetic only in terms of how its imagery and symbolic structures matched the ideological subject-position espoused by each of them. Such subject definitions are simplistically constructed in terms of self and other set in binary opposition: Yeats, through the construction of his theatrical movement, was attempting to complicate this paradigm of identity.

That such art was transformational is a *sine qua non* of Yeats's theme, specifically in urban areas where political and cultural opinion would be formed:

In the town, where everybody crowds upon you, it is your neighbour not yourself that you hate, and if you are not to embitter his life and your own life, perhaps even if you are not to murder him in some kind of revolutionary frenzy, somebody must teach reality and justice. You will hate that teacher for a while, calling his books and plays ugly, misdirected, morbid or something of that kind, but you must agree with him in the end. (1964: 198)

For Yeats, the gradual development of the movement, a development replete with difficulty and political antagonism, allowed for the creation of a specific Irish representation of experience: 'we could experiment and wait, with nothing to fear but political misunderstanding' (1964: 199). The *Playboy* riots were the most controversial period of the theatre, but Yeats outlines an ongoing 'political hostility' (1964: 200), from diverse quarters.[12]

The reason that such attacks would be forthcoming are many and various, but specifically, complex expressions and images that are central to the aesthetic are much to be feared by ideologically motivated movements. To quote from Heaney's essay on Yeats again, 'we go to literature in general to be forwarded within ourselves' (1995a: 159), and it is here that Yeats's concept of a theatre could prove most dangerous to ideological positions. As Yeats put it:

> Every political party had the same desire to substitute for life, which never does the same thing twice, a bundle of reliable principles and assertions. Nor did religious orthodoxy like us any better than political; my *Countess Cathleen* was denounced by Cardinal Logue as an heretical play, and when I wrote that we would like to perform 'foreign masterpieces' a nationalist newspaper declared that 'a foreign masterpiece is a dangerous thing'. (1964: 201)

Perhaps the most important word here is 'orthodoxy': the aesthetic is setting out to deconstruct the fixed identificatory parameters of the times: text is transforming context through these interactions.

Another way to put this point, of course, would be to say that art should encourage a complexity of response, and here we are on familiar territory, as one of Heaney's first credos about poetry is, we remember, that it should not simplify. Speaking about the whole idea of identity politics in *Sweeney Astray*, Heaney made the allied point that, in terms of such a politics of identity, one function of a writer might be 'to disrupt all that. One of your functions is to say that your language and your consciousness are as wide as the world' (Murphy 2000b: 94). Thus, the Yeatsian influence becomes all the clearer in this particular aspect of Irish identity.

In his own Nobel lecture, Heaney makes direct allusion to his famous predecessor a number of times. Speaking about the difficulty of attempting to balance the negative and positive aspects of the political situation, Heaney adverts specifically to the similar dilemma faced by Yeats 'half a century before', namely, 'to hold in a single thought reality and justice' (1995b: 17). We have already seen the context of this quotation from Yeats, and noted the imperative towards transformation of the cultural psyche which Yeats, and by extension Heaney, see as part of the *telos* of the aesthetic. In a longer exploration of Yeats's own Nobel lecture, Heaney cuts to the core of the exemplary role which Yeats plays in his own specific poetic context.

Heaney reminds the audience of the context of the Irish Civil War, which had ended in May 1923, some seven months before Yeats delivered his Nobel lecture. Heaney focuses on Yeats's lack of overt reference to the civil war, while agreeing that nobody understood better than Yeats the 'connection between the construction or destruction of state institutions and the founding or foundering of cultural life'. It is in the context of this 'connection' that Yeats chose his lecture topic:

> His story was about the creative purpose of that movement and its historic good fortune in having not only his own genius to sponsor it, but also the genius of his friends John Millington Synge and Lady Augusta Gregory. He came to Sweden to tell the world that the local work of poets and dramatists had been as important to the transformation of his native place and times as the ambushes of guerrilla armies. (Heaney 1995b: 24)

For Heaney, this sense of the redressive and restorative role of art is crucial. It places the aesthetic at a *point d'appui* in cultural and political discourse, as it sets out alternative definitions of selfhood and identity, definitions which necessarily complicate ideological positions.

We have already discussed, in Chapter 3, Heaney's own recounting of the cultural and political context within which his poems were written. Like Yeats, who spoke of ambushes and of murder answering murder, Heaney has told of the Kingsmills massacre, and highlighted the completely different relationships between self and other that were enacted on that dark night in County Armagh in Northern Ireland. In a manner analogous to Yeats, he is probing the value of art in such a context: he is reluctant to justify an aesthetic escape route which has little or no purchase on actuality. While willing to value the transcendent, he will not sanction any such movement which is not, in some way, grounded in the immanent, and it is this requirement for art to be engaged with both dimensions that underscores his thought process in *Crediting Poetry*.

Speaking of his early childhood in Mossbawn, he tells of how, when a 'wind stirred in the beeches, it also stirred an aerial wire attached to the topmost branch of the chestnut tree' (1995b: 9), the self-same tree of which we spoke in Chapter 5. Here, the dialectic of presence and absence, of self and other, is enacted as it was through this aerial that the voices of alterity entered his early consciousness and he began his journey 'into the wideness of the world beyond' (1995b: 11). The concreteness of place becomes transformed into the ethereality of space (indeed, he uses the term 'space station' a few sentences later). He traces this journey, as Yeats traced the development of the Irish Dramatic Movement, in the context of the complex issues of identity and belonging which would constitute the contextual framework which would circumscribe his work:

> The child in the bedroom, listening simultaneously to the domestic idiom of his Irish home and the official idioms of the British broadcaster while picking up from behind both the signals of some other distress, that child was already being schooled for the complexities of his adult predicament, a future where he would have to adjudicate among promptings variously ethical, aesthetical, moral, political, metrical, sceptical, cultural, topical, typical, post-colonial and, taken all together, simply impossible. (1995b: 13–14)

Heaney, all too aware of the pain and suffering of the actual, of, in Yeatsian terms, the 'stricken' rabbit's cry, strove to grant the reality of the immanent: 'bowed to the desk like some monk bowed over his *prie-dieu*, some dutiful contemplative pivoting his understanding in an attempt to bear his portion of the weight of the world' (1995b: 19–20).

There is a chronological tracing here of the development of the poet's aesthetic epistemology, a parallel structural paradigm with Yeats's Nobel lecture, and it is at this point that the ideas of the field of force, of art as embodying a dialectical relationship between the different strands of experience, and as setting out the interstices of that complex relationship, become central to his writing. He notes that there must be a sense of encompassing the totality of the experience. His notion of the field of force comes into play here, in that he now sets out a dialectical relationship between the transcendent and the immanent, a relation that is analogous to Blanchot's definition of the term in the aesthetic process:

> Limiting ourselves to a rather imprecise outline, we could say that it is according to this dialectic that the work moves from the erected stone, from the rhythmic and hymnlike cry where it announces the divine and makes the gods real, to the statue where it gives them form, to the productions in which it represents men, before becoming a figure of itself. (Blanchot 1982a: 231)

Heaney develops this theme of dialectical interaction in the later stages of the lecture. As he puts it:

> Then finally and happily, and not in obedience to the dolorous circumstances of my native place but in despite of them, I straightened up. I began a few years ago to try to make space in my reckoning and imagining for the marvellous as well as for the murderous. (1995b: 20)

Yeats as example hovers over this part of the lecture: the desire to express the full complexity of experience, and the reluctance to cede the task of defining Irishness to the politicians and the paramilitaries. At this juncture, Heaney is voicing the primacy of the poetic as a redressive force to that of the political. Poetic form is seen as an important element of complication: it no longer needs to mimic the actual: it can now reimagine the actual through a series of dialectical relationships and anastomoses:

> Poetic form is both the ship and the anchor. It is at once a buoyancy and a steadying, allowing for the simultaneous gratification of whatever is centrifugal and whatever is centripetal in mind and body. And it is by such means that Yeats's work does what the necessary poetry always does, which is to touch the base of our sympathetic nature while taking in at the same time the unsympathetic nature of the world to which that nature is constantly exposed. (1995b: 29)

For Heaney, this is the shape that poetic writing takes. Yeats as example serves to underline the complexity and dynamism of the epistemology of poetry. The metaphors of shape that Heaney uses foreground the increasingly complicated sense of poetry that Heaney has been developing.

His lecture closes with a discussion of the shape of writing in section six of Yeats's 'Meditations in Time of Civil War', entitled 'The Stare's Nest by the Window'. He speaks of the rhyme and structure of Yeats's lines, about the repetition of the refrain 'Come build in the empty house of the stare', with its 'tone of supplication, its pivots of strength in the words "build" and "house" and its acknowledgement of dissolution in the word "empty"' (1995b: 28). He goes on to speak of a similar complex formal dynamic in the 'triple rhyme of "fantasies" and "enmities" and "honey-bees", and in the sheer in-placeness of the whole poem as a given form within the language' (1995b: 29). It is the relational qualities at the level of signifier and signified that strike him as important in the work of Yeats. These relational structures embody much that is central to Heaney's own aesthetic, and I would argue that the growing influence on Heaney's career is the work of Yeats, in both poetry and prose. It is often forgotten that Yeats has produced a truly formidable range of writing, on various topics, in prose, and Heaney too, as we have seen, has amassed an impressive range of essays and lectures wherein an increasingly complicated epistemology of the aesthetic is enunciated. The ideas of reality and justice to which both men aspire, are expressed through this highly formal, complicated and carefully crafted poetic language.

In this reading, the Yeatsian example has underlined the full scope and power of poetic language. Blanchot, writing about Hölderlin, makes a parallel point about the encompassing nature of the poetic:

As early as 1804, in the hymn *Germania*, in lines that have a splendid rigor, Hölderlin had formulated the task of poetic language, which belongs neither to the day nor to the night but always is spoken between night and day and one single time speaks the truth and leaves it unspoken. (1982a: 276)

Heaney would agree, and his placing of Yeats at an important structural point of his own Nobel lecture underlines the influence of Yeats on his work, and on his epistemology of poetry: 'It is at once a buoyancy and a steadying, allowing for the simultaneous gratification of whatever is centrifugal and whatever is centripetal in mind and body' (1995b: 29).

Conclusion

In the preface to *Finders Keepers*, his selection of prose writings spanning the 30 years from 1971 to 2001, Heaney makes the following point:

> Some words I wrote in the Foreword to *Preoccupations* still apply to what is going on in the following pages: 'the essays selected here are held together by searches for answers to central preoccupying questions: how should a poet properly live and write? What is his relationship to be to his own voice, his own place, his literary heritage and his contemporary world?' (2002: x)

That this quotation should be so central to his work is significant in terms of the argument which we have traced through this book. The searches for answers which are implied in this quotation comprise a seminal aspect of Heaney's project, in poetry, prose and drama.

That poetry has an important role in cultural and political discourse is not in question: what is in question, however, is the modality of that role. Throughout this work, it has been argued that much of Heaney's thinking on these matters is paralleled by the work of Derrida. I am aware that this is a connection that is unusual in that Heaney and Derrida are seldom seen as coming within the same conceptual ambit. However, I think that once we move beyond the simplistic receptions of both writers – Heaney as writing about the bucolic and sensual, and Derrida as a relativist debunker of Western thought – and examine the actual writings, then a growing adequation and articulation of their thought can be seen to arise.

Heaney's sense of transcending the binary opposition of selfhood and alterity in the 'through-other' has strong theoretical resonances with the work of Derrida and Levinas. The sense that selfhood is necessarily shot through with alterity is clear from both writers, as is the ongoing necessity for analysing the anastomosis between any text – literary, cultural, ideological or subjective – in order to come to some understanding of the constituent factor of identity and ideology.

For Heaney, the whole process of writing involves this desire to reach a 'further language' through which some form of transcendence can be found with respect to the relationship between self and other. Much of his project has been grounded in the notion that we should strive to go beyond those attenuations of which we spoke at the beginning of this discussion: it is not that one should choose either the words 'God Save the Queen' or the shamrock on Catherine Bradley's sampler, but that one should focus on the dialectical and economic relationship between these iconic signifiers of selfhood and alterity. As Heaney has put it, in an interview with Karl Miller: 'no-one is entirely defined by their ethnicity or their gender: in fact, as a species we are defined by our ability to go beyond that' (Miller 2000: 52), and it is the effort of going 'beyond all that' that has been traced in this discussion. Similarly, for Derrida, the relationship between language and identity is concomitantly complex, as by defining itself in language, the 'I' is defining itself with respect to alterity:

> This *I* would have formed itself, then, at the site of a situation that cannot be found, a site always referring elsewhere, to something other, to another language, to the other in general. (Derrida 1998: 29)

For Heaney, it is this relationship between self and other, the 'through-other' that is crucial to the role of poetry. For Derrida, language in general is predicated on this sense of through-otherness:

> I have only one language and it is not mine; my 'own' language is, for me, a language that cannot be assimilated. My language, the only one I hear myself speak and agree to speak, is the language of the other. (1998: 29)

It is the exploration of this relationship between self and other, a relationship defined in language, that has been central to Heaney's searches for answers. The modalities of the field of force, the dialectical relationship, the space that is specific to literature, the deconstruction of simplistic enunciations of language, identity and place, the quincunx, and the role of Yeats as an avatar of this type of cultural work, have all been adduced in our attempt to understand some of the complex formulations that have arisen in response to his attempt to answer those self-posed questions as to the role of poetry.

That he comes to no simplistic conclusions is not to be wondered at, given his desire for a complex understanding of both the autotelic value of poetry as well as its value in broader socio-cultural terms.

As Heaney puts it elsewhere: 'I credit poetry...for being itself and for being a help' (1995b: 11), and it is this field of force wherein the epistemological structure of writing is measured both in terms of its own inherent value, as well as in terms of its connection with other areas of our life, that makes Heaney's work so culturally significant. The field of force is metonymic of the necessary complexity and hybridity of the knowledge that is to be found in literature, all part of the process of searching for answers: 'poetic form is both the ship and the anchor' (1995b: 29). The paradigm of knowledge within which both the questions and answers are formulated is transformational in mode and in operation:

> I wanted to affirm that within our individual selves we can reconcile two orders of knowledge which we might call the practical and the poetic; to affirm also that each form of knowledge redresses the other and that the frontier between them is there for the crossing. (1995a: 203)

As Derrida has put it, 'we have to cross the border but not to destroy the border' (1993: 33). Indeed, for Derrida, the whole notion of identity and home is predicated on a path towards the other:

> In order to constitute the space of a habitable house and a home, you also need an opening, a door and windows, you have to give up a passage to the outside world [*l'etranger*]. There is no house or interior without a door or windows. The monad of home has to be hospitable in order to be *ipse*, itself at home, habitable at-home in the relation of the self to itself. (Derrida 2000b: 61)

Both writers, then, look for a transforming of experience through the interaction and interpenetration of versions of selfhood and those of alterity. As Heaney has remarked: 'the older I get the more I want to be at home and away in myself, to allow every linguistic link and chink and loophole to bring me through to something uncensored, some gleam of self-extinguished thought flaring up' (Brown 2002: 79). Here, selfhood is being defined in terms of that opening to the other of which we have been speaking. It follows that any relationships between that selfhood and alterity will be predicated on such an anastomosis between self and other. It is this interpenetration which leads to the 'through-other' and is enunciated through the 'further language' which is the medium, and perhaps a crucial part of the message, of Seamus Heaney's searches for answers.

Notes

CHAPTER 1 – 'PREOCCUPYING QUESTIONS': HEANEY'S PROSE

1. Indeed, there is a book, Rand Brandes and Michael Durkan's *Seamus Heaney: A Reference Guide*, published in 1994, which attempts to compile a complete bibliography, though given the almost exponential rate of study, and review, this task would seem to be Sisyphean in scope.

2. However, this book makes what is probably the most concerted study of Heaney's prose in order to explore his attitudes to place, politics, language and other more general concerns. The format of the series is somewhat restrictive in terms of allowing Andrews to analyse in full the ramifications of these thoughts.

3. Murphy begins his book using the opening essay from *The Government of the Tongue*, 'The Interesting Case of Nero, Chekhov's Cognac and a Knocker'. He discusses the opening of this essay, recalling the decision of Heaney and the musician David Hammond, to cancel the making of a tape of songs and poems in response to the sound of explosions as they travelled to the studio. Murphy, correctly in my view, sees this as embodying a central responsibility in Heaney's writing, to remain faithful to the demands of both art *and* life, song *and* suffering.

4. Of the 30 books devoted to Heaney's work, only Neil Corcoran's has a chapter exclusively devoted to his prose. This is the best exploration of essays and lectures currently available, dealing mostly with *The Government of the Tongue* and *The Redress of Poetry*, with *Preoccupations* being covered incidentally. He deals with the books thematically, as opposed to chronologically, and this strengthens the chapter. He uses the headings of 'Exemplars', 'Unspoken Background', 'Home' and 'Listening' as rubrics through which to focus on the major themes. I would argue with his programmatic description of the writing as literary criticism, as this often leads him to see the aim of the essays as being simply to supply 'critical admiration' of other writers (Corcoran 1986: 231). To my mind, this categorisation is a limiting factor in the valuation of Heaney's writing. There are discussions of individual books in two collections of essays. Tony Curtis's *The Art of Seamus Heaney* (2001) has an essay by Anne Stevenson on *Preoccupations*, and one by Bernard O'Donoghue on *The Government of the Tongue*. Stevenson sees his poetry and prose as 'branches from the same tree' (2001b: 132), and spends most of the essay setting up contrasts and comparisons between Heaney and Eliot, a tactic which, while revealing certain connections, takes away from a real engagement with the book as a whole. O'Donoghue's essay is prescient, tracing connections between *Preoccupations* and *The Government of the Tongue*, as well as noting that Heaney's essays are not literary criticism *per se*, but instead, are nearer in 'critical theoretical terms' to Coleridge's view of imagination and poetry. He also notes,

correctly in my view, Heaney's practice 'of letting the language lead ety-mologically where it wants' in a manner 'curiously akin to deconstructive criticism' (1994: 189). I would question the adjective here, as I feel that a sustained study of the prose makes this connection obvious. This essay appears as a final chapter in O'Donoghue's book on Heaney, *Seamus Heaney and the Language of Poetry*, published in 1994. Michael Allen's *New Casebook* (1997) on Heaney also includes individual essays, in particular a review of *The Government of the Tongue* by Thomas Docherty, which sees the collection as focusing on twin threads of ethics in terms of the 'I–Thou' relationship of Buber, and the identity-difference dialectic which he sees as a concern which 'often crosses with the first' and 'warps its possibility of articulation' (1997: 148). This is a fine piece of writing, which fully engages with the complexity and sophistication of the per-spectives enunciated in that book. Stan Smith, in 'The Distance Between', and Richard Kirkland, in 'Paradigms of Possibility' both write about the prose though not exclusively. However, both writers deal with the com-plexities of the essays, and see the writing as theoretical in that it attempts to study the practice of writing itself, Kirkland seeing a modernist reading of Heaney as encouraging the 'play of meaning' (1997: 261), while Smith sees the relation between 'place and displacement' as the 'very ground of his writing' (1992: 249).

5. This essay on Heaney's *The Government of the Tongue* is broadly reprinted in O'Donoghue's *Seamus Heaney and the Language of Poetry* (1994), a closely argued and intelligent study of Heaney's language.

6. I do not mean to disparage this use of Heaney's essays and lectures. Many of the studies of Heaney's poetry are enriched and deepened by being read in the light of particular explications of individual poems, or of thematic overviews of literary or societal problems. Neil Corcoran (1986) makes especially adept use of the prose in this manner, while both Andrew Murphy (2000a) and Elmer Andrews (1988) also demonstrate the explicatory value of his prose, as already noted. However, what is being argued is that these essays are deserving of a sustained analysis in their own right.

7. This quotation is slightly different to the point made in the original essay, which appeared in *The Art of Seamus Heaney*.

8. Corcoran's book on Heaney, *The Poetry of Seamus Heaney: A Critical Study* (1986 [1998]) recently reissued, retitled and updated, is one of the best critical studies on Heaney currently available. The original book was published as part of a 'student guides' series, but this was very much to undervalue the level of sophistication which Corcoran brought to his readings of Heaney's work. He offers intelligent readings of the poems, and places them in thematic arrangements which illustrate the thematic integrity of Heaney's work.

9. I use this term as an extension of its context, which describes the encounter and debate between Jacques Derrida and Hans-Georg Gadamer, in April 1981, in the Goethe Institute in Paris. This encounter between both thinkers, symptomatic of an encounter between decon-struction and hermeneutics, is dealt with in Michelfelder and Palmer's book, *Dialogue & Deconstruction: The Gadamer–Derrida Encounter* (1989).

10. John Barrell and John Bull (eds) (1975) *The Penguin Book of English Pastoral Verse*. Harmondsworth: Penguin.

11. Raymond Williams wrote of pastoral poetry and conventions in broadly similar terms in his *The Country and the City* (1975), and Heaney sees this book as in many respects a 'companion volume', incorporating 'most of the texts he refers to and underlining or extending his discussion of them' (1980: 174). This aside demonstrates one aspect of the literary-political *nous* that becomes all the clearer as we read the essays and articles; he is ever-aware of the complications and connections between the world, the text and other critics.

12. An exception to this lack of discussion is to be found in Hart's (1992) book, where there is a two-page exploration of this essay (pp. 10–11), in a chapter entitled 'Pastoral and Anti-Pastoral Attitudes' (pp. 9–31). This chapter uses notions of pastorality as a framework through which to discuss Heaney's early poetry.

13. J. Hillis Miller's Joycean example of 'underdarkneath', in *The Ethics of Reading* (1987: 6), captures concretely the interpenetration of one word by another; the traces of the original ontologies of the words, and the neologistic relationship which is brought into being between syntax and semantic value through the anastomosis in question. He sees this as one of the generating linguistic tropes which brings about the crossings, displacements and substitutions between the non-linguistic and language (1987: 7).

14. The Bakhtin quotation comes from *Marxism and the Philosophy of Language* (Volosinov 1973: 471).

15. Strictly speaking, context is a cognate of text, but I feel that the example is still a valid one, working as it does both syntactically, semantically and etymologically with 'text' deriving from the Latin for fabric or structure while 'context' derives from the Latin for 'to weave together' or 'compose' (Myers and Simms 1985: 307).

16. In later essays, the whole issue of translation is discussed in similarly complex terms, especially in the context of translations from the Irish language; see *The Government of the Tongue*, *An Duanaire*, and also translations from Eastern European poetry.

17. Ronald Tamplin has an interesting discussion of this poem, and the attendant linguistic and cultural contexts in his book on Heaney (Tamplin 1989: 40–4).

18. This point, made in the 'Afterward' of *Limited Inc.*, is part of what can be seen as a redefinition of one of deconstruction's central axioms '*Il n'y a pas de hors-texte*' (Derrida 1976: 158) as '*Il n'y a pas de hors contexte*' (Derrida 1988: 136). Simon Critchley has an informative discussion of this point in his *The Ethics of Deconstruction* (Critchley 1992: 31–43).

19. In Heaney's case, these include different languages, different traditions and conventions, as well as the contexts which help to create the texts in question. Heaney is involved in a dialogisation of these facets, in the sense that the specifically English appropriation of pastoral generic and conventional aspects is de-privileged and is made aware of competing definitions (Bakhtin 1981: 427).

20. In a parenthetic aside, directly after mentioning Synge's text he notes '(prose, granted)', a point which underlines my own view that prose, while generically distinct, should not be factored out of any equation in terms of the study or analysis of a writer who is more celebrated within a different generic frame. If Heaney sees the prose of Synge, a playwright, as being important, this bolsters my own case for seeing the prose of Heaney as being worthy of a central place in his canon. It is also a further example of his stretching the borderlines of the book under review by questioning the automatic association of the pastoral with poetry.

21. Henry Hart makes a similar point in connection with Heaney's volume of prose poems, published in 1975, entitled *Stations*, in his book *Seamus Heaney: Poet of Contrary Progressions* (Hart 1992: 99–118). I would argue that this *modus agendi* of Heaney's can be seen as a driving force in all of his work. Hart's study, which is an excellent, theoretically aware reading of Heaney's poetry, pays comparatively little attention to his prose.

22. Derrida's essay 'Living On: Borderlines' is an involved discussion of the permeability of limits in terms of text and context, specifically dealing with Shelley's *The Triumph of Life* but progressing onto notions of limitation in general.

23. As we shall see, there are often more than two terms brought into the equation.

CHAPTER 2 – 'CONTINUOUS ADJUDICATION': BINARY OPPOSITIONS AND THE FIELD OF FORCE

1. Interestingly, country butter in those days was often printed with a design – there were woodcut stamps with different embossed patterns, and after the butter had been shaped with butter paddles, it was stamped with an image. To continue the metaphor, because the printed medium of the butter is malleable, the indentation can be changed, erased or added to. As such, it is an interesting multivalent image of a surface upon which there can be multiple imprints.

2. This term will immediately bring Heaney's work into connection with structuralist and poststructuralist discourse, and I would argue that his writing has much in common with a particular strain of such discourse, especially the writing of Jacques Derrida.

3. Corcoran has anthologised more postmodern readings of Heaney in his *The Chosen Ground: Essays on the Contemporary Poetry of Northern Ireland*, (1992: 153–67). He also adverts to Thomas Docherty's 'Ana-; or Postmodernism, Landscape, Seamus Heaney', in Anthony Easthope and John O. Thompson (eds) *Contemporary Poetry Meets Modern Theory* (1991: 68–80). This essay is also anthologised in Michael Allen's *Seamus Heaney* (1997: 206–22).

4. He does, at this stage, enter the caveat 'however much they [i.e., Heaney's conceptions of poetry] have been put through a Modernist or, in some respects, a post-modernist filter' (1986: 229). Given that the purpose of a filter is to make what has passed through purer, by removing certain aspects of what is being filtered, one might ask whether Corcoran is

suggesting that Heaney's conceptions of poetry are purer, more true and more accurate by virtue of the action of this postmodernist filter on these 'conceptions'. The difficulty of unpacking this metaphor points to its inapplicability in terms of a consideration of Heaney's work, and possibly, in a deconstructive irony, suggests the impossibility of classifying Heaney's writing as being part of any particular tradition. One might see the conceptual difficulty encountered by this metaphor as a resistance to any form of attenuation of Heaney's own writing.

5. This book has been the subject of much misreading, being seen as 'speaking the language of the tribe, brutal though that language may be....It is one of several points in *North* where one feels that Heaney is not writing these poems, but having them written for him, his frieze composed almost in spite of him by the "anonymities" of race and religion' (Morrison 1982: 68). Other critics, most notably Ciarán Carson, Conor Cruise O'Brien and Edna Longley, have made much the same point. However, I would argue that this is to misread the polyglossic range of voices and perspectives that are enunciated in *North*. For a contrastive reading, focusing on the polyglossic, and ultimately ethical, force of this book see my '*North*: The Politics of Plurality' in *Nua*, Vol. II, Nos 1 & 2 (Spring 1999): 1–19.

6. This was the Second John Malone Memorial Lecture, delivered on 9 June 1983 at Queen's University, Belfast and published by the John Malone Memorial Committee. In 1958, Heaney had taken up a teaching position at Orangefield School, under the headmastership of Malone (Parker 1993: 54) whom he praises both as an educator and a reader who valued the role of the writer as a 'fact of the usual life' (1983a: 1). Michael Parker's (1993) book on Heaney from which this note, and indeed this study, draws significant detail is an excellent critical biography of Heaney's life and work.

7. This professor, Heaney notes, is alleged to have confessed to being the first of his family to 'have gone into trade' (1983a: 7).

8. The United Irishmen were a group, led by Theobald Wolfe Tone, and strongly influenced by the French and American Revolutions, who revolted against Britain in 1798. Robert Emmett was another historical figure who led a rebellion against the British in 1803. Both roles place Heaney firmly within the nationalist Catholic camp.

9. In this context, it is no accident that one of Heaney's better-known poems from *North*, where he questions his outlook and attitudes to the social and political situation in Ireland in the 1970s, is called *Exposure*.

10. *Fear a' tigh* translates literally as 'man of the house' and denotes a master of ceremonies figure who calls out the name of the dances at the *ceilidh*, an evening of dancing at which only Irish dances could be performed. The organisation in charge, the GAA, was the Gaelic Athletic Association, which fosters Irish games and cultural pursuits. Its membership and ethos are predominantly Catholic and nationalist.

11. This phrase appears in the first of the Glanmore Sonnets in *Field Work*, as well as being the title of Heaney's collection of poems celebrating his 30 years of writing, *Poems: 1966–1996*, and is an example of how persistent this theme is in Heaney's writing. '*Opened Ground*' is precisely what the

activity of digging (both actual and metaphorical) produces, and it is a clear symbol of what his searches for answers can produce. Interestingly, this very title was the original title that Andrew Motion and Blake Morrison were going to give to their collection *The Penguin Book of Contemporary British Poetry* ('to think the title *Opened Ground* / Was the first title in your mind' (1983b: 8). Heaney gave his reaction to being called 'British' in *An Open Letter*, a text which is far from an anti-British diatribe. Michael R. Molino provides probably the most in-depth discussion of this text in his *Questioning Tradition, Language & Myth* (1994: 118–25).

12. Hart's (1992) book contains a chapter aptly entitled 'Deconstructions' which demonstrates effectively that Heaney's work does have some affinities with deconstruction as it has come to be defined. I would be wary of some of Hart's definitions of deconstruction, which tend to be along the accepted lines of Derrida's early critique of logocentrism and intentionality in terms of language. I feel that deconstruction now is far more ethically driven, and indeed, projects a similar complexity of thought with respect to interrelationships of different aspects of reality to the work of Heaney himself, as I hope to show.

13. Caputo's books clearly demonstrate this broadness of deconstructive criticism already mentioned in the previous note.

14. The influence of ethics within the field of literary studies has been a feature of the theoretical discourse of the last 20 years. A recent special topic edition of *Proceedings of the Modern Language Association* has been devoted to ethics, and the introductory editorial essay 'Introduction: In Pursuit of Ethics', by Lawrence Buell (1999), provides a thorough overview of the different strands of ethics that have become a prominent aspect of literary studies.

15. This was the Pete Laver Memorial Lecture, delivered at Grasmere, on 2 August 1984, and published in 1985 by the Trustees of Dove Cottage. The subtitle *Recent Poetry of Northern Ireland* interacts with the binarism of the title, *Place and Displacement*, to demonstrate the importance of his dialectical mode of enquiry in terms of his location, and his vocation. The writing of place, if it is not to be subverted by the centripetal pulls of gravity and atavism, must displace these locations, and their ideological baggage, so as to rewrite them.

16. The religious subtext that is connoted by the adjectives 'pious and passionate' is relevant here, as it allows Heaney to equate the politics of identity with a strong religious dimension of identity. In Northern Ireland, the political and the religious are intertwined as signifiers of belonging to one tradition or the other. This is true in terms of the almost 100 per cent adequation of Catholic with nationalist and of Protestant with unionist, but it is also true in terms of a transgressive influence of the *doxa* of religion on the *episteme* of politics. The criterion of belief in identity as a form of religion (etymologically connected with the notion of 'binding fast') means that those who disagree are, in some respects, unbelievers, with all the pejorative and historical associations of that term in religious persecutions throughout the world.

17. One might note the generic use of the masculine pronoun in this passage, which suggests that all of the typological figures in this essay are seen as

masculine. Some critics have written about a gender-bias in Heaney's writing. One of the best such critiques is that of Patricia Coughlan in '"Bog Queens": The Representation of Women in the Poetry of John Montague and Seamus Heaney', originally published in *Gender and Irish Writing* (eds T. O'Brien Johnson and D. Cairns, 1991), and anthologised in Michael Allen's *Seamus Heaney* (1997: 185–205). Catherine Byron has made a similar point in her book *Out of Step: Pursuing Seamus Heaney to Purgatory*, noting that the poem seemed to subscribe to a 'patriarchal, men-only version of the world' while seeming to ascribe to a universalist position (1992: 234). There is a thorough discussion of the issue of gender in Heaney's writing in Elmer Andrews's *The Poetry of Seamus Heaney* (1988: 126–41). There has also been some controversy over the eloquent silence in terms of the presence of women in the *Field Day Anthology of Irish Writing*, Edna Longley having taken the directors of the company, including Heaney, to task.

18. Interestingly, Heaney will further interrogate notions of knowledge and experience in *Electric Light* in a poem which takes the title 'Known World' (Heaney 2001: 19).

19. In 1971, 170 people were killed in the fighting in Northern Ireland, compared with 24 in 1970 and 16 in 1969. The following year would see 472 people killed in the violence, the highest total in all of the years of conflict in Northern Ireland (Sutton 1994: 206).

20. There is a concise but accurate discussion of Aristotle's theory of tragedy with particular respect to the notions of pity and terror to be found in *Shakespearean Tragedy*, edited by John Drakakis (1992: 5–7). Indeed, the introduction to this volume provides a conspectus of the different theorizations of tragedy up to the present day (pp. 1–35).

21. This is not to say that Heaney is in any way apologising for the sectarian violence in Northern Ireland, or that he is becoming here the voice of his tribe, what Ciarán Carson terms 'a laureate of violence – a mythmaker, and anthropologist of ritual killing' (1975: 183). What is being enunciated in *North*, is a multiperspectival voicing of what motivates people to kill each other in Northern Ireland. The voices in *North*, and they are many and varied, evince their motivations and atavisms, as if the poet has heard them all and is attempting to open a window onto the motivations that drive people to sectarian hatred and killing. The mythico-religious ideology of 'Kinship' captures the garbled mindset that causes people to kill in the name of religion, ideology.

22. For a more detailed discussion of the notion of the power of literature to achieve such mythological mystifications, specifically in an Irish context, see my *The Epistemology of Nationalism* (2002b).

23. Bernard O'Donoghue has drawn attention to the prevalence in Heaney's writing, in *The Government of the Tongue*, of words and phrases which derive from legislative discourse. He cites 'dispensation', 'the right to govern', 'authority', 'jurisdiction' (1994: 136).

24. In the context of this essay, Heaney had been speaking of a poem he wrote in *Door into the Dark* entitled 'Requiem for the Croppies', which was written for the 1916 commemoration ceremonies. It is typical of Heaney's complicated perspective that he celebrates 1916 in a poem about the

United Irish rebellion of 1798, a rebellion which was certainly more pluralist in tenor than that of 1916. One of the credos of the United Irishmen was the substitution of the common name of Irishman for Catholic, Protestant and Dissenter, and it is this crossing and dialectical relationship with notions of religion and identity that attracts Heaney to this rebellion as opposed to the far more Catholic and sectarian one of 1916.

25. Ironically, the sectarian homology that Heaney describes here Protestant: Catholic :: yeoman: rebel is not strictly accurate, as the vast majority of the leaders of the United Irishmen were Presbyterians and Protestants. See Marianne Elliot's *Partners in Revolution: The United Irishmen and France* (1982), and *Wolfe Tone: Prophet of Irish Independence* (1989). For a discussion on the pluralist nature of the United Irishmen and their Enlightenment *Weltanschauung*, see my *The Question of Irish Identity in the Writings of William Butler Yeats and James Joyce* (1998: 64–83).

26. The categorisation of 'Easter 1916' as a 'celebration' of the 1916 rebellion is not altogether as simple and straightforward as it might seem. A reading of the poem itself, as opposed to the critical commentary, demonstrates that for Yeats, the rising, while heroic, is not something to be granted unqualified approval. The climactic adjective 'terrible' has an ambiguous resonation, connoting both negative and positive meanings. The same qualification can be found in the comparison of a 'heart' which has been 'enchanted to a stone', a comparison which is life-denying in the sense that whereas a stone may last longer, it is neither sentient nor alive. The imagery of life and change which surrounds the stone, in the 'living stream' also conjures up some questioning as to whether Yeats is actually celebrating the rising, or posing a series of questions about the *mentalité* of its leaders. To read the simile at another level, a heart which has become a stone can no longer function as a pump for the body, and necessarily implies death to the organism. The question posed near the end of the poem: 'Was it needless death after all / For England may keep faith / For all that is done and said' (Yeats 1979: 204). I would submit that Yeats's position in this poem is far more complicated than a straightforward celebration of the rising; what is being offered is a series of questions which are asked, and then followed, not by any form of direct answer, but by the rhetorical figure of aposiopesis, a breaking off of syntax and a change in the direction of the poem. This process comes to a climax in the lines: 'We know their dream; enough / To know they dreamed and are dead'. The final lines are equally ambiguous, with approval or praise being avoided through the performative of naming the leaders and stressing the notion of change.

27. Though in the light of what I have termed the many misreadings of this project in *North* (see note 5, this chapter), such identifications are deeply embedded in the Irish psyche, and attempt to captate any other reading into a restatement of the *mythos* itself.

28. This view of nationalism as flawed in terms of vision achieves its apotheosis in the *Cyclops* chapter of *Ulysses*, wherein Irish nationalism, in the persona of the monocular 'citizen', and by extension, the essentialist nationalist ideology of Irish identity, is being placed under critique.

29. Adorno discusses the concept, coined by his friend and fellow member of the Frankfurt School in *Negative Dialectics* (1973: 162–6). There is an interesting account of the different uses and developments of this term in Simon Jarvis's study: *Adorno: A Critical Introduction* (1998: 173–17).
30. 'Anadiplosis' is a rhetorical figure wherein the final element of one syntactic, semantic or poetic unit is repeated at the beginning of the next unit.

CHAPTER 3 – 'WRITING IN THE SAND': POETRY AND TRANSFORMATION

1. Heaney has written frequently on Yeats. In *Preoccupations*, he has an essay entitled 'Yeats as an Example', while in *Among Schoolchildren* and in *The Place of Writing*, there are a number of discussions of Yeats's work. In *The Redress of Poetry*, he compares the eschatological approaches of Yeats and Larkin in 'Joy or Night: Last Things in the Poetry of W. B. Yeats and Philip Larkin'.
2. The original source of this quotation is *A Vision* (1937 [1962]: 24–5). Heaney's attraction to these Yeatsian systems should be apparent given that Yeats's systems and gyres are analogous attempts to define structures which can encompass, without completely reconciling, oppositional forces, and which allow for frequent multidimensional changes in terms of time and space.
3. The source for this recollection is *Letters on Poetry from W. B. Yeats to Dorothy Wellesley* (Raine 1940: 195).
4. This phrase figures as the subtitle of one of Heaney's important essays in *The Place of Writing* – 'Cornucopia and the Empty Shell: Variations on a Theme from Ellmann'. These essays were the inaugural lectures in the 'Richard Ellmann Lectures in Modern Literature', published by Scholar's Press, Atlanta, Georgia, for Emory University, with an introduction by Ronald Schuchard, in 1989.
5. Bernard O'Donoghue has traced the development of this particular essay in his book on Heaney (1994: 165). He notes that this essay was first published as 'The Interesting Case of John Alphonsus Mulrennan' in *Planet* 1978, 34–40. It was then adapted as a lecture to the Royal Dublin Society in 1986, before being published under its present title in *Shenandoah*.
6. The term 'answer' has a specific meaning in English as it is spoken in Northern Ireland. As Heaney puts it in *The Redress of Poetry*: 'if you say in Northern Ireland that a thing answers, it means that it is up to the mark, fit for the job, has passed itself' (1995a: 194).
7. It is worth mentioning that Heaney tends to place great weight on his introductions to his prose collections, using them to stake out the ground in terms of the issues which are to be addressed in the following essays and lectures. 'Mossbawn' and 'Belfast' served as introductions to *Preoccupations*, and the importance of these essays is clear from our discussion. Indeed, one might well argue that in the 'fixed words' of these titles are the poles of the dialectical oscillation through which the

poet journeyed during weeks at Queen's and weekends in County Derry. The introduction to *The Government of the Tongue*, 'The Interesting Case of Nero, Chekhov's Cognac and a Knocker' has also been discussed, and the introduction to *The Redress of Poetry* is, as we will see, equally as important.

8. Herbert's poem, 'The Pulley' is the subject of the opening essay of *The Redress of Poetry* while his 'Squarings' sequence is to be found in *Seeing Things* (1991: 53–108).

9. Interestingly in the context of this discussion which sees Heaney and Derrida as pursuing parallel courses of interpreting socio-cultural structures in their writing, Derrida's essay, a seminal text in the reception history of deconstruction which was delivered at a symposium at Johns Hopkins University entitled 'The Languages of Criticism and the Sciences of Man' (Hahn 2002: 1) in 1966, has as its epigraph a quotation from Montaigne: 'We need to interpret interpretations more than things' (Derrida 1978: 278).

10. Hart's notion of Heaney as a poet of contrary progressions, arriving at some form of *via negativa* is, I think, one of the better strategies for coming to terms with what is being attempted in Heaney's work.

11. This idea first appeared in the title of a poem 'From the Frontier of Writing', in *The Haw Lantern* (1987: 6).

12. This essay is to be found in Pinsky's *Poetry and the World* (1988).

13. John Wilson Foster, in his *The Achievement of Seamus Heaney*, makes use of this notion of redress as a structuring principle of his third chapter, entitled 'Heaney's Redress' (1995: 25–59).

14. The original source of this quotation is Stevens's *The Necessary Angel* (1965: 31).

15. The original source is Weil's *Gravity and Grace* (2002: 2–3).

16. The original source is Weil's *Gravity and Grace* (2002: 151).

17. This hunger strike was part of a campaign initiated in the Maze prison in County Antrim on 27 October 1980, as part of a demand for political status to be granted to IRA prisoners. Bobby Sands, elected MP for Fermanagh–South Tyrone while on hunger strike, was the first of ten to die between 20 April and 10 August 1981. The strike was called off in October of the same year. Francis Hughes was the second man to die.

18. For a more thorough definition of this term, which is seminal in terms of Derridean deconstruction, see *Margins of Philosophy* (1982: 3–27) and *Positions* (1981a: 8–9, 26–9, 39–41).

19. In the closing months of 1975, there had been a number of sectarian killings where groups on different sides singled out Catholics or Protestants and shot them in revenge for similar killings. The Kingsmills massacre took place on 5 January, and on the previous day, six Catholics had been killed in sectarian attacks – three at Whitecross, County Armagh, and three more at Ballydougan, near Gilford, County Down.

20. Malcolm Sutton, in his exhaustive listing of the victims of violence in Northern Ireland, makes the point that the killers of the ten Protestant workers in Kingsmills were 'The Republican Action Force', and goes on to see this as one of several *nommes de guerre* used by the Provisional IRA in the late 1970s to claim different killings (1994: viii).

CHAPTER 4 – 'SURVIVING AMPHIBIOUSLY': POETRY AND POLITICS

1. This collection, divided into three sections, contains a number of essays and reviews and marks Heaney's first significant intellectual excursion beyond mainstream Irish and British literature into the European ambit. It also signals an ethical turn as he begins to ponder the vexed but necessary relationship between poetry and politics.

2. In August 1970, a new nationalist party, The Social and Democratic Labour Party (SDLP) was formed, led by Gerry Fitt, with John Hume as deputy leader, to voice nationalist opinion. In March 1971, Brian Faulkner replaced James Chichester-Clark as Prime Minister. During these riots, the IRA demand for a united Ireland was rekindled, with a resulting split of the IRA, into the Official IRA and the Provisional IRA in December 1969. The more militant PIRA received arms and money from sympathisers in the Republic and in America. They targeted policemen and became increasingly involved in civilian demonstrations and riots. In 1970, 25 people were killed and 174 in 1971. By mid 1970, the PIRA were believed to be around 1,500 strong, and their economic war meant that there were 153 explosions in 1970, escalating to 304 explosions in the first six months of 1971. On 6 February Gunner Robert Curtis became the first soldier to die in the Troubles. In response to this campaign, internment was introduced in August 1971, with 342 people arrested and taken to internment camps. There was widespread violence in response to this initiative, and 17 people were killed in the next 48 hours, with some 7,000 people forced to flee their homes. Internment continued until 1975, with 1,874 Catholics/republicans, and 107 Protestants/loyalists being detained. In September of 1971, a further splintering in the unionist community took place, with Ian Paisley and Desmond Boal founding the Democratic Unionist Party (DUP).

3. In an essay entitled 'Belfast', in *Preoccupations*, a subsection entitled 'Christmas, 1971' describes Long Kesh internment camp, noting that it must be: 'literally, the brightest spot in Ulster. When you pass it on the motorway after dark, it is squared off in neon, bright as an airport. An inflammation on the black countryside. Another of our military decorations' (1980: 32).

4. In this poem, the area is not mentioned, merely being referred to as 'a wall downtown'. However, the epigraph reappears, almost word for word, as the final section of 'Whatever You Say Say Nothing' in *North* (1975: 57–60). In this version, the graffiti is located in Ballymurphy, a nationalist enclave in West Belfast: 'Is there life before death? That's chalked up / In Ballymurphy' (1975: 60).

5. This essay is repeated in his latest selection of prose *Finders Keepers*. All quotations from his prose will be taken from the original books, and only material that is new will be cited from *Finders Keepers*.

6. This term refers to the Provisional Irish Republican Army.

7. For a discussion of this poem as emblematic of the difficulties associated with issues of identity in Northern Ireland, see Scott Brewster's '"The Other Side": Proximity, Poematics, Northern Ireland' (forthcoming 2004).

8. For some interesting discussions on the issue of sanitising cultural and ideological difference see Cathy Wells-Cole's 'Disputed Territory: Heritage and Poetry in Northern Ireland' (1995: 136–43) and Richard Kirkland's *Literature and Culture in Northern Ireland since 1965: Moments of Danger* (1996).

9. I am indebted to Scott Brewster for bringing this essay to my notice, and also for informing my own views of Heaney in terms the work of Emmanuel Levinas.

10. I would proffer some form of connection here between Levinas's notion of *'saying'* as ethical openness, which in some way refuses the monological certainties of ontology, and Derrida's notion of *hauntology* which in an analogous manner, disseminates the certainties of ontology through the spectral presence of its other or others.

11. *Seamus Heaney and the Place of Writing* (O'Brien 2003), Chapter 2, *passim*.

12. This essay by James Simmons, 'The Trouble with Seamus', while I would disagree with many of its premises, is one of the better negative interrogations of Heaney's work. Simmons probes a number of Heaney commonplaces and asks some interesting questions about Heaney's politics, and the cultural contexts of that politics.

13. See *Seamus Heaney: Creating Irelands of the Mind* (O'Brien 2002a: 30–45); '*North*: the Politics of Plurality' (O'Brien 1999).

14. These opinions of Conor Cruise O'Brien are cited by Longley (1986).

CHAPTER 5 – 'A BRIGHT NOWHERE': THE DECONSTRUCTION OF PLACE

1. See O'Brien, *Seamus Heaney and the Place of Writing* (2003), *passim*.

2. Interestingly, a recent documentary on Derrida's life and work prioritises his fluid concept of place and space – *Derrida's Elsewhere*. A film by Safaa Fathy.

3. This interview 'This Strange Institution Called Literature', is published in Derek Attridge's *Acts of Literature* (Derrida 1992a), an excellent collection dealing with the interaction of Derrida's work with the institution and practice of literature.

4. Derek Attridge provides a translator's note to this quotation, stressing that *'Tout dire'* embodies the sense of both to 'say everything' with the sense of exhausting a totality, and to 'say anything', that is, to speak without constraints on what one may say (Derrida 1992a).

5. This refers to a British Army/RUC checkpoint which was situated at Toomebridge during the ongoing violence in Northern Ireland. Many of these checkpoints were discontinued in the aftermath of the Good Friday Agreement in 1998.

6. Roddy McCorley was a Presbyterian from Duneane. He took part in the Battle of Antrim, during the 1798 rebellion, and went into hiding after it. After a year in hiding he was betrayed, tried in Ballymena and hanged in Toome on Good Friday 1799.

7. This tag has become one of the most contested items in the discussion of deconstruction. Derrida, basically, is stressing the constructedness of

almost all socio-cultural and linguistic structures, and adducing the need for interpretation and contextual placement if interpretative activities are to have any sense of closure.

8. I have dealt with the linguistic and ideological implications of this placename and its dissemination through Heaney's different works in more detail in *Seamus Heaney and the Place of Writing* (O'Brien 2003: chapter 2, 31–64, *passim*).

9. Colin Graham's book *Deconstructing Ireland: Identity, Theory, Culture* (2001), is a formidable discussion of different strands in the politicisation of the notion of 'Ireland' across different historical and generic works. It sets out an agenda which, I would suggest, is paradigmatic of the direction which Irish Studies will need to follow in the coming years. His work, along with Gerry Smyth's *Space and the Irish Cultural Imagination* (2001), provide interesting points of reference in the current debate.

10. For a more thorough definition of this term, which is seminal in terms of Derridean deconstruction, see *Margins of Philosophy* (Derrida 1982: 3–27) and *Positions* (Derrida 1981a: 8–9, 26–9, 39–41).

11. There would appear to be definite connections between the theme of this poem and that of the thirteenth-century Middle English lyric 'Sumer is icumen in'. I am indebted to Tony Corbett for pointing out this connection to me, as well as for other cogent suggestions in the writing of this book.

CHAPTER 6 – 'THROUGH-OTHERNESS': THE DECONSTRUCTION OF LANGUAGE

1. In a clinker-built hull, the boards are bent over a frame and pinned or nailed down. Each plank overlaps with the next. The result is a tense construction which could fly apart, but which is also flexible and durable, waterproof and seaworthy, as long as it is maintained correctly. In other words, it is a type of field of force.

2. Daniel Corkery, professor of English at University College, Cork, wrote *The Hidden Ireland* (1925), in which he attempted to define the essence of the Gaelic literature of the eighteenth century and make that the basis for a quintessentially Irish spirit.

3. For a fuller discussion of this concept, see *Of Grammatology* (Derrida 1976: 65–73).

4. Heaney quotes the first three lines of this quotation in his essay 'Something to Write Home About', as he is discussing 'Terminus', with its image of stepping stones and water.

5. In the context of Derrida's foregrounding of the trope of citation as part of the differential imperative that defines the play of language, it is interesting to remark that Heaney's initial citation of the signifier '*lachtar*' is highlighted by the use of quotation marks. It is also germane to point out that these quotation marks are there to indicate the different linguistic and socio-cultural contexts with in which this particular signifier is being invoked.

6. In this case, the 'context' or 'code' would be the Irish language.

7. There has been much discussion as to whether O'Neill was, in fact, educated in the Devereux house at Penshurst. Hiram Morgan, in a comprehensive study of O'Neill's life, suggests that there is no evidence that O'Neill was ever actually educated in England (Morgan 1993: 8–10).

8. O'Neill would be defeated in two years' time at the battle of Kinsale, while Essex, returning from the Irish campaign in failure, would be executed as a traitor by Elizabeth.

9. This essay was originally given as an invited lecture to the Research Institute of Scottish and Irish Studies, at the University of Aberdeen, in Scotland in February 2001.

10. I have discussed this structure at length in *Seamus Heaney and the Place of Writing* (O'Brien 2003).

11. These towers were the central plank in Britain's Napoleonic defences – the chain of 103 Martello Towers stretching from Seaford in the west to Aldeburgh on the East Anglian coast which was built between Spring 1805 and 1812. These squat, ovoid-shaped brick-built towers were modelled on a gun tower at Martella, Corsica that had caused the Royal Navy much trouble in 1794. Martello Towers were the idea of Captain William Ford of the Royal Engineers and they were sited roughly 600 yards apart and each mounted a long-range 24-pounder cannon. The aim was to cover the most likely landing beaches and to confuse any French landing while British reserves and Royal Navy ships were rushed to the area.

12. The *Cyclops* chapter in *Ulysses* is a comic masterpiece of this type of commentary.

13. In this context, it is noteworthy that 'bleeding', as applied to colours, is a printing term. So, as well as the obvious signification of blood spilled over contesting identities and ideologies, there is also the suggestion that writing may transform both meaning and signification of this form of bleeding.

14. This book is entitled *The British Isles. A History of Four Nations* (1995).

15. This book is a sequel to *The Rattle Bag*, an anthology which the two poets also co-edited.

CHAPTER 7 – NOBEL CAUSES: HEANEY AND YEATS

1. These books are an invaluable source of information on Yeats's life and work: William Butler Yeats (1970) *Uncollected Prose. Volume 1. First Reviews and Articles 1886–1896*. Edited by John P. Frayne. New York: Columbia University Press; and William Butler Yeats (1975) *Uncollected Prose. Volume 2. Reviews, Articles and Other Miscellaneous Prose 1897–1939*. Edited by John P. Frayne. New York: Columbia University Press.

2. There has been much discussion as to whether these questions are, in fact, rhetorical, or not. For a contrastive reading of these questions, and of this poem, see Paul de Man's *Allegories of Reading* (1979), specifically the essay 'Semiology and Rhetoric'.

3. 'Prog' is a dialect term meaning to gain or profit in a bargain.

4. These lectures were presented at the inauguration of the Richard Ellmann lectures in Modern Literature, and published by Scholars Press as part of the Emory Studies in Humanities series, under the title *The Place of Writing*.

5. The actual connection is the citing of Yeats's lines from 'The Tower': 'or death / of every brilliant eye / That made a catch in the breath', and then connecting these lines with Raftery: 'One brilliant eye which had made a catch in the breath in nineteenth-century Ballylee was the beauty Mary Hynes, celebrated in song by the blind poet Anthony Raftery'. Both of them are invoked in an earlier part of 'The Tower'.

6. Heaney's final lecture in *The Place of Writing* takes this comment as its theme: 'Cornucopia and Empty Shell: Variations on a Theme from Ellmann'.

7. Heaney's long preface to his translation of *Beowulf* contains one of his most revealing accounts of the vexed, and sometimes chiasmatic relationship between identity, tradition, language and poetry to date.

8. In a long introduction to a recent selection from Yeats's work by Faber, Heaney offers an overview of Yeats's work. This essay is a revised version of the introduction to the selections from Yeats's work which he provided for Volume II of *The Field Day Anthology of Irish Writing*, in 1991.

9. For an overview of the history of the conflict in Northern Ireland, see *The Omagh Bomb and the History of Northern Ireland* (O'Brien 2000).

10. This interview with Seamus Deane, 'Unhappy and At Home', in *The Crane Bag*, has been one of the most quoted in Heaney studies. A recent in-depth interview between Heaney and Karl Miller (Miller 2000) offers one of the more acute contemporary conversations where Heaney discusses his work to date. Interestingly, there is still comparatively little interest in his prose in all of these interviews.

11. Interestingly, in the context of this discussion of the parallel projects of Yeats and Heaney, Heaney has an essay on Burns in *Finders Keepers*, entitled 'Burns's Art Speech' (2002: 347–63).

12. For a comprehensive discussion of the riots that accompanied early productions of Synge's *The Playboy of the Western World*, see *Anglo-Irish Theatre and the Formation of a Nationalist Political Culture between 1890 and 1930: 'Did that play of mine...?'* by Georg Grote (2002).

Bibliography of Seamus Heaney's Works

Heaney, S. (1966) *Death of a Naturalist*. London: Faber.
—— (1969) *Door into the Dark*. London: Faber.
—— (1972) *Wintering Out*. London: Faber.
—— (1975) *North*. London: Faber.
—— (1979) *Field Work*. London: Faber.
—— (1980) *Preoccupations: Selected Prose 1968–1978*. London: Faber.
—— and T. Hughes (eds) (1982) *The Rattle Bag*. London: Faber.
—— (1983a) *Among Schoolchildren*. Belfast: Queen's University.
—— (1983b) *An Open Letter*. Derry: Field Day.
—— (1983c) *Sweeney Astray*. Derry: Field Day.
—— (1984) *Station Island*. London: Faber.
—— (1985) *Place and Displacement*. Grasmere: Trustees of Dove Cottage.
—— (1987) *The Haw Lantern*. London: Faber.
—— (1988) *The Government of the Tongue: The 1986 T.S. Eliot Memorial Lectures and Other Critical Writings*. London: Faber.
—— (1989) *The Place of Writing*. Atlanta: Scholars Press.
—— (1990) *The Cure at Troy*. London: Faber.
—— (1991) *Seeing Things*. London: Faber.
—— (1995a) *The Redress of Poetry: Oxford Lectures*. London: Faber.
—— (1995b) *Crediting Poetry*. Oldcastle, County Meath, Ireland: Gallery Press.
—— (1996) *The Spirit Level*. London: Faber.
—— (1997) '"All Ireland's Bard". A Review of *W. B. Yeats: A Life. Volume 1. The Apprentice Mage*'. *The Atlantic Monthly*, Vol. 280, No. 5 (November): 155–60.
—— and T. Hughes (eds) (1997) *The School Bag*. London: Faber.
—— (1999) *Beowulf*. London: Faber.
—— (2000a) *The Midnight Verdict*. Oldcastle, County Meath, Ireland: Gallery Press.
—— (2000b) Introduction to *W.B. Yeats: Poems Selected by Seamus Heaney*. London: Faber.
—— (2001) *Electric Light*. London: Faber.
—— (2002) *Finders Keepers*. London: Faber.

General Bibliography

Adorno, T. (1973) *Negative Dialectics*. Translated by E. B. Ashton. London: Routledge & Kegan Paul.

Allen, M. (ed.) (1997) *Seamus Heaney*. New Casebook Series. London: Macmillan.

Andrews, E. (1988) *The Poetry of Seamus Heaney: All the Realms of Whisper*. London: Macmillan.

—— (ed.) (1998) *The Poetry of Seamus Heaney*. Icon Critical Guides Series. Cambridge: Icon Books.

Annwn, D. (1984) *Inhabited Voices: Myth and History in the Poetry of Geoffrey Hill, Seamus Heaney and George Mackay Brown*. Somerset: Bran's Head Books.

Ashcroft, B., G. Griffiths and H. Tiffin (eds) (1989) *The Empire Writes Back*: *Theory and Practice in Post-Colonial Literatures*. London: Methuen.

Bakhtin, M. (1981) *The Dialogic Imagination: Four Essays*. Translated by C. Emerson and M. Holquist. Austin: University of Texas Press.

Barrell, J. and J. Bull (eds) (1975) *The Penguin Book of English Pastoral Verse*. Harmondsworth: Penguin.

Barthes, R. (1979) 'The Death of the Author', in D. Lodge (ed.) (1988) *Modern Criticism and Theory*. Essex: Longman, pp. 167–75.

Benjamin, W. (1977) *The Origin of German Tragic Drama*. Translated by J. Osborne. London: New Left Books.

Bennington, G. and Derrida, J. (1993) *Jacques Derrida*. London: University of Chicago Press.

—— (1997) *Politics and Friendship: A Discussion with Jacques Derrida*. <www.sussex.ac.uk/Units/frenchthought/derrida.htm>

Bernhart, C. L. (ed.) (1972) *The World Book Dictionary*. Two volumes. Chicago: Doubleday.

Bhabha, H. K. (1994) *The Location of Culture*. London: Routledge.

Blanchot, M. (1981) *The Gaze of Orpheus*. Translated by L. Davis; edited by P. Adams. New York: Station Hill Press.

—— (1982a) *The Space of Literature*. Translated by A. Smock. Lincoln: University of Nebraska Press.

—— (1982b) *The Siren's Song*. Edited by G. Josipivici. Brighton: Harvester Press.

—— (1995) *The Work of Fire*. Translated by C. Mendell. Stanford: Stanford University Press.

Brandes, R. and M. J. Durkan (1994) *Seamus Heaney: A Reference Guide*. New York: G. K. Hall.

Brewster, S. (forthcoming 2004) '"The Other Side": Proximity, Poematics, Northern Ireland', in M. McQuillan (ed.) *Emergencies: Politics, Deconstruction, Cultural Studies*. Leeds Studies in Cultural Analysis. London: Routledge.

Broadbridge, E. (1977a) Radio interview with Seamus Heaney, published in *Seamus Heaney Skoleradioen*. Copenhagen: Danmarks Radio, 5–16.

—— (ed.) (1977b) *Seamus Heaney: Skoleradioen*. Copenhagen: Danmarks Radio.

Brown, R. (1992) 'Bog Poems and Book Poems: Doubleness, Self-Translation and Pun in Seamus Heaney and Paul Muldoon', in N. Corcoran (ed.) *The Chosen Ground: Essays on the Contemporary Poetry of Northern Ireland.* Bridgend, Mid Glamorgan: Poetry Wales Press, pp. 153–67.

Brown, J. (2002) *In the Chair: Interviews with Poets from the North of Ireland.* Cliffs of Moher, County Clare, Ireland: Salmon Publishing.

Buell, L. (1999) 'Introduction: In Pusuit of Ethics', *Proceedings of the Modern Language Association,* Vol. 114, No. 1 (January): 7–19.

Burris, S. (1990) *The Poetry of Resistance: Seamus Heaney and the Pastoral Tradition.* Athens: Ohio University Press.

Byron, C. (1992) *Out of Step: Pursuing Seamus Heaney to Purgatory.* Bristol: Loxwood Stoneleigh.

Caputo, J. D. (1993) *Against Ethics: Contributions to a Poetics of Obligation with Constant Reference to Deconstruction.* Bloomington: Indiana University Press.

—— (1997) *Deconstruction in a Nutshell: A Conversation with Jacques Derrida.* Edited with a commentary by J. D. Caputo. New York: Fordham University Press.

Carson, C. (1975) 'Escaped from the Massacre?', *The Honest Ulsterman,* Vol. 50 (Winter): 183–6.

Cookson, W. and P. Dale (1989) *Agenda: Seamus Heaney Fiftieth Birthday Issue.* Vol. 27, No. 1. London: Agenda and Editions Charitable Trust.

Corcoran, N. (1986) *Seamus Heaney.* Faber Student Guides series. London: Faber. Republished 1998 as *The Poetry of Seamus Heaney: A Critical Study.* London: Faber.

—— (ed.) (1992) *The Chosen Ground: Essays on the Contemporary Poetry of Northern Ireland.* Bridgend, Mid Glamorgan: Poetry Wales Press.

Coughlan, P. (1997) '"Bog Queens": The Representation of Women in the Poetry of John Montague and Seamus Heaney', in M. Allen (ed.) *Seamus Heaney.* New Casebook Series. London: Macmillan, pp. 185–205. Originally published in *Gender and Irish Writing* (1991), eds T. O'Brien Johnson and D. Cairns. Milton Keynes: Open University Press.

Critchley, S. (1992) *The Ethics of Deconstruction: Derrida and Levinas.* Oxford: Basil Blackwell.

Crotty, P. (2001) 'All I Believed That Happened There Was Revision', in T. Curtis (ed.) *The Art of Seamus Heaney.* Fourth revised edition. Dublin: Wolfhound Press, pp. 191–204. Originally published by Poetry Wales Press, 1982.

Cruise O'Brien, C. (1975a) 'An Unhealthy Intersection', *New Review,* Vol. 2, No.16 (July): 3–8.

—— (1975b) 'An Unhealthy Intersection', *Irish Times,* 21 August.

Curtis, T. (ed.) (2001) *The Art of Seamus Heaney.* Fourth revised edition. Dublin: Wolfhound Press.

Deane, S. (1977) 'Unhappy and At Home: Interview with Seamus Heaney', *The Crane Bag Book of Irish Studies.* Dublin: Blackwater Press, 1982, pp. 66–72.

— (1985) 'Seamus Heaney: The Timorous and the Bold', in S. Deane, *Celtic Revivals.* London: Faber, pp. 174–86.

de Man, P. (1979) *Allegories of Reading.* New Haven: Yale University Press.

Derrida, J. (1973) *Speech and Phenomena and Other Essays on Husserl's Theory of Signs*. Translated by D. B. Allison. Evanston: Northwestern University Press.

—— (1976) *Of Grammatology*. Translated by G. Chakravorty Spivak. London: Johns Hopkins University Press.

—— (1978) *Writing and Difference*. Translated by A. Bass. London: Routledge.

—— (1981a) *Positions*. Translated by A. Bass. London: Athlone.

—— (1981b) *Dissemination*. Translated by B. Johnson. First published in Paris (1972). Chicago: University of Chicago Press.

—— (1981c) *Deconstruction and the Other*, in R. Kearney (ed.) (1995) *States of Mind: Dialogues with Contemporary Continental Thinkers*. Manchester: Manchester University Press.

—— (1982) *Margins of Philosophy*. Translated by A. Bass. Chicago: University of Chicago Press.

—— (1985) *The Ear of the Other – Otobiography, Transference, translation: Texts and Discussions with Jacques Derrida*. Translated by A. Ronell; edited by C. V. McDonald. New York: Schocken Books.

—— (1986) 'But, Beyond...', *Critical Inquiry*, Vol. 13 (Autumn): 155–70.

—— (1987) 'Living On: Borderlines' in H. Bloom, P. de Man, J. Derrida, G. Hartman, and J. Hillis Miller, *Deconstruction and Criticism*. New York: Continuum Press, 1992 edition, pp. 75–176.

—— (1988) *Limited Inc*. Translated by S. Weber and J. Mehlman. Evanston, Illinois: Northwestern University Press.

—— (1989a) *Of Spirit: Heidegger and the Question*. Translated by G. Bennington and R. Bowlby. Chicago: University of Chicago Press.

—— (1989b) *Mémoires: For Paul de Man*. Translated by C. Lindsay, J. Culler and E. Cadava. Revised edition; first published 1986. New York: Columbia University Press.

—— (1989c) 'Biodegradables. Seven Diary Fragments', *Critical Inquiry* (Summer) Vol. 15, No. 4 (Summer), 'On Jacques Derrida's "Paul de Man's War"': 812–81.

—— (1992a) *Acts of Literature*. Edited by D. Attridge. London: Routledge.

—— (1992b) *The Other Heading: Reflections on Today's Europe*. Translated by P. A. Brault and M. Naas. Bloomington: Indiana University Press.

—— (1993) "On Responsibility." Interview with J. Dronsfield, N. Midgley and A. Wilding in *Responsibilities of Deconstruction: PLI – Warwick Journal of Philosophy* (edited by J. Dronsfield and N. Midgley), Vol. 6 (Summer 1997): 19–36.

—— (1994) *Specters of Marx: The State of the Debt, the Work of Mourning & the New International*. Translated from the French by P. Kamuf. Introduction by B. Magnus and S. Cullenberg. London: Routledge.

—— (1995) *Points...Interviews, 1974–1994*. Translated by P. Kamuf and others; edited by E. Weber. Stanford: Stanford University Press.

—— (1997a) *Politics of Friendship*. Translated by G. Collins. London: Verso.

—— (1997b) *Deconstruction in a Nutshell: A Conversation with Jacques Derrida*. Edited with a commentary by J. D. Caputo. New York: Fordham University Press.

—— (1998) *Monolinguism of the Other; or, The Prosthesis of Origin*. Translated by P. Mensah. Stanford: Stanford University Press.

—— (1999) *Adieu To Emmanuel Levinas*. Translated by P. A. Brault and M. Naas. Stanford: Stanford University Press.

—— (2000a) *Demeure: Fiction and Testimony*. Translated by E. Rottenberg. Stanford: Stanford University Press.

—— (2000b) *Of Hospitality: Anne Dufourmantelle Invites Jacques Derrida to Respond*. Translated by R. Bowlby. Stanford: Stanford University Press.

Docherty, T. (1991) 'Ana-; or Postmodernism, Landscape, Seamus Heaney', in A. Easthope and J. Thompson (eds) *Contemporary Poetry Meets Modern Theory*. Hemel Hempstead: Harvester Wheatsheaf, pp. 68–80.

—— (1997) 'The Sign of the Cross: Review of *The Government of the Tongue*', in M. Allen (ed.) *Seamus Heaney*. New Casebook Series. London: Macmillan, pp. 147–54.

Drakakis, J. (ed.) (1992) *Shakespearean Tragedy*. Longman Critical Readers Series. General editors R. Selden and S. Smith. London: Longman.

Eagleton, T. (1991) *Ideology*. London: Verso.

Eliot, T. S. (1963) *Collected Poems 1909–1962*. London: Faber.

Elliot, M. (1982) *Partners in Revolution: The United Irishmen and France*. New Haven: Yale University Press.

—— (1989) *Wolfe Tone: Prophet of Irish Independence*. New Haven: Yale University Press.

Fennell, D. (1991) *Whatever You Say, Say Nothing*. Dublin: ELO Publications.

Foster, R. F. (1993) *Paddy & Mr. Punch*. London: Allen Lane.

—— (1997) *W. B. Yeats: A Life. Volume 1: The Apprentice Mage 1865–1914*. Oxford: Oxford University Press.

Foster, T. C. (1989) *Seamus Heaney*. Dublin: O'Brien Press.

Gadamer, H.-G. (1981) 'Text and Interpretation', translated by D. J. Schmidt and R. Palmer, in D. P. Michelfelder and R. E. Palmer (eds) (1989) *Dialogue & Deconstruction: The Gadamer–Derrida Encounter*. New York: State University of New York Press, pp. 21–51.

Graham, C. (2001) *Deconstructing Ireland: Identity, Theory, Culture*. Series title – Tendencies: Identities, Texts, Cultures. Edinburgh: Edinburgh University Press.

Grote, G. (2002) *Anglo-Irish Theatre and the Formation of a Nationalist Political Culture between 1890 and 1930: 'Did that play of mine...?'*. Lampeter, Wales: Edwin Mellen Press.

Haffenden, J. (1981) 'Meeting Seamus Heaney: An Interview', *Viewpoints: Poets in Conversation*. London: Faber, pp. 57–75.

Hahn, S. (2002) *On Derrida*. Wadsworth Philosophers Series. Wadsworth: Belmont, California.

Hart, H. (1992) *Seamus Heaney: Poet of Contrary Progressions*. New York: Syracuse University Press.

Jarvis, S. (1998) *Adorno: A Critical Introduction*. London: Routledge.

Jay, M. (1984) *Adorno*. Fontana Modern Masters. General editor F. Kermode. London: Fontana.

Joyce, J. (1916) *A Portrait of the Artist as a Young Man*. 1993 edition, edited by R. B. Kershner. Boston: Bedford Books of St Martin's Press.

Kearney, H. (1995) *The British Isles. A History of Four Nations*. Cambridge: Cambridge University Press.

Kiberd, D. (1995) *Inventing Ireland: The Literature of the Modern Nation*. London: Jonathan Cape.

Kirkland, R. (1996) *Literature and Culture in Northern Ireland since 1965: Moments of Danger*. London: Longman.

—— (1997) 'Paradigms of Possibility: Seamus Heaney', in M. Allen (ed.) (1997) *Seamus Heaney*. New Casebook Series. London: Macmillan, 252–66.

Lacan, J. (1977) *Écrits – A Selection*. Translated by A. Sheridan. London: Tavistock.

Levinas, E. (1969) *Totality and Infinity: An Essay on Exteriority*. Translated by A. Lingis. Pittsburgh: Duquesne University Press.

—— (1981a) *Ethics and the Infinite*, in R. Kearney (ed.) (1995) *States of Mind: Dialogues with Contemporary Continental Thinkers*. Manchester: Manchester University Press.

—— (1981b) *Otherwise Than Being Or Beyond Essence*. Translated by A. Lingis. The Hague: Nijhoff.

—— (1989) *The Levinas Reader*. Edited by S. Hand. Oxford: Basil Blackwell.

—— (1994) *Beyond the Verse: Talmundic Readings and Lectures*. Translated by G. Mole. London: Athlone Press.

Lloyd, D. (1993) '"Pap for the Dispossessed": Seamus Heaney and the Poetics of Identity', in *Anomalous States: Irish Writing and the Postcolonial Moment*. Dublin: Lilliput, pp. 13–40. Article originally published in *Boundary*, Vol. 2 (Winter 1985): 319–42.

Lodge, D. (ed.) (1988) *Modern Criticism and Theory*. London: Longman.

Longley, E. (1986) *Poetry in the Wars*. Newcastle: Bloodaxe Books.

—— (2001) '*North*: "Inner Emigré" or "Artful Voyeur"?', in T. Curtis (ed.) *The Art of Seamus Heaney*. Fourth revised edition. Dublin: Wolfhound Press, pp. 63–95. Originally published by Poetry Wales Press, 1982. Also collected, in expanded form, in E. Longley (1986) *Poetry in the Wars*. Newcastle: Bloodaxe Books, pp. 140–69.

McDonald, P. (1997) *Mistaken Identities: Poetry and Northern Ireland*. Oxford: Clarendon Press.

McQuillan, M. (ed.) (2003) *Emergencies: Politics, Deconstruction, Cultural Studies*. Leeds Studies in Cultural Analysis. London: Routledge.

Mathews, S. (1997) *Irish Poetry: Politics, History, Negotiation: The Evolving Debate, 1969 to the Present*. London: Macmillan.

Mendelson, E. (1988) 'Review of *The Government of the Tongue*', *Times Literary Supplement*, 1–7 July, p. 726.

Michelfelder, D. P. and R. E. Palmer (eds) (1989) *Dialogue & Deconstruction: The Gadamer–Derrida Encounter*. New York: State University of New York Press.

Miller, J. Hillis (1987) *The Ethics of Reading: Kant, de Man, Eliot, Trollope, James, and Benjamin*. The Wellek Library Lectures. New York: Columbia University Press.

Miller, K. (2000) *Seamus Heaney in Conversation with Karl Miller*. London: Between the Lines.

Molino, M. (1994) *Questioning Tradition, Language and Myth: The Poetry of Seamus Heaney*. Washington DC: Catholic University Press.

Morgan, H. (1993) *Tyrone's Rebellion*, Woodbridge, Suffolk: Boydell Press for The Royal Historical Society.

Morrison, B. (1982) *Seamus Heaney*. London: Methuen.

Murphy, A. (2000a) *Seamus Heaney*. Writers and Their Work Series. Plymouth: Northcote House in association with the British Council.

—— (2000b) *Reading the Future: Irish Writers in Conversation with Mike Murphy*. Dublin: Lilliput Press, pp. 81–98.

Myers, I. and Simms, M. (1985) *Dictionary and Handbook of Poetry*. London: Longman.

Norris, C. (1991) *Spinoza and the Origins of Modern Critical Theory*. Oxford: Basil Blackwell.

O'Brien, E. (1998) *The Question of Irish Identity in the Writings of William Butler Yeats and James Joyce*. Lampeter, Wales: Edwin Mellen Press.

—— (1999) 'North: The Politics of Plurality', *Nua*, Vol. II, Nos 1 & 2 (Spring): 1–19.

—— (2000) *The Omagh Bomb and the History of Northern Ireland* in M. O'Meara (ed.) *History Behind the Headlines*. Detroit: Gale Publishing Group, Volume 2: 221–35.

—— (2002a) *Seamus Heaney: Creating Irelands of the Mind*. Contemporary Irish Writers Series. Dublin: Liffey Press.

—— (2002b) *Examining Irish Nationalism in the Context of Literature, Culture and Religion: A Study of the Epistemological Structure of Nationalism*. New York: Edwin Mellen Press.

—— (2003) *Seamus Heaney and the Place of Writing*. Gainesville: University Press of Florida.

O'Donoghue, B. (1994) *Seamus Heaney and the Language of Poetry*. Hemel Hempstead:

—— (2001) 'Heaney's ars poetica: The Government of the Tongue', in T. Curtis (ed.) *The Art of Seamus Heaney*. Fourth revised edition. Dublin: Wolfhound Press, pp. 179–90. Originally published by Poetry Wales Press, 1982.

Parker, M. (1993) *Seamus Heaney: The Making of a Poet*. Dublin: Gill and Macmillan.

Pinsky, R. (1988) *Poetry and the World*. New York: Ecco Press.

Raine, K. (ed.) (1940) *Letters on Poetry from W. B. Yeats to Dorothy Wellesley*. London: Oxford University Press, 1964.

Randall, J. (1979) 'An Interview with Seamus Heaney', *Ploughshares*, Vol. 5, No. 3: 7–22.

Rapaport, H. (2003) *Later Derrida: Reading the Recent Work*. London: Routledge.

Simmons, J. (1992) 'The Trouble with Seamus', in E. Andrews (ed.) *Seamus Heaney: A Collection of Critical Essays*. London: Macmillan, pp. 39–66.

Smith, S. (1992) 'Seamus Heaney: The Distance Between', in N. Corcoran (ed.) *The Chosen Ground: Essays on the Contemporary Poetry of Northern Ireland*. Bridgend, Mid Glamorgan: Poetry Wales Press, pp. 35–61.

Smyth, G. (2001) *Space and The Irish Cultural Imagination*. Basingstoke: Palgrave.

Spivak, G. Chakravorty (1976) Translator's Preface, in J. Derrida (1976) *Of Grammatology*. Translated by G. Chakravorty Spivak. London: Johns Hopkins University Press.

Stevens, W. (1965) *The Necessary Angel*. New York: Random House.

Stevenson, A. (2001a) 'Stations: Seamus Heaney and the Sacred Sense of the Sensitive Self', in T. Curtis (ed.) *The Art of Seamus Heaney*. Fourth revised edition. Dublin: Wolfhound Press, pp. 45–51. Originally published by Poetry Wales Press, 1982.

—— (2001b) 'The Peace Within Understanding: Looking at *Preoccupations*', in T. Curtis (ed.) *The Art of Seamus Heaney*. Fourth revised edition. Dublin: Wolfhound Press, pp. 129–37. Originally published by Poetry Wales Press, 1982.

Sutton, M. (1994) *Bear in Mind These Dead...An Index of Deaths from the Conflict in Ireland 1969–1993*. Belfast: Beyond the Pale.

Tamplin, R. (1989) *Seamus Heaney*. Milton Keynes: Open University Press.

Tóibín, C. (1988) 'Review of *The Government of the Tongue*', *Sunday Independent*, 10 July.

Tobin, D. (1998) *Passage to the Center: Imagination and the Sacred in the Poetry of Seamus Heaney*. Lexington: University Press of Kentucky.

Vendler, H. (1998) *Seamus Heaney*. London: HarperCollins.

Volosinov, V. N. (1973) *Marxism and the Philosophy of Language*. Translated by L. Matejka and I. R. Titunik. New York: Seminar Press.

Wade, S. (1989) 'Creating the Nubbed Treasure (*Station Island*)', in W. Cookson and P. Dale (eds) *Agenda: Seamus Heaney Fiftieth Birthday Issue*. London: Agenda and Editions Charitable Trust, pp. 62–71.

—— (1993) *More on the Word-Hoard: The Work of Seamus Heaney*. Nottingham: Pauper's Press.

Weil, S. (2002) *Gravity and Grace*. London: Routledge.

Wells-Cole, C. (1995) 'Disputed Territory: Heritage and Poetry in Northern Ireland', *Critical Survey*, Vol. 7, No. 2: 136–43.

Williams, R. (1975) *The Country and the City*. Oxford: Oxford University Press.

Wilson Foster, J. (1995) *The Achievement of Seamus Heaney*. Dublin: Lilliput Press.

Wolfreys, J. (1998) *Deconstruction • Derrida*. Transitions Series. London: Macmillan.

Yeats, W. B. (1937) *A Vision*. London: Macmillan, 1981.

—— (1962) *Explorations*. Selected by Mrs W. B. Yeats. New York: Macmillan.

—— (1964) *Yeats: Selected Criticism and Prose*. London: Pan Classics, 1980.

—— (1970) *Uncollected Prose. Volume 1. First Reviews and Articles 1886–1896*. Edited by J. P. Frayne. New York: Columbia University Press.

—— (1975) *Uncollected Prose. Volume 2. Reviews, Articles and Other Miscellaneous Prose 1897–1939*. Edited by J. P. Frayne. New York: Columbia University Press.

—— (1979) *The Collected Poems of William Butler Yeats*. London: Macmillan.

Young, R. (1995) *Colonial Desire: Hybridity in Theory, Culture, and Race*. London: Routledge.

Index